The Thirteen AMERICAN *Arguments*

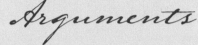

* * *

ENDURING DEBATES THAT DEFINE AND INSPIRE OUR COUNTRY

* * *

HOWARD FINEMAN

2009 Random House Trade Paperback Edition

Copyright © 2008, 2009 by Howard Fineman

Published in the United States by Random House Trade Paperbacks,
an imprint of The Random House Publishing Group, a division of
Random House, Inc., New York.

RANDOM HOUSE TRADE PAPERBACKS and colophon are trademarks of Random House, Inc.

Originally published in hardcover and in slightly different form in the United States by Random House,
an imprint of The Random House Publishing Group, a division of Random House, Inc., in 2008.

LIBRARY OF CONGRESS CATALOGING-IN-PUBLICATION DATA
Fineman, Howard.
The thirteen American arguments: enduring debates that define and
inspire our country/Howard Fineman.
p. cm.
ISBN: 978-0-8129-7635-9
1. National characteristics, American.   2. United States—Politics and government.
3. Political culture—United States.   4. United States—Civilization.   I. Title.
E169.1.F524 2008   973—dc22   2007045133

Printed in the United States of America

www.atrandom.com

11 13 15 17 19 18 16 14 12

Book design by Casey Hampton

To Amy Lee,
who makes everything possible

CONTENTS

The Thirteen
AMERICAN
Arguments

FOR THE SAKE OF
ARGUMENT

First, I owe you a definition, then an explanation. You will see the word "argument" throughout this book. By "argument" I mean something besides shouting or name calling, though both often are part of the transaction. I mean a clash between at least two people (or regions, political parties, candidates, or economic interests) over facts and ideas in the search for answers—in this case, answers to questions about the future and fate of America. The gist (the "argument," if you will) of this book is:

We are the Arguing Country, born in, and born to, debate. The habit of doing so—the urgent, almost neurotic need to do so—makes us unique and gives us our freedom, creativity, and strength. By my count, there are thirteen foundational arguments that comprise our public life—hence the title of this book. Rather than argue too much, which is the conventional wisdom's critique, we in fact do not argue enough, about the fundamentals. If we fail to draw strength from our argumentative nature, we risk losing what made us great and gives us hope. Our disputes are not a burden, but a blessing.

Who am I to make such sweeping declarations? After all, I am neither a scholar nor a historian. I am a reporter, however, and I have been around—literally and figuratively. Long ago, a favorite professor of mine at Columbia reduced his journalistic advice to two words: "Go there." I have tried, reporting in and about forty-nine of the fifty states (I'm saving what I expect to be the best, North Dakota, for last). I have covered every presidential campaign and major candidate since 1983. I have covered leaders and stories in other fields as well, from business and entertainment to the environment and communications. Inside the Beltway, I have come to know all quadrants, from the White House to Congress to K Street to the think tanks to the hallways of the federal bureaucracy. I also have learned about America by leaving it, traveling in more than forty countries in Europe, Asia, and Latin America. I have woven my own reporting from the campaign trail and from Washington into the history I have picked up along the way and discovered as I worked on this book. I came to see a pattern.

Generalizations are imperfect, admittedly, but they can be useful in sorting out the tribes and nations of the planet. The United States stands out in sharp relief for one reason.

We are an endless argument.

Even as we arrived we were asking ourselves: What was the destiny of this place? Was this to be a Christian New Jerusalem, a Dutch speculation, or an English shire? Was everyone welcome, and welcome to be free, or were merely the Old World chosen? Were there to be borders, or none, central authority, or none, a continental nation, or none, a currency and market to call our own—or none? Was the virgin earth a hedged-in garden to be tended in perpetuity, or a limitless, disposable commodity? Was this place a coastal outpost of a global elsewhere, or a new type of nation, its self-sufficient identity waiting to be forged in the woods above the fall line?

We forget—or fail to realize—how unlike most of the world we are in this essential characteristic. In China, when Mao died, there was no debate over his legacy; schoolchildren were commanded to put their heads down on their desks and cry. In the name of jihad, the Al Qaeda training manual dismisses all "Socratic debates, Platonic ideals, and Aristotelian diplomacy." In America, by contrast, we have been debating our very identity from the first days of our existence.

The Thirteen American Arguments bitterly divide us, but they also define, inspire, and ultimately unite us by bestowing legitimacy on hard-fought deals. They are the force that makes us whole and who we are. They produced a civil war, the still-smoldering embers of racial tribalism and pitiless economic competition; but they also produced the freest of societies, an ongoing (if imperfect) accommodation between capital and community, and a Constitution that stands as a beacon to the world even if we sometimes honor it in the breach. Arguing keeps us moving fitfully forward—toward being worthy of the gifts God gave us.

I began my education in the American character—in Arguing America—as a cub reporter for *The Courier-Journal* in Louisville. I was eager for any assignment that would send me out into Kentucky. I believed then, and still do, that the "real" country was "out there" somewhere, which is how I came to cover the Mountain Laurel Festival in eastern Kentucky. Every Memorial Day weekend, the town of Cumberland, far up in the mountains, staged a parade and beauty pageant to welcome the spring and its flowers. The governor would fly down to preside. As the Commonwealth's only statewide paper, one with a deep commitment to Appalachia, *The Courier-Journal* felt obliged to publish its own (not from a wire service) picture and story.

Only one problem: No one on the city or state desk wanted to waste his precious holiday on what seemed a merely ceremonial assignment. I did, of course, if for no other reason than that I would get to fly to Cumberland in the paper's own twin-engine airplane, piloted by the legendary Billy Davis Jr. For decades, Billy had been documenting the region from the air. Flying low, he would throw open the window on the pilot-side door, bank to the left by steering with a special set of foot pedals, and aim his huge Graflex camera at whatever story was down below. In the late 1960s, that story was strip-mining, and the ravages of what was then a fast-growing—and largely uncontrolled—part of the coal industry. No one had ever photographed the devastation so dramatically: the scarred hillsides, the rubble in the creeks, the vegetation shriveled by acid drainage. Billy documented it all, which was one reason why the paper had won a Pulitzer Prize for its coverage of the issue.

Looking back, I regard Billy as a journalistic role model. He took pride in a landscape he viewed as his own, if for no other reason than that he had seen it all. On the way back, he added another leg to the itinerary. "Howard," he said with a flourish. "Let's go see the Cumberland Gap!" Even a rookie from Pittsburgh by way of New York understood the significance of that declaration. I was about to see, from a unique vantage point, one of the most historic features of the American landscape, the dip in the Appalachians through which Daniel Boone led his band in 1775.

We flew southeast across an undulating carpet of green, the folds of mountains highlighted by shadows in the low-angled late-afternoon sun.

Soon enough, our destination loomed ahead: a long, hammock-shaped dip in the line of hills. The Gap looked like the place God had put His boot on a fence and told His flock to cross. I could see why Boone and his Transylvania Company had come this way. It was the only way they *could* come—through the Khyber Pass of a New West.

I assumed we would get a look from well above the Gap, but Billy had a different flight plan in mind. "Hang on!" he cried as he nudged the controls forward. Down we went, to just above the treetops. "Now *this* is the Cumberland Gap!" he said as we roared through. There was no time for a picture and no need.

Boone had been heading to a place of new beginnings, one that was simultaneously connected to, and cut off from, the established towns of the coast. The Gap was a signal geological feature of what became (and remains) an age-old, bitter tug-of-war, between the Old Ways of the ocean-facing, Europe-oriented East and the New Ways of a frontier in which all the reference points were purely, inwardly American. The land Boone settled became a fertile ground for agitation, change, controversy, and war. The sons of the pioneers who settled Kentucky and Tennessee drew from their frontier experience radical new ideas of national destiny and popular participation: Henry Clay's "national system" of federal public works, which challenged the role of the then-dominant states; Andrew Jackson's new "populist" theory of direct democracy, including the chrysalis of modern campaign politics.

I got a sense of the ardor of that "frontier" politics later, when I covered the coal industry in the same mountains over which Billy Davis had flown me. When the United Mine Workers of America went on strike, the rank and file in eastern Kentucky were among the most reluctant to make a deal. In a nasal twang, they sang the folk song "Which Side Are You On, Boys?" The title expressed their combative worldview. They were suspicious of the "coal operators," of course, but more so of the distant companies Up East that owned the mineral rights and traded the stock that controlled the mines.

The East-West (or local versus national) divide symbolized by the Cumberland Gap is only one of the many fault lines that run through our public life and history. In the early days of the twenty-first century, the newest Cumberland Gap was not geological but digital—yet another virgin territory fertile with freedom and ferment, this one called the Internet. Conflict is built into the very landscape of our country, and into the character of the people who inhabit it.

So what are the Thirteen American Arguments? Drop a pebble into a pond (Walden Pond would be an appropriate one) and the perpetual disputes radiate out in concentric waves. At their core, they were set in motion by a Declaration of "self-evident truth" that every person is entitled to freedom and respect. Our first Argument, therefore, always is: Who is a "person"? Next we want to know who can *become* an American person. Then we argue about what Americans can be told to believe as a matter of faith rather than reason; what they can know and say; and what responsibilities they have to each other in terms of behavior, material wealth, and social welfare. Moving outward, ring by ring, the next set of arguments is about the shape and rules of government: how we choose the priests of our secular faith, the law; how we define money and manage debt; the conflicts between regions and between local and national power (such as the frontiers of Kentucky and Tennessee versus the powers Back East); and the relative strength of the president in a federal scheme dedicated to finding the midpoint between monarch and mob. In the next circles, we argue about our relationship to the world: the role of trade, war and diplomacy, and the environment. The last and perhaps most vehement argument is over the distance we still must travel to reach the "more perfect union" the Founders claimed to have established. Lincoln called us the "last best hope of earth." Have we redeemed that promise? If arguing is our saving grace, everyone must feel they have a voice and a chance to be heard. Do they?

How were we born and bred to argue? To understand our nature—and to sustain it—we need to appreciate the lucky mix of accident and intention that made us who we are. Here, in sum, is how it happened:

THE FADING OF TOP-DOWN AUTHORITY

As we were rising in the New World, unquestioned authority—the kind you risk your life to oppose—was dying in the Old. In England in the early seventeenth century, King James I decreed that he ruled by divine right. The fact that he felt it necessary to commit this idea to writing was proof enough that the concept was crumbling beneath his throne. As in politics, so in religion. In the late sixteenth century, Martin Luther had loosed a war of theology, ideas, and blood in defiance of the Catholic Church. For more than a millennium, Rome had held sway in Christendom, but the Reformation had eroded its authority by the time the first settlers left Europe for our shores. In one way or another, to one degree or another, most of our first founders were dissenters: initially, Protestants dissenting from the Vatican, then from the successor orthodoxies of a nominally Protestant official church. Robert Browne, an early dissenter, wrote that the church should be guided not by bishops but by "the voice of the whole people." Our forefathers, by and large, had the habit of and even a theological need for disputation.

NO GOLD

Even if royal (and ecclesiastical) authority had remained supreme, it would have been hard to feel the weight of their command if you were an average person in early America. For most of our first 180 years, the powers that be in London (or, for a brief time, Amsterdam) paid relatively little attention to what was going on in their rather obscure and distant American colonies. We were afterthoughts, essentially commercial franchises, a way to show the flag without draining the treasury. Inattention amounted to freedom to argue with (local) authority.

And there was no glittering treasure to draw royal attention. The Founders would later remark that it was our good *political* fortune to have been bereft of gold, the ravenous mining of which had led the Spanish to exert a much tougher and more dictatorial reign over their New World possessions. (We can be thankful that the California Gold Rush didn't begin until the United States was sixty years old.) Americans got used to a light administrative hand, which led to revolution and war when the grip tightened in the late eighteenth century.

THE BIRTH OF FREE INQUIRY

If neither the pope nor the king had the power to explain the world and to rule it, who did? America's founding coincided with the dawn of an age in which leading men first began to suggest a shattering new answer to that question: the free mind and soul of Man. With a printed Bible in one hand (written, for the first time, in his local, native language) and a telescope or microscope in the other (through which he could observe real-world phenomena with his own eyes), Man could understand the world, and forge his own destiny rather than merely accept it.

Now, understanding would require argument in the scientific sense. Ironically, but appropriately, the dawn of this new era effectively was in 1620, the year the Pilgrims landed at Plymouth Rock and Sir Francis Bacon first propounded the theory of the scientific method, which required close observation and open-minded experiment. Soon after, John Milton proposed a new method of inquiry into questions about God and Man—in free speech. The unencumbered play of argument was the point of his *Aeropagitica,* published in 1644 and read with great interest in America. "And though all the winds of doctrine were let loose to play upon the earth," he famously wrote, "so Truth be in the field, we do injuriously by licensing and prohibiting to misdoubt her strength. Let her and Falsehood grapple; who ever knew Truth put to the worse, in a free and open endeavor." The majestic cadences echoed across the Atlantic, and still do. The Founding Fathers knew the passage by heart. Key word: "grapple."

THE FREE FLOW OF INFORMATION

From the beginning, America was made for that Miltonian contest. We are the first nation—arguably the only nation—in which top-down control of the flow of ideas and information never was seriously attempted. The British weren't eager to import printing presses to the colonies, understanding the risk of doing so, but by the early eighteenth century a robust, coffeehouse-and-pamphlet culture was thriving in cities such as Boston, Philadelphia, and New York. If there was "grappling" to be done, these were the places.

Attempts to dam the flow of information were proximate causes of our national existence. The Stamp Act Congress, which convened in New York in October 1765, is generally considered the first official act of what ultimately became the United States, and its Declaration of Grievances our first collective political utterance. What followed was perhaps the most intense period of public debate in our history, as we argued about how to establish a government. Thomas Paine's *Common Sense,* published in 1776, sold an astonishing 600,000 copies in a country of 3 million.

ISAAC NEWTON'S CONSTITUTION

What Bacon had begun, Sir Isaac Newton brought to fruition, and the Founding Fathers who drafted the Constitution were steeped in respect for his successful experiments. Our Founders inherited a belief in scientific method, and several of them—Benjamin Franklin, Thomas Jefferson, even George Washington—were men of science, a gentleman's credential in the America of the late eighteenth century. Newton's discoveries in physics were echoed in public life in a search for laws of mass and motion in human affairs.

The Constitution they drafted was Newtonian clockwork, a wheel-within-wheel of countervailing gravitational forces. Those wheels—we call them "checks and balances"—were designed to encourage the release of energy while at the same time preventing political passion from tearing us apart. Historian Michael Kammen calls it "A Machine That Would Go of Itself." We are still going.

In the most famous of all of the *Federalist Papers, No. 10,* the intellectual architect of the Constitution, James Madison, proposed that the multiplicity of "faction" was essential to a just and equitable society. The more factions, the more disputes—and the less chance for tyrannical rule, either from moblike majorities or power-mad politicians.

LAWYERS AND LEGAL ARGUMENTS

Lawyers launched a "nation of laws" in the language of legal procedure. The Declaration of Independence was written in the prescribed form of ancient common-law pleading known in *Blackstone's Commentaries* as "The Argument"—that is, the motion in court that states the plaintiff's civil claim. The Declaration is a list of grievances against King George: our causes of action for the case we were about to argue. And the Declaration launches itself in the form of a court-rendered judgment in a case: "We *hold* these truths to be self-evident. . . ." In other words, in the court of human morality, we handed down an a priori judgment that we would cite in our new case.

The Constitution is not in pleading form, but it was fashioned in a legal environment of fifty-five men gathered behind closed doors in Philadelphia in 1787. Of that group, thirty-three—a working majority—were lawyers. How could we be anything other than the Arguing Country? And the result of their deliberations was not a Code in the Roman (or later, Napoleonic) sense. It was, in classic common-law fashion, the shortest distance between two points, dealing only and precisely with the problem at hand: how to assemble in the most efficient and durable way one country from thirteen fractious colonies. The "brevity and precision" of the document, wrote Lord James Bryce, emphasizes its "definiteness of principle," which in turn leads to endless arguments over its application—which is the whole point. And the more arguers the better.

HOW TO MAKE A NEW EDEN?

Wherever we have come from, whatever we have come for, most of us view America as a clean slate of fresh possibilities. We tend to regard ours as the first and only perfectible nation. Our ancestors, burdened as they were by a prehistory of tribal warfare, beset by the need for mere survival and territorial coherence, rarely dared to pursue—and could not conceive of—the idea of societal perfection. We did, and do. The idea burned bright on the *Mayflower*. "They were not ordinary pilgrims," wrote historian Paul Johnson, a Brit with a keen eye for his cousin country. "They were, rather, pilgrims, setting up a new, sanctified country which was to be a permanent pilgrimage, traveling ceaselessly toward a millenarian goal."

THE BLACK EXPERIENCE

We aim high, which makes our failures dramatic—which spurs arguments about them. No one can see the contrast or feel the pain of it more sharply than African Americans, who, as slaves, literally built the Capitol in which laws were enacted to keep them in chains. But it was also in that very building where other, later laws were enacted to bring them to full personhood. Cornel West, the Princeton professor, captured the duality that fosters argument, and change. "To accept your country without betraying it," he wrote, "you must love it for that which shows what it might become. America—this monument to the genius of ordinary man and women, this place where hope becomes capacity, this long, halting turn of the 'no' into the 'yes'—needs citizens who love it enough to re-imagine and remake it." So we try, fitfully, and argue about how to remove the burden that history gave to us all.

COMPETING COLONIAL MODELS

When we remember the Founders, we tend to think of the Pilgrims: the grim theocrats of Plymouth and Boston, censorious Puritans who gave us our communitarian idealism and our bristling impatience with those who do not share our ideals. But as historians have unpacked and repacked the past, they have come to see a more varied landscape and a greater variety of social frameworks that jostled each other up and down the Atlantic Coast. These existed, and thrived, for up to *180 years* before the convention in Philadelphia. (And that's not counting Spanish explorers, who crisscrossed the continent and established a smattering of settlements in the sixteenth century.) Each of these colonial frames—in New England, Virginia, and the Middle Colonies—began with its own blend of attitudes toward the fundamental forces in human affairs. Boston was communitarian and theocratic, Virginia a reconstituted English countryside. In Philadelphia and New York, the market ruled.

Each of these three colonial models was utopian in its own way, but each envisioned a different kind of Elysium. They clashed from the start, and still do.

UTOPIAS IN A LIMITLESS ELSEWHERE

When our country was confined largely to its east-of-the-Appalachians configuration—a period that lasted roughly from 1609 to 1784—the West gave unimaginable room in which to imagine more new beginnings. We could get away from each other; each succeeding group of Israelites could build its own version of a Promised Land. The paradoxical result was *more* friction, and more numerous arguments, as the proponents of each fresh utopia worked themselves into a lather of unquestioned righteousness in the wilderness. Since they never had to look at the world through someone else's eyes, they were all the more uncompromising about their own.

Roger Williams fled Boston to establish his own ideas in Rhode Island. His flight path was replicated endlessly in a big continent that was, for the most part, undefended. The Scots, venturing west over and through the Alleghenies, established a live-free-or-die society that only President George Washington himself could tame. Mormons, beset in the East, and facing cruelty and bloodshed as they trekked through Missouri and Illinois, finally found their utopia near the Great Salt Lake. The newest West for freedom-seeking utopians doesn't exist on the land; it is not beyond the Alleghenies, or in the vastness of the Far West. It's a truly limitless place: cyberspace, where gunslinging bloggers vie for attention with the hucksters from Back East. "It's wild and wide-open," said Arianna Huffington, a Los Angeles activist and writer who used that latitude to turn her eponymous website from a start-up to a must-read.

IMMIGRANTS' EYES

Immigrants revere America with a fervor few natives can match, yet no one can see the contrast between American ideals and street-level reality more quickly or vividly. (Huffington, for example, a native of Greece, exhibits both qualities.) That shock can strike a spark of recognition and anger, and a consequent urge to demand change. Immigrants, or more usually their children, generate waves of idealism and indignation that fuel the never-ending debate over the distance between the "more perfect union" and its sometimes grim shortcomings. From early in the nineteenth century on, the Irish faced discrimination and scorn, but they eventually fought back by creating the big-city political machine that brought with it the Catholic social-welfare ideals of Europe. Coming to America with their own hopes for American society, the Jews of New York argued for a place at the table—and for social justice—in a movement that helped consummate Franklin Delano Roosevelt's New Deal. Now Latinos, Asian Americans, and Muslim Americans are stepping into the arena. What will they say? We need to hear it, and we will. Whatever it is, they will join in and help sustain the Thirteen American Arguments that have—and still can—define and inspire us.

What do I hope to achieve by writing this book? Here is my to-do list:

SEEING PATTERNS

American democracy is not tidy, but it is understandable—and certainly worth trying to understand. My first goal is to cut through the noise of the day and try to show you a comprehensible and nonpartisan overview of our public life and how it works. The earthquakes and lava eruptions we see and hear every day, whether at *Daily Kos* or the *Drudge Report,* whether on O'Reilly or NPR, are merely the visible expressions of deeper forces. If you have a map of the tectonic plates and know the terrain, as Billy Davis Jr. did, you know where you are, you know where the next story is coming from, and you can separate what is useful from what is mere bombast and entertainment. I call that map *The Thirteen American Arguments*. You can see evidence of them every day on the home page of your favorite news website (or if you insist, on the front page of your local newspaper).

In his *The Cycles of American History,* Arthur Schlesinger Jr. summarizes America as an ebb and flow in attitude toward the role of government "as the best way of meeting our troubles." He's right, but only partially. The arguments are more numerous and, in some cases, more fundamental.

To understand them, what matters is not the name of the package, but its contents. The labels change, but the issues—the arguments—remain constant. In the past century, for example, the Republican Party has been the party of high trade barriers and low; the tribune of emancipation for African Americans and a barrier to civil rights and affirmative action; the bastion of the industrial North and of the rural South. The Democrats have been the party of Bible-toting teetotalers, and the libertines of New York and San Francisco; the "peace" party opposed to the use of military force in foreign affairs and the "hawk" party agitating for wars; the supporters of "states' rights" and the champion of expanded federal power. The labels don't matter, the Arguments do. You won't see me using the words "conservative" and "liberal," or "left" and "right" very much. They are functionally meaningless, especially in America. We are not a country of rigid ideologies, but of real, permanent conflicts.

THE RISKS OF FAILING TO ARGUE

My second goal is to remind us that arguing is good—in fact, indispensable. The process can seem so nasty, petty, and personal. But the harshness literally comes with the territory. Here is the paradox in Arguing America: The process that makes us so fragile also makes us durable. The machinery of our life is complex, deliberately so, and always in danger of corrosion and collapse from lack of maintenance. We need education if we are to argue; but we need emotion if we are to want to. I hold no brief for the haranguers of radio or flamers of the Web, but when they mention facts (which they sometimes do) or argue from the heart (which they often do), they are essential. Our constant challenge is to harness the often passionate energy of our arguments to the useful deals that can result, without tearing ourselves apart. The word "but," I realized long ago, is the most important one in any speech, and in public life it is the moment an argument begins.

We are the sum of the resulting achievements and accommodations. We make progress that way. The "mixed" American economy is the legacy of the never-ending negotiation among the fundamental forces of the Market and the State. For all of its shortcomings, it has been, so far, the largest generator of wealth in the world and the most productive economy in history. It took a depression to weave a "social safety net." Though frayed, it achieved its primary goal—the amelioration, through Social Security and Medicare, of dire poverty and untended disease among the elderly. It took a civil war to free the slaves, and another century to ensure their civil rights, but no country has emerged more genuinely committed to the ideal of individual freedom for all—in part because we had to shed so much blood for that prize. The never-ending argument over our relationship to the rest of the planet—do we want to merely survive in it or change it?—led us to achieve both in World War II, the "good war" if there ever was one.

Silence is a greater risk than tumult. Many would regard the all-too-smooth road to war in Iraq as a grim example of that risk. Congress did not do its part in arguing over our course; neither did the press, the author of this book included. The president was free to propound, with little debate, a new doctrine of preemptive war—a radical change to our theory of the use of military power and foreign involvement. Pro-life activists from a generation ago regarded the Supreme Court's 1973 decision on abortion the same way, as a radical change in policy made without the grand public debate it deserved. Argument requires voices. Progress requires that they be heard, even if they are not obeyed.

The absence of vehemence is one risk; the failure to recognize the validity of vehemence is another. The multifaceted debate over the question of who controls the genetic destiny of mankind—God, or society and science—is a vivid example. Those who worry about the morality of embryonic stem-cell research are not necessarily ignorant; those who put their fierce faith in the life-saving possibilities of such research are not godless heathens. Each side needs to accept the other's humanity, and understandable emotional intensity, so the debate can really begin. For argument is inert without a measure of goodwill. Our Declaration of Independence, after all, was written in the name of "a decent respect for the opinion of mankind."

IMPEDIMENTS TO ARGUMENT

Next, I want to sound an alarm. Like a reciprocating engine or a human heart, our country can produce energy only if the valves flow freely. In the early twenty-first century, the obstacles have thickened. We have clotted the arteries of the American body politic.

One impediment often is the presidential selection process, which the political parties have turned over to primary voters. The objective was a noble one: to foster democratic participation. But often the result is the opposite, exaggerating the clout of small groups of single-issue activists and rapacious consultants at the expense of the larger electorate. Rather than addressing each other, the candidates (even in the general election) tend to stand back-to-back, gesticulating in the direction of their own "base." It's "why Americans hate politics," as author E. J. Dionne once put it.

Rather than lubricating the engine of argument, the media—old and even new—often jams the gears. The Internet exponentially has expanded venues for free expression, but at the same time encourages like-minded people to cling together, talking to each other rather than engaging the world outside of their digital enclave. As the University of Pennsylvania's Kathleen Hall Jamieson has shown, TV ads often obscure more than they reveal. In the "free" media, the hunger for ratings reduces the ratio of real argument to mere rant. We are left to operate in a miasma of what comedian Stephen Colbert calls "truthiness."

In the post-9/11 world, war has further clogged the arteries of argument. In the name of security, officials withhold information. It often is difficult, if not impossible, to debate the actions of government if we have no idea what government really is doing. In his first six years as president, George W. Bush was free to maneuver without strict oversight from a largely compliant, Republican-led Congress. Yet even the fitfully aggressive Democrats, who took charge in 2007, have been largely unable to closely inspect, let alone redirect, Bush's national-security policies. A generation ago, as the Cold War began, a venerable Republican senator declared that, at such times, political debates should stop "at the water's edge." What Senator Arthur Vandenberg meant was that we should vigorously debate our course here at home, then present a united front to the world. But his dictum has been turned inside out in the post-9/11 era. If there is no "water's edge" at all, there is no safe place for free debate.

GET INTO AN ARGUMENT

The impediments to argument are daunting, but not insuperable. All it takes—but what it requires—is involvement. My fourth aim is to encourage voters to commit the most American of acts: to take part in the arguing. The era of proxy participation in public life is over; a new era of direct action has begun.

It is no accident that, as the Web rises, the traditional political parties decline. As the 2008 presidential election approached, there were as many voters registered as "independents" or "unaffiliated" as Democrats or Republicans. Voters have become wary of one-size-fits-all, prix fixe party agendas. Americans pick and choose. I have tried to lay out the menu of arguments as they exist in nature, if you will, independent of the parties that, over the years, have taken (all) sides in them. The political parties have shriveled as conduits for "collective expression," a phrase that has a deservedly musty, twentieth-century feel to it. In the new millennium, voters are taking it upon themselves—and must take it upon themselves—to make their own case. Think of this as a briefing book for a nation of citizen-candidates. The Internet is their campaign trail, *YouTube* their advertising campaign.

Involvement is also an antidote to media "truthiness." As Jamieson of Penn points out, the Internet is allowing a speedier response to false claims in TV ads and false reports on the news. In this new era, everybody is her own fact-checker.

WE'VE BEEN HERE BEFORE

My fifth goal is to offer a sense of perspective in the midst of what, to many, seems like a gloomy period in our national life. The lesson of looking at the Thirteen Arguments and their history is sobering, to be sure: They have a sense of inescapability that can be unnerving, like a political version of Bill Murray's living nightmare in *Groundhog Day*. Immigration is perhaps the most vivid these days, but all of the arguments are alive on the front page. It will always be that way.

On the other hand, it is comforting and inspiring to know, in essence, that We Have Been Here Before—that we have been in similar predicaments and not only survived, but triumphed, working out ways to preserve freedom and yet inch ever closer to the ideals of justice. We have felt overwhelmed by immigrants before, and survived. We have felt threatened by overbearing, secretive presidents in wartime, and survived. We have erupted in bellicosity toward the world, and survived. We have laid waste to our environment, and *it* has survived. The economy and the dollar have been devastated before, and *they* have survived. What is required to move forward is something more than luck. What is required is that we dig deep down into our history to find the countervailing insights and rediscover the enduring ideas that can set us right. It's all in our DNA— the double helix of our contentious and complex history. "There is nothing wrong with America that cannot be cured by what is right with America," Bill Clinton said in his first inaugural address—and he was right.

BE THANKFUL

Last, we need to appreciate our uniqueness, and strive to be worthy of it. We have been blessed with history's best chance to live in the space created by equipoise among the brute forces that forever vie for dominion over mankind in society. In shorthand, they are the State, the Church, the Market, the Tribe, and the Academy (Science). Balance among them produced the golden ages in the history of mankind. But let any of these five forces achieve untrammeled control, and slavery is the inevitable result. So far, we have avoided the fate of Stalin's Soviet Union, the Taliban's Afghanistan, Dickens's London, the Mob's Sicily, or Huxley's Brave New World. Our best hope lies in keeping each of the basic forces forever in countervailing conflict with one another. Let them make accommodation; never let them collude. Freedom exists in the space created by equipoise among them.

There is no such equipoise on most of the planet. From the great cities of China to the mountain caves of Afghanistan, there is no faith in the idea of argument. Most of humanity pays allegiance to only One Eternal

Answer, whether it is a sacred text or a "revolutionary" party. I first saw that dangerous allegiance as a student on a visit to the old Soviet Union in 1970. On my first night in Kiev I checked into a hotel. The spartan room had a desk with a lamp and a modern-looking radio. As I examined the radio more closely I noticed something odd—and chilling. It had no dial, only an "on/volume" switch. I was in a country with only one voice—the government's.

In the never-ending aftermath of Al Qaeda's 9/11 attack, we face constant reminders of the hatred and ferment that face us. Yet in spite of the bloodshed—indeed, because of it—we have to remain willing to argue in good faith among ourselves. We have to prove (again) that argument is strength, not weakness, and that freedom and security can live together.

How do we do so? By making sure that people know they have a chance to be heard. The American way breeds unsettling conflict, but argument is what leads to consent, and consent is what leads to legitimacy. People accept outcomes that they deplore, because they think the process gives their point of view a chance.

As long as we argue, there is hope, and as long as there is hope, we will argue. In *Democracy in America,* Alexis de Tocqueville saw genius in this. "To take a hand in the regulation of society," he said, was our "biggest concern and, so to speak, the only pleasure an American knows." This "ceaseless agitation," he wrote, creates an "all-pervading and restless activity, a superabundant force, and an energy which is inseparable from it and which may, however unfavorable circumstances may be, produce wonders. These," he concluded, "are the true advantages of democracy."

The "ceaseless agitation" is what this book is about. It's the story of the Thirteen American Arguments.

One

WHO IS A PERSON?

The sky was cloudless that sunny morning in Springfield, the air was so brutally cold it felt almost viscous—so cold you could barely think. As far as Senator Barack Obama of Illinois was concerned, the temperature did not matter. He was oblivious to it in his elegant wool overcoat. Springfield, capital of Illinois, was where he wanted to be—needed to be—on that frigid February 11, 2007. It was there, he knew, that he had begun his political career as a state legislator only a decade earlier. It was there, he knew, that another Illinois legislator, Abraham Lincoln, had asked a question that ultimately led to the deadliest, most profound argument in American history: Is everyone, including a black man, a person? And it was there, in Springfield, that Obama hoped to begin a quest that would answer the question emphatically by making him the first African American to win the White House.

In a personal sense, Obama's trip to Springfield was a political homecoming. A mixed-race son of Kenya and Kansas, he had lived in many places—Hawaii, Indonesia, Los Angeles, New York City, and Cambridge—before finally finding love and identity on the South Side of Chicago in the security and striving of its fabled black community. His wife, Michelle Robinson, was a Princeton-educated pride of the neighborhood and, like Obama, a graduate of Harvard Law School. He settled down to build the foundation of a political career as a community organizer, civil rights lawyer, and law professor. In 1996, he was elected to the state senate from the South Side, and quickly made a name for himself in

Springfield. Like Lincoln, he was a tall, gangly fellow with a wry sense of humor and a knack for speeches, deals, and poker.

But was he like Lincoln in other ways? Did he in fact need to be? Now, after spending a mere two years in the U.S. Senate, Obama was back in Springfield with a message of national unity. He wanted to make racial history, but this time, paradoxically, by ending our national preoccupation with it once and for all.

The story of Springfield gave reason for both hope and caution. In Springfield, Lincoln had transformed himself from an easygoing shopkeeper into an inspiring politician. As a state legislator, he had become a champion of a cause—the Cause—of ending a system of slavery that, at its root, denied the basic, elemental humanity of the people it enslaved. With increasing sophistication and determination, he argued that slavery, as entrenched and familiar as it was, violated the central idea upon which this country had been founded: that all souls—not just white male citizens of the United States of America—were entitled to personhood, dignity, and the respect of their fellow men. This is our first and most fundamental American Argument: Who, in our constitutional scheme, is a "person"?

Lincoln won the cause and the war that flowed from it, but not necessarily the hearts of the country. Springfield's story was sometimes as ugly as it was uplifting. Forty-three years after Lincoln's death it was the scene of a shocking, murderous race riot. In the fall of 1908, a black man accused of having raped a white woman was spirited out of town by local police worried for his safety. News of his transfer spread to an angry crowd, which metastasized into a mob that rampaged through the city. The crowds overwhelmed the police; the governor sent in the Guard to restore order. At least four blacks died.

This Springfield story alarmed the country: a race riot in Lincoln's hometown in the historically antislavery state of Illinois. The lesson was clear. While civil rights for blacks existed in theory, they did not exist in fact. A few months later, spurred by the Springfield riot, a new civil rights group held its first full organizational meeting. The National Association for the Advancement of Colored People (NAACP) dates its founding in 1909 from Lincoln's birthday, February 12.

Now, on the eve of Lincoln's birthday, Obama stepped forward. The spot he chose was the lawn of the old state capitol, a Greek Revival edifice of worn golden sandstone. His advance team built a stage that would allow him to be framed in the morning light against the backdrop of the templelike building. They cordoned off the streets to squeeze the crowd—most of it young, much of it adoring—against the office buildings and storefronts on the capitol square.

When it came time for the speech, the candidate appeared with his wife and two little girls at his side. "Lincoln's will and his words," Obama said, "moved a nation and freed a people. It is because men and women of every race, from every walk of life, continued to march for freedom long after Lincoln was laid to rest, that today we have the chance to face the challenges of this millennium together, as one people—as Americans." Cheers echoed off the flag-draped buildings.

Once again, the people of Springfield were witnesses to the history of an ongoing American Argument. This new chapter had less to do with Obama's campaign per se than with the larger narrative that it evoked, and the question that it asked once again. Obama did not stress his own racial heritage. He was not running a "race-based" campaign—just the opposite. Nevertheless, in earlier times, a man who looked like Obama might well have been chased down the streets of Springfield. A war had been fought in the name of assuring him, and those like him, equal rights. And yet here he was, in effect, asking the crowd and the country: "Are we really 'one people'?" That Obama was the candidate posing the question showed how far we had come. That he was posing it at all showed how far we still needed to travel.

Ann Richards, the treasurer of Texas, prided herself on being one imperturbable lady. She wore her silver hair in a mile-high beehive and cloaked herself in the distantly amused, I've-seen-it-all-before demeanor of a truck stop waitress in Waco, where she grew up. And yet here she was, at fifty years of age, in the back row of the Texas delegation to the 1984 Democratic convention in San Francisco—crying. Rivulets of tears streamed down her face as she waited for what she knew would be a historic moment. The lights dimmed in the hall. *Chariots of Fire* music washed over the crowd. Suddenly, out of the darkness, a lively blonde with a winsome smile materialized onstage. She wore an elegant white suit, which made her more visible and somehow almost sacramental as she stood alone in the blue-white glare of the spotlights. She waved as the party faithful set up a thunderous cheer and an announcer said: "The next vice president of the United States, the Honorable Geraldine Ferraro!"

More cheers—and more tears in the Texas delegation. "I didn't think I'd live to see this," Richards said to no one in particular. "Lordy."

Ferraro, a New York congresswoman, went on to lose, of course, the lower half of a Democratic ticket with Walter Mondale that was flattened (losing forty-nine of fifty states) by Ronald Reagan's "Morning in America" reelection campaign against what he called "the San Francisco Democrats." Still, Ferraro's star turn was a milestone reached and a fire lit. She was the first woman on a major ticket in American history, and she inspired a new wave of women to enter politics and to move fully and finally out of electoral shadows and into the sunlight of full legal and political personhood in the American scheme of things. Among the women inspired by Ferraro that night were a San Francisco party activist named Nancy Pelosi and the spouse of the governor of Arkansas, a lawyer named Hillary Rodham Clinton. As for Richards, within six years of that night in San Francisco, she was sworn in as governor of the great state of Texas. "But nothing topped that Ferraro night," she told me.

For women, it had been a long road from the Philadelphia of the Founders to the Bay Area of the 1980s. Whatever the men who gathered in the State House in 1776 thought about women, the Founding Wives thought it was rather less than full personhood in the eyes of the law and the country. In early America, as in England, women could not vote and a married woman in particular was lacking in legal rights, unable to control property or even her own marital destiny in most cases in most courts. Women were essentially barred from a college education or much education at all.

This did not sit well with, among others, Abigail Adams, whose husband, John, was helping to forge the country's independence in 1776. "[I] would desire that you remember the Ladies," she tartly wrote him in Philadelphia, "and be more generous and favorable to them than your ancestors." Her plea came with a sharp warning. "If particular care and attention is not paid to the Ladies," Abigail wrote, "we are determined to foment a Rebellion, and will not hold ourselves bound by any Laws in which we have no voice or representation." Those were fighting words, and it was a long fight. In fact, it took nearly a century and a half for women to win a constitutional right to vote, and nearly that long for them to fully escape the bonds of legal tradition and social custom that viewed them as children, or chattel, or both.

No sooner had one fight essentially ended than another one began.

For many women, a logical and necessary feature of American person-hood was the right to control the functioning of their own bodies—even and especially as that related to childbearing. But when their theory was accepted by the U.S. Supreme Court in *Roe v. Wade* in 1973, a new cultural war arose, this one between abortion-rights supporters (among them Richards, Ferraro, Pelosi, and Clinton) and the foes of the medical procedure, who insisted that life (and personhood) began at conception, and abortion was a form of murder. In the end, science may moot the issue by making the termination of a pregnancy almost instantaneous, self-administered, and virtually undetectable. In the meantime, however, advances in science and genetics are raising an equally profound question: Who controls, and who *should* control, the genetic destiny of mankind?

Those questions were distant thunder on the day that the San Francisco matron—now Rep. Nancy Pelosi of California—was sworn in as the first female Speaker of the House in January 2007. Viewed from the press gallery in the House of Representatives, the event looked like Washington's largest family reunion, as Pelosi's extended family and other children gathered around her on the Speaker's rostrum. "This is an historic moment," she said, "for the women of this country. It is a moment for which we have waited more than two hundred years. For our daughters and granddaughters, today we have broken the marble ceiling. For our daughters and granddaughters, the sky is the limit." Two weeks later, an Arkansas political spouse—now Senator Hillary Clinton of New York—announced her candidacy for president and later told students at her alma mater, Wellesley College, that she was "ready to shatter the highest glass ceiling." Soon after that, Ferraro—long since retired, but still active—endorsed Hillary. By electing the senator from New York, she declared, "we can smash the ultimate glass ceiling once and for all." As she campaigned for the nomination, Hillary targeted female voters—now a 54 percent majority of the electorate—and moved around Iowa and New Hampshire with her mother and daughter in tow. Clinton did not have to talk about abortion rights. None of the Democrats did: They all agreed that such rights were enshrined in the Constitution. (The Republicans did not discuss the issue either: Every one of their candidates was "pro-life.")

Had she lived, Richards would have been out there campaigning for Hillary Clinton. The former governor passed away only a few months before the senator launched her bid. At the funeral services in Austin, folksinger Nanci Griffith sang "Across the Great Divide." Richards had crossed several in her life, and there was not a dry eye in the place. Even Hillary shed a tear, a friend later said, and that was rare.

Who is a person? As the first country created by "the People" in the name of "the People," our first question (even if we do not always acknowledge it) is: Who is entitled to be regarded as a full-fledged human being within the meaning of our law?

Our first founding document requires us to ask, answer, and argue this question. In the Declaration of Independence, Thomas Jefferson anchored a new nation on the rock of a single, revolutionary, but to him "self-evident" truth: that all men are created equal. This was not self-evident to everyone, however, and we have always debated—and even gone to war over—the proposition. As devoted as we claim to be to the Jeffersonian ideal, America has an equally deep penchant for denying what we now call "human rights." In the search for profit or political power, in the fervency of faith and fear, we have limited or ignored the legal personhood—even the elemental humanity—of a long list of people, from Native Americans to alleged terrorists.

It's a paradox that fires this first American Argument. Jefferson himself was the living embodiment of it. Who is a "person" in our eyes and Constitution? As a leader, Jefferson said "everyone," and yet as a slave master, he said "not everyone." In 1857 the U.S. Supreme Court ruled that slaves could not be persons in the eyes of the Constitution, sparking a civil war that lasted, in cultural form, until at least a generation after Martin Luther King Jr.

Other, newer versions of the age-old argument arose, and arise still. Were women entitled to full personhood in the eyes of the law? It took them generations to progress from what amounted to legal chattel to full-fledged citizens. Are you fully a person if you are not allowed to "marry" in the eyes of the law? Are corporations "persons" with legal rights? Perhaps only in America, the land that puts "personhood" at the center of the universe, would that be a question. The answer: Yes, corporations *are* persons in American law. Do we really want to be "one America," as Obama put it?

What about groups for whom personhood is a settled issue, at least in terms of the law? Do we owe them for their suffering? Do we owe them preference in hiring or education? And what do we do when some persons insist on their claim to separateness—which used to be considered a sure mark of inferiority? What happens when a focus on human rights turns into the kind of "identity politics" that dwells on differences of race, gender, ethnicity, or sexual orientation? Don't our founding ideals require that we ignore such distinctions? Is there such a status as personhood-plus? Are we really "one America"?

We the People wrote our own earliest guiding documents: the statutes drafted in Jamestown, Virginia, in the summer of 1619, and the compact written on the high seas as the *Mayflower* sailed the Atlantic in 1620. They were not dictates or directives, but rather the product of the collective judgment of individuals, voluntarily assembled. A century and a half later, the Declaration of Independence, the Constitution, and the Bill of Rights established the world's first government predicated upon the freely given consent of the People—not upon the dictates of a church, royalty, plutocrats, or conquering tribes.

But not every "self" could participate in self-government. There were, from the start, others who did not count, who could not be part of the community, who were not fully human or at least capable of receiving God's grace. Each of the fundamental forces of society had its own reasons for deciding who was, or was not, a person.

In much of New England, the Church took that decisive role. In the Massachusetts Bay Colony, only Protestant Christians could live in Winthrop's City on a Hill. The Bay Colony's roster of laws, written in 1641, rang with impressive declarations of individual rights, but they applied only to members of that specific religious community. You faced death if you were found praying in an unapproved way. It was not until the Constitution was ratified that the Church in the broadest sense was barred from exercising legal authority in the debate.

Most colonies were in the main commercial ventures (or so their sponsors hoped), and in them the Market played the largest role in defining personhood. Market forces encouraged men to mortgage their freedom in exchange for their labor. The indenture was at least theoretically voluntary, and had an end point. "Chattel" slavery—"chattel" as in the old legal meaning of "personal goods" that could be sold, mortgaged, or destroyed— was something else entirely. Slaves, who first arrived in Jamestown in 1619, quickly became the foundation of plantation economies of tobacco, rice, and cotton. The men who enslaved them usually considered them to be little more than units of energy, alive but all but insensate.

Tribal instincts have shaped the meaning of personhood, too. The idea of the tribe was well known, even sacred to the first European immigrants, not to mention the Native Americans who came across the land bridge from Asia thousands of years earlier. Our ancestors studied the tribes, the Iroquois Federation in particular, for clues on how to organize a government in the wilderness. They revered the Old Testament, with its stories of the Twelve Tribes of ancient Israel.

There was nobility and respect in tribal thinking, but also the seeds of what we came to call racism. We were among the first modern nations to sort people by skin color—white, red, black, brown, and yellow—and to decide which colors were entitled to legal respect. The decision often was a brutal "none." We invented dismissive names for the rejects, from "red savages" to "coolies" to "wetbacks."

In the South, especially, the forces of the Market and the Tribe combined to enshrine race-based attitudes. In 1640, the "border" colony of Maryland became the first to formally enshrine chattel slavery. But the South was not alone. In 1641, Massachusetts—two centuries later the home of the abolition movement—gave credence to slavery by agreeing that slaves could be purchased there and kept as such. In typically high-minded fashion, the *Massachusetts Body of Liberties* declared that slaves would have "all the liberties and Christian usages which the law of God established in Israel concerning such persons doth morally require." In other words, the Bible had rules about the handling of slaves. We will follow them, which means that, in practical terms, slavery is acceptable to us, too.

Slavery was the snake in the garden of freedom, as Tocqueville put it. It produced arguments—and rebellions—from the beginning. In 1676, a group of black and white bonded laborers rebelled against the planter class in Virginia, shutting down tobacco production. After the revolt was crushed by a British naval bombardment, a new British policy emerged, dividing laborers into two groups: whites who could earn their freedom and blacks who could not. Author Theodore Allen saw this as the key moment in what he labeled "the Invention of the White Race." The tribe that ran the economy, so Allen's argument went, had to find a theory by which to declare forced labor an acceptable burden for an *un*human other tribe. It was the only way to square the moral circle of slavery in a free society, and a way to divide working men against each other.

A century after Bacon's Rebellion, the Founders in Philadelphia drafted a Constitution in the name of "We the People." But it excluded more than a million souls from the legal rolls of humanity. For the purposes of counting the census (and apportioning the power of the states in the union), the Founders decided that each black would count as three-fifths of a person. Academics furiously debate the political intent of this deal. Was it to limit the power of Virginia and the rest of the South, or to enhance it? But the threshold question of whether slaves were to be considered citizens was never considered inside the State House. The silence said everything. The deafening explosion occurred eighty years later in the Civil War. Nearly a million people were killed or wounded or died of disease—an odd, eerie balance in the arithmetic of human sympathy.

It fell to Lincoln to lead the prewar debate, when it finally materialized, in all of its deadly intensity. In Springfield, in the 1850s, he found his voice as he stood up to, and against, the most popular and powerful politician in the state at that time, Democratic senator Stephen Douglas. Their dispute seemed, at first glance, almost a technical one. Trying to bridge growing gaps in his party between Democrats in the slave-owning South and white farmers elsewhere in the country, Douglas argued that each new state had the right to exercise its own "popular sovereignty" on the question of whether it would allow slavery to exist within its borders. It was a clever and powerful argument, based, as it seemed to be, on the will of the people.

Lincoln worked hard to prepare an answer. He unveiled it at the fairgrounds in Springfield in the fall of 1854, and two weeks later in a speech in Peoria. Lincoln was no radical; he wasn't an "abolitionist," in the sense that he did not suggest that slavery be ended in the slaveholding states. He expressed sympathy for the South. But in opposing Douglas he was forced to (and perhaps wanted to) make a far more sweeping argument. It was within Congress's power—indeed, its moral duty—to ban slavery in new states. Why? Because Jefferson's Declaration said so.

In Lincoln's view, Jefferson was First Among Founders. To Lincoln, the Old State House in Philadelphia was a sacred place not because the Constitution had been written there, but because Jefferson's Declaration had been launched from there. "I have never had a political feeling," Lincoln said in Philadelphia in 1861, "that did not spring from the sentiments embodied" in the Declaration that had been announced in that city.

The essence of the Declaration—and, therefore, of America—was its statement about universal personhood. Against that, Douglas's view could not stand. "The doctrine of self-government is right," Lincoln agreed, but not in the case of slavery. The just application of it, he said, "depends on whether a negro is *not* or *is* a man. . . . If the negro *is* a man, why then my ancient faith teaches me that 'all men are created equal,' and that there can be no moral right in connection with one man's making a slave of another."

That was the question: Who was a man? Who was a person? All the rest flowed from that. Nine years after Springfield and Peoria, when Lincoln rose to address the mourners at Gettysburg, he did not date the birth of the nation to the ratification of the Constitution. "Four score and seven years" meant 1776.

The civil rights movement of the 1950s and 1960s ensured that the legal promises that had been made a century earlier—full citizenship rights for blacks—would become reality nationwide. In terms of constitutional rights and practice, the argument over black personhood is settled, though even now the detritus of slavery remains, whether in the dismal health and education statistics of the Cotton Belt or northern inner cities. By the 1980s, a new generation of African Americans had arisen, products of the nation's finest universities. Some of them chose to work in those downtrodden places. One of them—educated at Columbia and Harvard Law—was Barack Obama.

The way things work in America, no sooner do we settle one version of an Argument than another emerges. The question, so essential to our society, remains the same. These days Science, not Tribe, drives the debate, and the central actors are not African Americans, but women.

As science enabled women to gain control of their own bodies, including control over pregnancy—and as women in general began insisting on equal rights—abortion emerged as our most emotional personhood dispute. Some think that abortion has divided American society as deeply as slavery once did. That is an overstatement, but to the extent that it is true, it is because both issues touch on the most fundamental question of American society, individual rights.

In the 1973 case of *Roe v. Wade,* Supreme Court Justice Harry Blackmun grounded a woman's access to an abortion in the idea that the Constitution contained a right of individual privacy. Included within that, he wrote, was her right to control her own physical being under most circumstances. To those who supported the Court's decision, nothing could be more obvious. For women to enjoy their full rights as human beings, they necessarily were entitled to full control over their person, to put it literally.

But what if *two* persons were involved? Rather than *oppose* the rights of women per se, anti-abortion activists spawned a "pro-life" movement to support a concept they regarded as not only noble but constitutionally required: rights for the "unborn," whose "right to life," in most circumstances, took precedence over the privacy rights of the mother. In the eyes of pro-lifers, the more than 40 million abortions since 1973 add up to an unprecedented slaughter.

To buttress their case, they drew a parallel between *Roe* and the Supreme Court's infamous *Dred Scott* decision of 1857, which declared that, at the time of the ratification of the Constitution, slaves were, in the words of Justice Roger B. Taney, "a subordinate and inferior class of beings, who had been subjugated by the dominant race . . . and, therefore, remained subject to their authority and had no rights or privileges." *Dred Scott* had long since been discredited as a low point in America's moral and political life. *Roe,* the right-to-lifers argued, should, and one day would, be seen in the same light.

Abortion supporters noted that the Court had for many decades recognized that the State had an interest in controlling pregnancies—at least of the mentally incapacitated. "Three generations of imbeciles are enough," Justice Oliver Wendell Holmes had famously declared. But the very coldness of that statement—and the hint of eugenics theory that lay behind it—did the pro-choice advocates little good.

Thus began a new Civil War, not as bloody as the first, but in some ways just as urgent and divisive. Science affords us the power to see into the womb and manipulate what is going on there, and in so doing makes the dispute more acute. The "pro-life" movement made the suddenly, vividly visible fetus the focus of their attention. Abortion-rights advocates invoke medical technology, too, observing that no early-term fetus—that is, one less than nineteen weeks old—has ever survived outside the womb. If you can't survive on your own, are you a person?

Pushed ahead by technology, new issues surface with blinding speed. Is a human blastocyst, the first tiny cluster of cells created by the fertilization of the egg, a person in any legal sense if it can be made to grow outside the womb for a while? Would not a cloned human being—more than a theoretical possibility at this point—be a person like any other, indeed exactly like another? New drugs can short-circuit pregnancy or prevent it altogether by preventing the fertilized egg from attaching to the wall of the uterus. Is a homeless blastocyst a person, too, or a person at all?

Now that science has unlocked the bond between reproduction and sex, and now that the human genetic code has been mapped, humankind has the godlike power to engineer its own biology. Who will control the *creation* of personhood? At the other end of life's arc, doctors now can keep alive indefinitely a soul in a "persistent vegetative state." When, if ever, does a person cease to be one? Science keeps shifting the ground beneath the personhood debate.

G ary Bauer is an owlish, gnomelike fellow from modest, blue-collar roots in Kentucky. But as meek as he looks, he is a lion in the ranks of longtime evangelical Christian activists. He worked as their liaison in the Reagan White House, pushing their uncompromising, faith-based views on the issues. He explained his positions in a mild, apologetic manner, but compromise was not his style. In 2000, he watched the field for the GOP presidential nomination shaping up without someone that he regarded as a staunch "pro-life" candidate. So he got into the race, presenting himself as the purest of the pure. He was an armadillo on the George Bush Highway, with a half million dollars to spend, compared with the Texas governor's $100 million. Bauer's candidacy literally flopped in New Hampshire when he fell from the stage during a pancake-flipping contest. He never did catch up with the pancake.

In the argument about personhood, however, Bauer was a pivotal figure, part of a cadre of "pro-life" conservatives who worked diligently to transport the language of civil rights—and the cause of individual rights—to the cause of the human "unborn." In the process, he helped turn the concept into political orthodoxy for millions of Americans, especially Republican politicians whose chances depended on the support of evangelicals and conservative Catholics.

Bauer's first and most potent ally in the crusade against abortion was President Reagan. Earlier in his career, the former governor of California had been better known for his other enemies-of-choice—taxes, the Soviet Union, student demonstrators at Berkeley—than for abortion. Still, Reagan and his advisers sensed the power of the issue at the GOP's grass roots in the aftermath of the *Roe v. Wade* decision in 1973. It was his supporters, not those of President Gerald Ford, who pushed the Republican Party to make its 1976 platform the first to call for a constitutional amendment protecting "the right to life for unborn children." Four years later, when Reagan won the GOP nomination, he insisted on only one condition when he offered the position of vice presidential running mate to George H. W. Bush. Reagan demanded that Bush switch his position on abortion from pro to anti. Bush complied.

As president, Reagan took on the role of pro-life mouthpiece in a series of writings geared to his reelection campaign. In 1983, a periodical called the *Human Life Review* published an essay, said to have been written by Reagan, which made the *Dred Scott* comparison and declared, "Make no mistake, abortion on demand is not a right granted by the Constitution." A "right to life," he added, was. Later that year, the essay was published as a book titled *Abortion and the Conscience of the Nation*. It remains the only book ever published by a president while in office. Bauer told me years later that he and other pro-lifers in the Reagan inner circle wrote most of the book, with Reagan serving in the role of editor, or, more accurately, speech-giver.

Bauer returned to the right-to-life theme in his short-lived campaign. He had just enough cash to shoot one TV ad in the run-up to the Iowa caucuses. It featured him standing alone in front of the Lincoln Memorial, cradling an infant in his arms. Lincoln had freed the slaves, Bauer said; now he, Bauer, would free the unborn to be born. "I really moved up quickly in the polls right after that ad," he insisted, though there is no record of such a surge. "Then I ran out of money."

Even so, the movement did not run out of clout—and neither did the other side. The abortion crosswinds can shred the career of politicians who try to satisfy both camps, especially if they try to move from one to the other. One such hapless character was Rep. Dick Gephardt of Missouri. He began as a foe of abortion, but over two decades in national politics, he inched his way to the other side. In the run-up to the 2000 Democratic presidential primary, he knew that he had to recant fully, unequivocally, to satisfy the pro-choice activists. He chose the right place to do it: the annual meeting in Washington of the National Abortion Rights Action League (NARAL).

Gephardt's performance was akin to that of a newly saved soul at a revival meeting, only a secular one. He was the sinner, onstage to confess the error of his ways, vowing to do right by the Lord, or in this case, the lord of women's rights as measured by abortion rights. "I have been on a path," he said with as much fervor as his staid Midwestern mien would allow. "It has taken me a long time to see that I was wrong." I half expected the audience to shout "Hallelujah!" Instead the crowd applauded politely, and turned their attention to candidates they regarded as the more pure of heart. Gephardt was the first Democrat to quit the race.

Yet another version of the personhood argument emerged after the terrorist attacks of September 11, 2001. The question this time was: Are "unlawful enemy combatants," the stateless, shadowy figures who perpetrated the crimes, "persons" in the eyes of American law and society? Once again, Americans felt an instinct to say no, this time not because the Market told us so, or because a Faith tradition did, but because our State and Tribal instincts did. We knew that the "combatants," the detainees, were not American citizens, but were they entitled to such rights as due process of law, habeas corpus, and a public jury trial? Indeed, could they be tried by a jury of their "peers" if we did not consider them persons?

The legal response of George W. Bush's administration to this nettlesome clutch of questions was blunt, swift, and sweepingly sure: Unlawful, "stateless" enemy combatants were not only beyond the reach of our constitutional law, but even (just for good measure) of international law as embodied in the Geneva convention, which, the administration argued, was designed to address the rights of traditional military forces in national uniform.

American courts, Bush's attorneys argued, had no jurisdiction over such people—only the president did, in his role as commander in chief or, through his authority, the United States military. The administration cited as precedent the actions of President Franklin Delano Roosevelt in World War II. He convened a secret military tribunal to hear the "case" of the German commandos who had stealthily come ashore from a U-boat in New Jersey in 1942. Their "trial" featured none of the usual procedural protections, and they were quickly executed. Bush claimed the authority, if necessary, to do the same thing.

The Supreme Court, in 2004 and 2006, said otherwise, insisting that the federal courts had the power to hear pleas from such "unlawful enemy combatants," who enjoyed at least minimal due-process rights. In other words, they were people, too. The Court ordered a reluctant Congress to decide how to proceed. The Congress did so, kicking the matter back to the military—but the point had been made.

Or so we think.

Like the universe, the meaning of personhood is expanding. We make progress fitfully. Sometimes we measure it in generations—by fathers and sons, among them the Reverend Jesse Jackson Jr. and Jesse Jackson III, a congressman from Illinois. The arc of their lives and minds shows how far we have come.

The father was on center stage in Washington for decades. He debuted on the Washington Mall in 1968 at the Poor People's March, eventually becoming the only presidential contender I ever covered who made the idea of self-worth—of full personhood in the eyes of the law and the country—his main message. In the fall of 1981, he had been invited to address a rally of labor union members, gathered on that same Washington Mall to protest what they regarded as the antilabor policies of President Reagan. Perhaps a half million—most of them male, most of them white, most of them middle-class steelworkers and carpenters and miners—had driven or been bused into the capital for a "Solidarity Day" rally.

Jackson was an unlikely figure to be addressing such a crowd. They distrusted him. He was, to begin with, black. Worse, from their point of view, he had a reputation as a loudmouth, and eagerly added to it whenever he could. Furthermore, Jackson was a professional agitator. Labor guys had once been agitators, too, but not this crew. By 1981 they had comfortable lives to protect: a middle-class wage, job security, maybe even a motorboat on a lake in the country. Worst of all, Jackson was not even a union member, and never had been. "Who invited *this* guy?" I remember one carpenter shouting to no one in particular.

To all of this, Jackson was oblivious. He was his own message. Head high, shoulders set, back arched, he strode gravely to the podium with a defiantly regal air. Commandeering the microphone, he bellowed his diatribe against the Reagan administration, denouncing it as a sweeping assault on the New Deal consensus that Labor had helped to construct and defend for half a century.

Then, pausing dramatically, he launched into a singsong of the civil rights era. "Now I want you to repeat after me," he shouted. " 'I AM . . . SOMEBODY!' That is right! 'I AM . . . SOMEBODY!' Say it with me now: 'I AM . . . SOMEBODY!' "

A confused, embarrassed silence ensued. The Pittsburgh steelworkers, blue-collar royalty, did not like the idea of being treated as if they
were invisible, oppressed nonpersons, in, say, Alabama. Jackson persisted.
Like any other successful and charismatic pol (a certain Arkansan comes
to mind), he was born without the gene that produces the emotion of em-
barrassment in the human soul. " 'I AM . . . SOMEBODY!' " he shouted. " 'I
AM SOMEBODY!' " Eventually, a smattering of laborers took up the chant.
Then more of them did, until, finally—against their will—steelworkers
were declaring what they already knew, but of which Jackson, deep
down, seemed never to have been quite sure.

Everyone was somebody.

A quarter century later, I visited his son, Jesse Jackson III, in his Capitol Hill office suite near that same Mall. The walls were covered from eye
level to ceiling with family photos, including images of the man he called,
with needling affection, "The Rev." His father had long since become an
Establishment figure, an icon to his admirers. His father was now comfortable financially, in part from the fruits of "advising" corporations
eager to keep racial peace with their employees and their customers. He
sent his sons to Washington's St. Albans, a private school that educated
many of the children of the capital's elite.

By 2006, the Poor People's March had long since come and gone
(though the disparity between incomes of whites and blacks remained
glaringly wide, and had even grown wider). In the years since Solidarity
Day, union membership had shrunk from a quarter of the American
workforce to barely 13 percent. In the meantime, a new black generation
had arisen, including "Jesse Junior." Others were rising fast: Mayor Cory
Booker of Newark, New Jersey, and Reps. Harold Ford Jr. of Tennessee
and Artur Davis of Alabama. Then there was Condoleezza Rice, secretary of state. There were Rhodes Scholars and graduates of Harvard,
Yale, Columbia, Stanford, and the universities of Pennsylvania and
Michigan. And, of course, there was Barack Obama, soon to be a senator,
and then the first truly major African American candidate for president
of the United States.

Besides their youth and, in some cases, Ivy League pedigrees, this new
generation had something else "the Rev" lacked: a sense of comfort in
their own skin. On my visit to Junior's office, he pointed to a picture from
his high school years at St. Albans. The thickly built younger Jackson was
in a football uniform, apparently after a winning performance. His

mother and sister were hugging and kissing him; the Rev was beaming with pride. It was a tableau of all-American acceptance. The picture was taken in the fall of 1981, the same season in which his father was down on the Mall, invoking the universal struggle to be "SOMEBODY."

In politics, Jesse Senior was the most visible American black figure of the late twentieth century, yet he embodied the striving to be seen, to be unarguably *there*—to be something more than the "invisible man" depicted by Ralph Ellison in his famous novel of that name. In 1981, the father had been repeating the mantra to himself—for himself. At least that is what his son thought. "What he said on the Mall was sad and amazing," Junior told me. "Here's my dad, 120 years after the Civil War, feeling the need to declare that he was a person. And he felt it and meant it: Until everyone can think of themselves as a person with a capital 'P,' we won't be there." Junior had arrived, or so it seemed, and so had Barack Obama.

But are we there yet?

Two

WHO IS AN AMERICAN?

The Republican senator was moving—fast—down a crowded hallway of the Omni Shoreham in Washington, D.C. He looked ill and under siege, his wife, a fellow fleeing refugee, at his side. Senator George Allen of Virginia was at the hotel for a routine drop-by with his Christian conservative allies. At the time, September 2006, he was the insiders' favorite for the GOP's 2008 presidential nomination. A former Southern governor with gruff charm and a hard-core voting record, Allen had a gift for talking football (he was the son of a famous coach), faith, and family. He was thought to be the Bush-like guy to carry the standard of George W. Bush.

Instead, Allen literally was being engulfed by crisis, and the Republican Party that Bush and Karl Rove had built suddenly wanted nothing to do with him. Allen's lofty political expectations were evaporating in the heat of a campaign-trail gaffe he had committed a few days before as he was campaigning in rural southwestern Virginia for reelection. It had not taken long for the press to bestow upon the event legendary status and a Ludlumesque name: "the 'macaca' incident." It would ruin Allen's career, but it had a deeper significance. It was a dramatic, instructive example of the power of an enduring American Argument over immigration.

At the start of the twenty-first century, the largest tide of immigration in a century—some 40 million souls arriving in a one-decade period, a third of them illegally—was inundating Virginia and the rest of America. Fear of the economic and social consequences, especially of "illegals," was rampant, but so, too, was the realization that the new wave of want-to-be Americans was our best hope for a new burst of creativity and a renewal of global competitiveness.

Allen seemed oblivious to all of this. His eventual demise was rooted in his failure to comprehend (or remember) how immigration had changed his state. For most of its four centuries, Virginia had been relatively isolated from waves of immigration. The first wave to reach the Old Dominion—starting in the seventeenth century with the English and continuing through the Scotch-Irish in the eighteenth—was basically the last. The other early wave, of course, was an involuntary one: African Americans who arrived in slave vessels. For most of its history, Virginia was a study in black and white, with the descendants of pioneers and slaves on opposite sides.

The state's demographics, however, had been transformed since the 1970s, especially in the burgeoning Washington suburbs. The first new arrivals were South Vietnamese, settling in what came to be called Little Saigon. They were refugees from the war we had waged and lost in their homeland. Next to arrive were educated Indians, Pakistanis, and other South Asians, drawn by a world-class high-tech Internet corridor spawned by the Pentagon and spin-off communications companies. Large numbers of Hispanic immigrants filled the growing ranks of service jobs needed to make the new suburbs livable.

This was the polychromatic Virginia Allen ignored when he appeared one late-August day at a sunny campaign picnic in the far southern corner of the state. A "tracker" was on his tail. In the high-def, handheld-video era, every campaign sent one to record the opposing candidate's every public utterance. The campaign of Allen's Democratic opponent, former Navy secretary James Webb, had done so. More interesting and, in the end, more fateful, was the identity of the "tracker" Webb sent: one S. R. Sidarth, a student at the University of Virginia. He was a math whiz, a political junkie, and, at 6′4″, a former defensive end on his high school football team. Sidarth had pursued his responsibilities so diligently throughout the campaign that he became a familiar figure on the trail, though Allen did not know his name.

He would learn soon enough. At the event near the Kentucky border, Allen decided to use the "tracker" as a stage prop, a foil for bolstering his credentials as an Old South "Southside" simpatico. Extolling the virtues of life in America, Allen pointed at Sidarth with a slightly menacing smile. "So, welcome, let's give a welcome to Macaca here! Welcome to America and the real world of Virginia!"

Here is a rule in politics: If you are going to say something suicidally insulting, do not do it while looking at a video camera operated by the person you're insulting, especially if that person works for the campaign of your opponent. Soon enough, the video was on *YouTube,* news websites, and every other place in Digitalia. Pressed to defend himself, Allen claimed he had no idea that "macaca" was a French colonial slur ("monkey") for dark-skinned locals in such countries as Tunisia, where, perhaps not coincidentally, Allen's mother had lived much of her early life. Not a lot of people believed the senator's explanation.

"I really didn't mean anything by it," he announced to no one in particular as he hurried along to his meeting of conservative activists. "I really didn't. I was just making what I thought was a joke. The media's made way too much of it, of course," he added with a bitter grimace. "I've apologized every way I can think of."

He had stepped on two land mines. One of them was race, of course. As it happened, Allen had a controversial history of fondness for the symbols of the Confederate South, particularly the Stars and Bars. Now he seemed to be making fun of "Sid" (which is what his friends called him), because of the color of his skin. But, more important, Allen had insulted the state's *immigrants*—specifically, the large, prosperous Indian American community in Washington's northern Virginia suburbs. And Sid, it turned out, was their unofficial favorite son.

It would have been hard to find someone who was a more appealing advertisement for the virtues of immigration or the promise of immigrants. Sid was a descendant of Indian political and business royalty. His great-grandfather had accompanied Mahatma Gandhi on missions to London. His grandfather was secretary of the World Health Organization in the 1990s. His father came to America in the early 1980s, and had become a successful investment banker. As for Sid, he had been an academic and athletic star at Thomas Jefferson High School in Fairfax County—one of the best science-oriented schools in the nation in one of the most affluent counties in the nation. He was the new Best and Brightest.

Ironically, the Republican Party had been making inroads in these communities, which tended to like GOP economic thinking and, if they were not Muslim, Allen's approach to the "war on terror."

Allen, realizing way too late that he couldn't have picked a worse target, frantically set about trying to make amends. He met with every Indian American and Asian American group in northern Virginia that would have him. He apologized publicly, and repeatedly.

Outreach didn't help. Nothing else did, either. On election day, Allen lost northern Virginia big, including the heavily immigrant Asian and South Asian precincts. "Sidarth was the kid next door," concluded the online magazine *Salon*. "He, not Allen, was the real Virginian."

Only a "nation of immigrants" could argue so earnestly and endlessly (and sometimes violently) about who can become one of its own. That is so even though—or rather, because—all of our ancestors arrived in some sense as foreigners. America has never had "open" borders, at least not intentionally. Sometimes the door slams shut. Through four hundred years, we have endeavored to shape and manage the flow of immigrants. As individuals, we want to protect our own identity, customs, and economic prerogatives. As Americans, we often take aggressive pride in them because they are so comparatively new; and yet, as a country, we have a ravenous hunger for new blood, new workers, new minds, and new perspectives.

The result is an enduring American Argument. From William Penn to George Bush, business-minded leaders have sought to open doors for market reasons—to deepen the pool of laborers and consumers. At the same time, observers and polemicists from Ben Franklin to Pat Buchanan to Lou Dobbs have warned that the resulting flood of foreign humanity threatens our purportedly (but not really) settled, solid, Anglo-American culture. Is a "Mayflower American" a more "genuine" American than a newly minted one? Of course not. Is it as American as apple pie to ask that question in a sneering voice? Of course it is. We live in the midst of a never-ending tension between needs: for periodic infusions of immigrant energy and idealism, and for lawful ways to forge one country from a babel of peoples. And since we are self-consciously a "nation of immigrants," we are the country that affords the most latitude to immigrants themselves to be part of that conversation. Only in America could "illegals" petition the courts and Congress to protect their "rights."

Until recently, most countries did not need to spend a lot of time debating who their citizens were, or could be. The French were French; the English were Gilbert and Sullivan. Countries with identities rooted in the mists of human prehistory were essentially a tribe, or a collection of tribes, writ large. Wars annealed those identities. Modern citizenship in most places grew from what the Germans call *Volk*—a mystical unity of a nation's people.

We were, and are, different. We are founded on ideas, not genetics; on aspirations, not the accidents of geography. We do not trace our nationhood to a tribal history, but to a concept of liberty and constitutional order that was unique in the world when it was first officially proclaimed in 1776. In theory, *anybody* could become an American—and most of the world has tried.

In theory, we love immigrants, or at least want to keep the doors open wide for their arrival. How could we think otherwise, since they literally, legally, built the country? Seven of the thirty-nine men in Philadelphia who signed the draft of the Constitution in 1787 were foreign-born, as were a tenth of the First Congress, a third of the first United States Supreme Court, four of the nation's first six secretaries of the Treasury, and one of its first three secretaries of war. Long before the gathering at the State House, immigrants had helped people the West, expanding trade and extending the pacifying reach of domestic life. Later, their toil literally assembled a nation, or knitted one together: the Irish who built the canals, the Chinese who built the railroads, the many Latinos who clambered over construction sites.

Immigrants come bearing not only muscle, but also fresh thinking and bursts of political energy. It was not just the Einsteins who brought valuable ideas when they arrived; every immigrant comes bearing a genetic inheritance waiting to be awakened and amplified by America. Immigrants bring something else, too: an idealized view of the country they suddenly call their own. "My mother always told me that, in America, anything was possible," recalls Madeline Kunin, who came to this country as a war refugee from Switzerland in 1940, "and I believed her." The result was a sterling career of public service that would make any Yankee proud: a stint as a popular governor of Vermont, as an assistant secretary of education, and, finally—fittingly—as the U.S. ambassador to Switzerland.

Immigrants are sometimes shocked by what they discover when they get here. They quickly learn that the streets are not really paved with gold. But the resulting dismay itself can be the immigrant's priceless contribution to his or her new country, because for every homegrown American who gives up on the Dream, there are scores willing to risk their lives for the chance to live it. For every American who can't be bothered with the task of weeding the garden of democracy, there is an immigrant—or an American-born child of immigrants—willing to bend to it. Immigrants' eyes are necessary mirrors: To see ourselves as they do is to see what is best about our country—and what must become better.

Still, there are limits even to this country's digestive power, especially in tight economic times. Not all fear of immigrants is irrational, let alone "nativist" or "racist." The concerns are genuine, sometimes justified, and, in any case, understandable and natural. Like new religious converts, the descendants of recent immigrants are often the first to want to pull up the drawbridge behind them. The waves of newcomers can drown working families in a riptide of risings rents and falling wages. Local, state, and federal governments, if they respond at all, can be overwhelmed—as they were in metropolitan cities of the late nineteenth century, and as they are in the Southwest, California, and many other places today.

Even if wages of existing citizens do not decline, their tax burden goes up. Voters can come to believe—often with good reason—that they are paying for the health care and education of the very people who are taking their jobs from them. The cultural fears are real, too, and sometimes justified. What country can endure the erosion of the language and culture that have formed its core for hundreds of years? Common language *is* indispensable glue. Buchanan, author, polemicist, and erstwhile presidential candidate, contends that the glue in America is English. A sense of common legal heritage is essential, especially if that heritage is the one we are privileged to possess: an eighteenth-century British model that, when decently administered, provides shock-absorbing flexibility and cultural neutrality.

When are we overwhelmed? When does the politics of immigration turn angry and urgent? There is a tipping point in tolerance: when immigrants become roughly 15 percent of the population. Each time that happened, in the nineteenth and early twentieth centuries, the result was a backlash—sometimes violent, and often producing draconian, racist limitations. In the spring of 2006, the country's demographic profile was approaching that number: an estimated 14 percent of a nation of 300 million was foreign-born (in Miami, more than half the residents were born elsewhere). Two other factors added urgency to the immigration debate. For the first time in American history, a visible part of the immigrant cohort (some 11 million souls) was admittedly—sometimes even defiantly—"illegal." Then there is "national security." We have fretted about it in the past—think of the "Red Scares" in World War I and during the Cold War. But the Al Qaeda attacks of 9/11 generated a whole new category of hysteria, and a whole new justification, or excuse, to slam the door.

There is another unsettling reason for concern. The new immigrant wave included many who were not really immigrants at all, in the traditional sense, but rather temporary sojourners whose hearts, minds, families—and bank accounts—remained elsewhere, in countries such as Mexico and the Philippines. Cheap phone services, satellite TV, and the Internet allowed them not just to keep in touch with their homeland, but keep their hearts and minds there as well.

The truth is, we have never really asked the world to give us *all* of its tired and poor. We always have been meticulous, often racially so. From the seventeenth century on, Americans shaped the flow of immigrants to suit their needs and alleviate their fears. We have oscillated between opening the gates and slamming them shut as business interests, ethnic groups, and political parties maneuver for advantage. It has not always been a pretty or inspiring national history.

You can see the conflicting attitudes memorialized almost side by side in Philadelphia. The statue of William Penn perches precariously atop City Hall. As one of our first real-estate developers, he traveled through the German Rhineland in 1686, pamphlets in hand, touting the attractions of his soon-to-be-created homeland. He calculated that his "Holy Experiment"—with its promise of Eden-like fertility and Enlightenment-style freedom—would lure Lutherans eager for a place to plow and pray as they saw fit. He was right. The farmers came, which is why the suburb of Germantown sits primly up the road.

But there was another side to this Philadelphia story. Penn remained steadfast in his appeal to newcomers, but not so one of his civic heirs and admirers, Benjamin Franklin. Modern Americans tend to think of Franklin as a kindly old fellow, the very soul of Enlightenment thinking, but he deeply feared that German immigrants would obliterate the city that he knew and loved. His angst echoes eerily through the ages, sounding, with a change of ethnicities, like what you can hear on any talk-radio show in America (including Philadelphia) today. The "swarthy Germans," said Franklin, would drown the rule of constitutional law in their beer, their strange tongue, and their authoritarian instincts.

From the start, racist thinking has been wound through our immigration policies like a poisonous thread. At one point or another, numerous states and the federal government have barred or severely limited, by name or by implication, by statute or treaty: free blacks, Roman Catholics, Chinese, Japanese, Jews, Italians, and Slavs. In the name of preserving America, we have barred, at various times: paupers, polygamists, epileptics, imbeciles, beggars, carriers of tuberculosis, anarchists, prostitutes, and pimps—and now, in the post-9/11 world, persons from certain countries suspected of terrorist tendencies. In 2008, the tide of restriction was rising along with the danger, and not all of this could be called hysteria. After all, none of the nineteen hijackers was American-born, or an American citizen.

From the outset, America needed people, and that insatiable appetite (still alive) has propelled one side of the argument for hundreds of years. Advertising and recruitment efforts began in the seventeenth century and continue to this day, communicated at first by printed pamphlets and now by the global reach of Hollywood, the Internet, and the alluring excellence of American universities, which enroll 600,000 foreign students a year. Penn's efforts are a representative early example. His father had been a major financial backer of King James II, who rewarded the son with the colossal land grant that became Pennsylvania. But even before the Royal Charter came through, the entrepreneurial Penn was hustling for business—in the form of immigrants—in person and in print. His targets were fellow Quakers in England and on the Continent, as well as free-thinking (and economically beset) German farmers in the Palatine Rhineland of Germany. "Come, come here," he wrote a friend, Benjamin Furley, "and serve God with me in a virgin wilderness, which already begins to blossom like a rose."

It is natural to think of the colonial continent—surrounded by vast oceans and sparsely settled land—as an empty quarter in which all the early outposts were eager, even desperate, to accept the arrival of any soul. But coming to America was never an uncontested journey, even in colonial times. Colonial Boston was a theocratic version of a Chicago clubhouse in the heyday of the Daley Machine. The Puritans did not want "no guy that no guy sent." That meant anyone who did not follow the Puritans' strict antiestablishment orthodoxy. Catholics and Jews were welcome—as long as they did not mind being burned at the stake. The cavaliers of Virginia were less fierce, but similarly inclined. Even the town of New Amsterdam, founded by Dutch merchants who saw profits in tolerance, turned exclusivist in tone when Peter Minuet arrived from Holland and began barring non-Protestant riffraff.

In early years, it was assumed that the arriving ship passengers were Protestant. Ships' captains could be charged a special tax for every Roman Catholic they accidentally deposited here. Skin color was another condition, assumed by the colonies, and written into law as one of the first acts of the federal government. In 1790, the First Congress passed a Naturalization Act limiting citizenship to "free whites of good moral character."

Though they were white, the Irish immigrants who came in waves before the Civil War were often not welcomed. In the eyes of the locals, they were good for digging canals and building bridges—but little else.

It took a civil war for Americans to decide that millions of involuntary immigrants—African slaves—were citizens, too. They were naturalized, in effect, by the Fifteenth Amendment, ratified by the states in 1870. Once that issue was settled, at least in theory, anti-immigration sentiment focused on the Chinese, who, starting in the 1840s, descended on the West to dig the mines and build the railroads generated by the discovery of gold in California. Labor-hungry employers accumulated this toiling army of near-slaves until, in the 1870s, Congress and the federal courts were moved to respond to rising anti-Chinese sentiment.

In California, especially, the Chinese were widely seen not just as "aliens" in law but in fact, mysterious opium-smoking heathens who would overwhelm even the remorselessly absorptive powers of America. Applying old naturalization laws, courts ruled that, since the Chinese were not "white," their importation was a violation of federal statute. Despite the ruling, riots broke out repeatedly in California cities. In the presidential election of 1880, the major-party platforms shouted a loud "no more!" to the Chinese. In 1882 Congress passed the Chinese Exclusion Act, the first (but by no means the last) federal statute to limit, by name, immigrants from specific ethnic groups.

The faster the flow of immigrants in the late nineteenth century, the nastier the politics became. In 1894, the Immigration Restriction League started a national drive for literacy tests. Congress listened, and enacted a literacy requirement in 1895, only to have it vetoed by President Grover Cleveland, who, uncharacteristically for a Democrat in those days, was trying to respond to industrialists who needed a continually expanding pool of cheap labor. Politically, it did not work. Cleveland was dumped by his own party in 1896, and in the general election that year the captains of industry got the man they really wanted, Republican William McKinley. After he was assassinated, however, the big shots got a very different—and, from their point of view, disturbing—sort of character as president: Teddy Roosevelt.

As he did on many issues, the passionately opinionated Roosevelt embodied both sides of immigration debate. An empire-builder by nature, an American's American, he sought not to curtail but to shape the turn-of-the-century tsunami of humanity. As a former police commissioner of New York, he saw the plight of those who had been herded into squalid tenements, and he spoke out for their fair treatment and for a welcoming attitude. He supported humane employment and social-welfare rules. His only condition was that the new Americans be required to learn to speak the English language.

But, at the same time, T.R. was picky—and even frankly racist—about whom to let in to begin with. "We can never have too much immigration of the right sort," he told the Knights of Columbus, with emphasis on "the right sort." They must not be "laborers who are ignorant, vicious and with low standards," he wrote at one point early in his career. From the beginning to the end of his public life, he felt no compunction about denying a welcome to the Chinese, in California or elsewhere. The "sound, proper attitude, an attitude which must be insisted upon," was to bar them altogether. In his view, they were simply incapable of becoming American. He favored immigrants with "the intelligent capacity to appreciate American institutions and act sanely as American citizens"—a pretty high bar that most of us cannot reach today.

By the end of World War I, Roosevelt's balancing act had collapsed under the weight of a powerful, grassroots slam-the-door campaign. It was driven by newly organized labor unions, pseudoscientific eugenists and unabashed bigots—all of whom argued that the country had been overrun by Mediterranean Roman Catholics and Russian Jews. Beginning in 1921, the United States essentially shuttered its ports to all except for a trickle from "Teutonic" places such as England, Scotland, Ireland, and Germany. For the first time, in fact, the answer to the question of who could be an American depended on the country of a new émigré's origin. The result, decades later, was hardship for millions, and death for untold numbers of Jews whose easiest route of escape from Nazi Germany had been blockaded in ways that even President Franklin Roosevelt was reluctant to try to change. As the nation approached midcentury, it had become, comparatively, a land of natives. The percentage of foreign-born dropped from 15 percent in 1910 to 4 percent by the turn of the 1960s.

The immigration debate endures because the needs and instincts that underlie it are so fundamental. No set of restrictions is ironclad. Eventually, inexorably, loopholes grow over time. The will of the world to make its way to America—and the need for this country to have the world do so—is too great. The laws of the 1920s shut the doors to the Jews, Italians, and Slavs, for example, but they opened them for immigrants from the Western Hemisphere, especially from Mexico. The 1920s laws specifically exempted the entire hemisphere from their reach, and in so doing, implicitly told the Latinos of the world that they belonged to a different, more American, destiny. In World War I, Mexican laborers—braceros—were allowed to enter (and in practice, to stay) to do the farmwork that the Doughboys left behind. Outside the Southwest, no one noticed at the time that the country had set the stage for the next great wave.

Slowed to a trickle, the flow of immigrants began rising to tidal levels again only after the New Frontier and Great Society, which redefined the meaning of opened doors to fit the 1960s-era commitment to civil, family, and human rights. That meant extending an official, permanent invitation to political refugees, as well as to family members of those already in America. Country-specific quotas were abandoned. If you had a blood tie or a just cause, you could come. Eager to fight the Cold War by attracting the best minds, government officials also changed laws to admit—even to lure—the brightest mathematicians, scientists, and engineers from a host of the "nonaligned" developing countries. Taiwanese and Koreans, who essentially had been barred to that point, found that they now had family ties and GPAs to draw upon. Refugees from Communist-era wars in Southeast Asia—Vietnamese, Laotians, and Cambodians—found a purchase on the new country's conscience. Graduate students from India, Pakistan, and Nigeria came to work—and to stay if they could manage to do so. (One of those brilliant students was Barack Obama Sr., the late father of the presidential candidate.)

Above all, the Mexicans came. Never barred by nationality, often brought across the border for stays as migrant workers—indeed, uniquely at home in reaches of the American Southwest that had been

part of their native country—the Mexicans came in unprecedented numbers: between 1970 and 2005, an estimated 20 million of them. In that
same span, the rest of Latin America sent another 20 million here. Taken
together, the mass migration has been the largest in recorded history of
one people from their homeland to that of another.

The problem: Perhaps as much as half of the total came here illegally.

In the Reagan years, an odd-couple alliance of conservative Republicans and Democratic union bosses joined hands in an effort to stop illegal
immigration. The resulting statute, signed into law by the president in
1986, for the first time made it a crime—although only a misdemeanor—
to be here without proper permission and papers. (For the previous 350
years or so of the continent's history, the only punishment for illegal entry
had been immediate deportation, but even that had rarely been enforced.)
The new law called for fines and even jail time for employers who knowingly employed illegal aliens. Surveillance was to be strengthened along
the borders, especially the 1,969-mile-long one between the United States
and Mexico. There was another side to the ledger. A new category was established to ease entry for immigrants with high-tech skills needed by the
newly emerging industries of Silicon Valley. And in the law's most fateful language, some 3 million illegals (most from Mexico) were granted
"amnesty"—a term adopted from human-rights law and now applied to
lucky souls who were not refugees from totalitarianism but merely people seeking a better life. "We thought that we finally had fixed the problem," said former representative Ron Mazzoli, an author of the 1986
legislation.

They had not. Employers looked the other way. Local police departments did not want to spend their time rounding up "illegals" on misdemeanor charges for their mere presence; indeed, the cops preferred that
these people feel free to come forward to testify about more serious crimes
in the community. The insatiable appetite in the United States for cheap
labor, coupled with the desperate need of immigrants for dollar-based
work in *El Norte,* rendered the 1986 law a dead letter within a few years.
The flow started again, and intensified. The Mexicans became the first
immigrant group to have come here en masse over land—indeed, literally
from next door.

That very proximity produced an explosion in California, the font of
all American political trends. The fuse was lit by Pete Wilson, the ultimate Anglo and former governor. Running for reelection in 1994, he

aired a now-infamous TV ad, a grainy, night-vision piece of video surveillance showing Mexicans swarming over a border crossing near Wilson's hometown of San Diego, where he had been mayor. The ad was linked to his support for a ballot proposition that called for denying education and health benefits to even the legal (that is, American-born) offspring of illegal parents. The ads shrewdly played to Anglo fear, and the measure passed. The fastidious Wilson, who looked like the still-trim father of a surfer, won reelection with overwhelming Anglo support.

It was a victory for him, but a Pyrrhic one for his Republican Party in California. Democrats easily painted him and the GOP as anti-immigrant, anti-Mexican, and, if not openly racist, certainly too retrograde to be trusted. Hispanic voters abandoned the GOP in droves. A few years later, Wilson's nascent presidential quest collapsed under the weight of criticism from rivals (including Texas governor George W. Bush), who portrayed him as a heartless immigrant-basher. Wilson defended his stance when I talked to him about it years later. "We couldn't and still can't afford the drain on our economy," he said. But Democrats saw their chances and took them. "Wilson set them back a generation," said Bill Carrick, a longtime Democratic strategist in California. "The Republicans still are paying in California for the Wilson campaign."

The backlash against Mexican immigrants that began in Southern California spread to the entire Southwest over the next decade. There, it was powered not so much by religion or race as by a sense of loss of territorial and linguistic integrity. It was also fueled by a sense that Mexicans, with a history of their own in North America and no ocean to cross, have obliterated the very idea of national borders—even nationhood—by their unwillingness to follow the rules for entering the country and acquiring citizenship, even as advocates demand full access to the benefits of the American welfare state. "I am not anti-immigrant!" Rep. J. D. Hayworth, a Republican from Phoenix, told me in the summer of 2006. "I am anti-illegal! These people are coming here, illegally, and they come with an assumption of entitlement that I find outrageous. We're talking about the rule of law." A large, beefy man with a stentorian voice, Hayworth said that business interests look the other way so they can expand the labor pool; Democrats want to bestow "amnesty" on 12 million undocumented illegals "because they think that they'll all end up voting Democrat! So the Corporate Right wants cheap labor and the Democrats on the left want cheap votes! Meanwhile, working Americans are shouldering an unacceptable tax burden for social services for people who have no legal right to be in the country!"

Hayworth, the author of a book called *Whatever It Takes,* outlined what it would take. As a first step, "We have to secure the border." Parting from conservative orthodoxy that dates back to fears of the standing British Army in colonial times, Hayworth called for stationing the U.S. Army along the Rio Grande "as a temporary measure." He was for building a physical and digital fence along the entire southern frontier. He was for making it a felony, not just a misdemeanor, for anyone to be in the United States illegally, and a felony for employers to knowingly hire illegals. He was for designating English the official language of the United States of America—something even Teddy Roosevelt didn't think to suggest a century ago. Hayworth wanted to require noncitizens to carry data-rich electronic identity cards. He was for reminding the Mexicans—and, while he was at it, Hugo Chavez of Venezuela—that the Gadsden Purchase and the Treaty of Guadalupe Hidalgo (by which the United States acquired sovereignty over the Southwest and California) were real events with real consequences. He cited what he regarded as an ominous number in a 2006 opinion survey by the Pew Hispanic Center. "It said that 58 percent of Latinos think the Southwest rightly belongs not to the United States but to Mexico!" (Actually, it turns out to have been a Zogby Poll from 2002, but the number is the number.) He was for repatriating as many illegals as possible, which he assumed meant many millions. "People want to call us xenophobes, nativists, racists," he said. "Well, we are none of those. They can call us what they want. We just don't want to lose our country, the rule of law, and our sovereignty."

By the summer of 2006, Hayworth's message had spread north and east to Pennsylvania, as local politicians grew tired of waiting for Congress and the federal government to crack down. The mayor of Hazleton, a gritty town in the anthracite region north of Philadelphia, convinced his city council to withhold any services to illegal immigrants over the age of eighteen, and charge them special fees. He drew nationwide publicity—and copycat mayors.

As for Hayworth, his anti-immigration rhetoric won him a following among hard-line activists. But his combative rhetoric cost him in Arizona, not just among Hispanic voters, but among middle-of-the-road suburban Arizonans who favored a balanced approach, feared being branded racists—and who liked the cheap, eager labor that had helped fuel a boom in the fast-growing region. Hayworth lost—big—to a Democrat who favored reform that included a "path to citizenship" for millions of illegals. Hayworth had a point. But the wrong point. In America, it is okay to be worried about the impact of "immigration"—but not of immigrants.

The tone was tricky, the politics treacherous. George Bush had made a career of successfully wooing Hispanic voters, and he made a centerpiece of his second term an effort to "reform" immigration policy. The essence of it was a "path to citizenship" for millions of illegals. But as the economy weakened, Anglo resentment grew, and passing a new bill became more difficult. Republicans such as Hayworth had played to that resentment—and lost. But by late 2007 most of the GOP's presidential candidates were sounding just like him. With the important exception of Senator John McCain, they competed with each other to see who could propose the harshest measures and use the nastiest language. Democrats, meanwhile, were being buffeted by the same crosswinds. Did they favor, for example, giving driver's licenses to the illegals, as, indeed, Governor Bill Richardson of New Mexico had done? Senator Barack Obama said yes; Senator Hillary Rodham Clinton at first said a qualified yes, then an emphatic no. It seemed like a trivial issue. It wasn't. A license, after all, was a golden ticket to national identity. With one, you were free to hit the open road. What could be more American?

You would have known that travel was freedom had you spent the time I did in Love Park in Philadelphia on a fine, clear April day in 2006. Some ten thousand souls had journeyed there to plead for an immigration deal in a park that stood within shouting distance of a Founding Father—William Penn—who spent his life luring immigrant settlers to his new paradise of Pennsylvania.

The rally was not about coming here, it was about *staying* here. That was the hope—and the problem. The hope was economic opportunity, the problem that many of the people in Love Park should not really have been there at all. By the estimate of an expert on the scene, an administrator of Catholic charities, perhaps two-thirds of those in the throng were illegals—or, to use his charitable phrase, "undocumenteds."

In any case, most Americans opposed the idea of quickly putting such immigrants on a path to citizenship. The protesters thought otherwise.

Politely, with smiles on their faces, they essentially said: No matter how we arrived, we are here now. We are here for good, in both senses of the term. We are so eager to be hardworking, law-abiding citizens that we left our workplaces and came by car, bus, and trolley to the center of a city that we now demand reflect its name, City of Brotherly Love. We should not be treated as criminals, but as new marchers in the struggle for civil rights.

The crowd was the New American polyglot: Colombians, Salvadorans, Brazilians, Koreans (with signs in Korean and English), Indians. Bangladeshis held aloft a carefully sewn banner advertising "The Bangladesh Community of Pennsylvania," whose members stood proudly, if a little sheepishly, beneath it. The Mexicans, criticized earlier that spring for carrying Mexican flags at such rallies, showed up draped in Old Glory, relegating the Mexican red, green, and white to their T-shirts.

But I saw evidence of Franklin's fearful view later that day during a trip to a holy local shrine—Geno's restaurant in the Little Italy section of South Philly. The countermen behind the service windows looked as if they had stepped out of a *Rocky* movie, and seemed as eager as Sly Stallone himself for combat in the cause of pride. I thought of their immigrant ancestors as I read a hand-lettered sign pasted to the serving window. It was a quote from a speech by Teddy Roosevelt a century ago. Citizenship, T.R. had said, was predicated upon the immigrant's "becoming in very fact an American, and nothing but an American. There can be no divided allegiance here. We have room for but one flag, the American flag. We have room for but one language here, and that is the English language." As a Geno's grill man in a white muscle-T slid my order through the window, I asked if the sign had been there long. "Put it up a few weeks ago," he said. "Some people around here need to read it, but they can't."

Every summer he was in the U.S. Senate, Tom Daschle of South Dakota made it his earnest business to visit all sixty-six counties of his state. That was a lofty goal, considering that South Dakota was 76,000 square miles of what often appeared to be forbidding emptiness. Daschle's staff would carefully "advance" each trip, calling ahead to the people and groups he was to meet: ranchers and health-care clinicians, weekly newspaper editors and senior citizens—the heart of everyday life on the Plains. Then Daschle would head out from Sioux Falls in a rented

Ford, music CDs racked up, a carefully handwritten and highlighted itinerary by his side.

I accompanied him on one such trip. We would drive the northeastern quadrant of the state, he said. Much of the area was old German country, where immigrant farmers had come a century earlier, many of them from ethnic enclaves in Russia. On the Great Plains, they had busted the sod and built homes with the very earth they had dug up. Small towns sprouted along the rough roads and railroad lines: tiny patches of civilization hunkered down against the winter winds and baking summer sun. The immigrants had thrived—at least until the Depression. Many of their descendants had long since moved on. But the pioneers had left behind evidence of their culture. In the dusty back rooms of small-town newspapers, decades of German-language editions stood stacked to the ceiling. In restaurants along the two-lane highways, you could still order sauerbraten and soup with heavy dumplings. You could still buy a special kuchen, a cake worshipped in north-central South Dakota with religious fervor.

The Germans were gone, but a new wave was coming, bringing both hope for renewal and the prospect of new problems to confront. In the small city of Aberdeen, the health clinic was a one-man operation run by an earnest—and very busy—Pakistani physician. He was indispensable, and beloved in the community. In the aftermath of 9/11, he explained, he was having trouble getting family members into the country, and worried that others like him were, too. The small town of Eureka, Daschle announced, was home to the world's best kuchen bakery. When we stopped at the shop, the bakery owner told us enthusiastically about her plan to use the Internet to generate mail-order sales among the German-Russian-American diaspora. As for the baking itself, that was mainly handled by a woman from the Philippines, who had married a South Dakotan and learned the secrets of the cake.

Then there were the bees. In the 1950s, agriculturalists discovered that the Plains of South Dakota, with their short but intense summer season, were ideal for producing honey. South Dakotans have international prizes to prove that their product, light and smooth, is among the best in the world. Bee farms enliven the summer landscape with fields of sunflowers. Swarming bees produce racks of combs laden with raw honey. Harvesting and cleaning the racks is hot, laborious work.

We stopped at a bee farm showplace on the way west. The owner showed us around. Daschle and I wandered out behind the barn. There, several Latinos were hard at work on a pile of racks. They shot us blank stares and then bent to their task. It was virtually impossible to find locals to do such work, the owner said quickly when he arrived. The beekeeper was clearly uncomfortable, and Daschle did not want to ask any questions. We hustled back to the car and were on our way.

That evening we reached Mobridge, a town of some significance, since it was one of only six places in South Dakota where a bridge crossed the wide, meandering Missouri River. I hurried down to the marshy riverbank before sunset. Two hundred years earlier, President Thomas Jefferson had sent Lewis and Clark this way, charging them to document the Louisiana Purchase—the new nation's vast new frontier—and search for a water route across the continent to the Pacific. In the summer of 1805, the explorers had passed the spot where I now stood. They were passing through, harbingers of settlers to come.

The man who sent Lewis and Clark was of two minds about people who wanted to come to America. Jefferson knew that we needed immigrants to fill the empty landscape—even before he doubled its size by the deal he cut with France in 1803. He fretted that the newcomers might destroy the essence of what made America American. "They will bring with them the principles of the government they leave," Jefferson said, "or, if they throw them off . . . it would be a miracle if they stopped precisely at the point of temperate liberty." The result, he said, would not be a country but "a heterogeneous, distracted mass."

Still, in his first message as president, Jefferson opposed the idea of restrictive residency requirements—fourteen years—for citizenship. "Shall oppressed humanity find no asylum on this globe?" he demanded to know. We should assume, Jefferson said, "the general character and capabilities" of those "manifesting a bona fide purpose of embracing his life and fortunes permanently with us." That was how South Dakota's "German Russians" thought of themselves, and how we thought of them. The same was true a century later for the Pakistani doctor and the baker from the Philippines. Would not that soon also be the case for the Latinos cleaning the beehives in the shed? Didn't they want to embrace "life and fortunes permanently with us"? Should we let them?

Three

THE ROLE OF FAITH

God in His infinite wisdom must have designed Tennessee as the ideal place in which to argue the role of faith in public life. In what sometimes is still called "the buckle of the Bible Belt," locals favor "strong preachin'," but also the evangelism of a secular gospel called Jacksonian Democracy. Nashville is home to the abstemious souls of the Southern Baptist Convention, but also to country singers keening over lives ruined by drink and dissolution. In 1925 the mountains of east Tennessee were the site of the infamous Scopes Trial, in which a teacher was sent to jail for teaching the science of biological evolution. Yet those same rugged mountains are home to the Oak Ridge National Laboratory, a leading center for advanced science, and to two nuclear power plants that operate on the physics venerated there.

So Tennessee was the appropriate launching pad for the political career of Senator William Frist, M.D.—and also the appropriate place for it to crash to Earth. In Tennessee, the senator had to fly through the crosswinds of cultural conflict, between the theories and demands of Bible Belt religion and of ivory tower science. The bumpy ride ultimately reduced his image from that of an idealistic, *Grey's Anatomy*–style "superdoc" and presidential possibility to a hopeless political hack. The trajectory of his public life illuminated the power of an essential American Argument. We are a prayerful, Bible-believing country, yet that same trait causes us to constantly fret—and argue—over the extent to which our faith should influence decisions about education, research, welfare, and other government activities.

Frist rose to prominence on the secular, science side of the argument. His first calling card was medicine. His father and uncle were prominent Nashville physicians who had made a fortune assembling one of the nation's first HMOs. He was a brilliant, meticulous student, excelling at Princeton, at Harvard Medical School, and in internships at Massachusetts General Hospital.

Frist had a need to exhibit his knowledge in dramatic circumstances. He became a renowned cardiothoracic surgeon famous for steely nerves and clinical derring-do, "cracking open chests," as he put it, thrusting his hands into thoraxes to remove diseased hearts and lungs. He owned a plane, which he kept gassed up and ready to fly so he could ferry in replacement parts—living hearts—for his patients. He piloted the plane, of course. He was forever experimenting with new surgical techniques, studying logistics, puzzling over the social consequences of the on-the-fly triage necessary to match salvageable patients with salvageable hearts. A committed runner, lean as a whippet, and blessed with an ability to concentrate in an operating theater, Frist slept only three or four hours a night. He used the wee hours to educate himself by writing medical tracts.

As he launched his campaign for the Senate in 1994, his religious faith was not a visible part of his public profile. He rarely talked about his standard-issue Presbyterianism, the denomination of choice among the Southern business establishment. Rather, he advertised the healing power of medicine. On the wall behind his desk, he tacked up a picture of a picnic he had organized and attended earlier that year. He was surrounded in the photo by a cheerful-looking throng of more than one hundred. Who were they? "Those are my former transplant patients," Frist said proudly. "I feel a deep bond with those people," he said. "I can't express it in words."

Even after he became a senator, Frist did not abandon his medical pursuits. He was an unofficial doctor-in-residence in the Capitol. After the 9/11 terrorist attacks, he used his late-night study vigils to produce a picture-and-text guide and instruction manual on how to treat injuries and contaminations that might follow a chemical or biological assault. He insisted that his full title be emblazoned on press releases and in brass on his office door: Senator William Frist, M.D.

When he began fashioning his political career, Frist had little contact with the Other Tennessee, the one controlled, or at least defined, by the Southern Baptists. The state's largest denomination, they had always set the tone politically, but not always directly. In pioneer days they were a liberating political force, opposed to hierarchical authority, especially an "established" church, of any kind. They promoted democratic ideals by insisting that man had free will, and by insisting that the route to salvation lay in the simple, straightforward act of reading and believing the Bible. Baptists had grown mighty on America's frontiers, where settlers had needed a portable, independent faith, one that validated their sense of freedom but also gave them confidence that they were doing the Lord's work in the New World.

At first, Baptists and their brethren wanted nothing to do with direct involvement in government, which they tended to fear—given their history in Europe and in much of colonial America—as an instrument of theological oppression. That attitude changed somewhat in the 1920s, as rural Americans came to feel themselves under assault by a new, metropolitan modernity. The battle was joined in Dayton, Tennessee, where a teacher named John Scopes was brought to trial for violating a state law against the teaching of evolution. Clarence Darrow, the most famous courtroom lawyer of his day, teamed up with an equally famous journalist, H. L. Mencken, to make a national laughingstock out of the law's chief defender, William Jennings Bryan, the "prairie populist."

And yet it was Bryan's side—the Bible-believing one—that won the case at trial and on appeal. In New York City, textbook authors were forced to delete evolution from their newest manuscripts. The Tennessee law remained on the books, banning instruction in "any theory that denies the story of the Divine Creation of man as taught in the Bible" or that suggests "man has descended from a lower order of animals." Similar laws existed in fourteen other states until the U.S. Supreme Court, in 1968, firmly and finally ruled that they were an unconstitutional imposition of sectarian dogma in secular classrooms.

The national ridicule engendered by the Scopes Trial drove two generations of Baptists out of the political arena. Despite their legal early "victory," the Southern Baptist leaders increasingly downplayed fundamentalist teachings, even if their congregants did not.

But by the time Frist was thinking of running for office, a new generation of hard-liners—more media-savvy and sophisticated, but no less dedicated to Scripture—had reasserted control of the denomination. Luckily for Frist (at least it seemed lucky at the time) the Baptists' leading political figure in the early 1990s was Dr. Richard Land, who had close ties to Karl

Rove, an ally of the late Lee Atwater's and the emerging kingmaker of the Southern-based Republican Party. Land headed the Southern Baptists' political and grassroots organizing arm. He was theologically devout, but had a doctorate from Oxford and enjoyed jousting with the Other Side. And maybe the Lord had a hand in bringing him to the campaign: Like Frist, Land was a Princeton man. He could educate Frist in the political ways of the Word.

It was a slow, careful process. In Frist's first campaign, in 1994, Land did not press his fellow Princetonian on faith issues. It wasn't part of the GOP's national game plan. Instead, the Republicans ran coast-to-coast on Newt Gingrich's determinedly secular "Contract with America," which studiously avoided social and theological issues and instead focused on anti-Washington themes: tax cuts, spending reform, and the iniquity of the new Clinton administration and the Democrats who had ruled the House of Representatives for forty years. Frist was anti-abortion—just about everybody in the new GOP was—but otherwise had felt little need to talk much about "the social issues."

Frist's focus changed once he arrived in Washington, especially after George Bush became president, the GOP took control of the Senate, and Frist, with a behind-the-scenes boost from the White House, became majority leader. Suddenly he was the man in the middle of an American Argument. Stem-cell research was the specific issue. Baptists and other fundamentalists joined with the Vatican hierarchy to oppose the use of human embryos in such research, even though many frozen embryos were being discarded by fertility clinics and most scientists thought research using cells from that source held great clinical promise in the search for cures to disease.

Frist proceeded to ambush himself on the issue. In 2001, he supported the president's decision to limit federally funded research to cultures from existing embryo "lines." But under pressure from his erstwhile colleagues in the medical community—not to mention former first lady Nancy Reagan, who saw stem-cell research as the route to a cure for Alzheimer's disease—Frist reversed course. Now, he said, he considered the existing "lines" inadequate, and would support the use of embryos that would otherwise be discarded by clinics and perhaps other sources as well. Since he was a doctor and potential presidential candidate, Frist's 2005 switch was major national news. "It's an earthquake," said his Republican colleague Arlen Specter of Pennsylvania at the time.

Frist garnered praise from the same medical and scientific community that had denounced him earlier. But the GOP's religious fundamentalists attacked him for supporting what they labeled "destructive embryo research." "To push for the expansion of this suspect and unethical science," said Dr. James Dobson, "will be rightly seen by America's values voters as the worst kind of betrayal of choosing politics over principle." Dr. Land had a simpler political reaction, but equally to the point. "I'm heartbroken," he declared.

And so it came to pass that Frist was politically doomed, even though he tried his best to reconnect with the "heartbroken" Land. The senator sought to placate his religious "base" by championing the anti-euthanasia cause of Terri Schiavo. Although he had not personally seen the bedridden and severely brain-damaged woman, he offered a long-range "diagnosis" of her condition, concluding that she was aware of her surroundings and thus should be spared. He did so after watching a video of her moving her eyes in what some had concluded was a purposeful, sentient fashion.

Then, as though burrowing into Tennessee's antimodern past, Frist showed up at a Rotary club in Nashville to talk about evolution. After the Supreme Court in 1968 invalidated statutes that had banned the teaching of evolution, Biblical literalists had developed a new strategy. Rather than opposing evolution per se, they supported the teaching of a theory they called "intelligent design." The idea was that human beings and other forms of life were so complex and elegantly arranged that only an intelligent "Creator"—that would be God—could have made them. Scientists generally dismiss the theory as nothing more than a faith-based tautology, an assertion beyond the reach of experimental, factual verification, and therefore not "science" at all.

But Frist was not one of those scientists. "I think a pluralistic society should have access to a broad range of fact, of science, including faith," he said. Exposing schoolchildren to intelligent design "doesn't force a particular theory on anyone," he said. A few months later, a federal judge in Pennsylvania disagreed. He struck down a local school-board policy that required that students be made "aware of the gaps/problems in Darwin's theory, and of other theories of evolution, including, but not limited to, intelligent design."

By then Frist had bowed out of that debate—and most others in the faith wars. He had said from the beginning of his political adventure that he would serve only two terms in the Senate, and as his second term drew to a close in the fall of 2006, the only remaining question was whether he would run for the GOP presidential nomination. He was not a deft politician—you could see the gears grinding with every move he made—but even a Lyndon Johnson would have had trouble surviving in the riptides of the faith-versus-science debate.

In his final few months, Frist almost literally wasted away, shrinking from lean to gaunt, his normally chipper surgeon's demeanor falling off into what resembled absentmindedness. On the Senate floor, he seemed almost lost. He had been chewed to pieces by the Eastern establishment that had credentialed him initially; he was almost too easy a target for *The New York Times*. At the same time, the Richard Lands of the world had given up on him, looking elsewhere for Republican presidential candidates to champion. Rove had once been a backer—he had led the effort to get him the majority leader's job—but Bush aides now privately derided Frist as a ham-fisted amateur who had never learned to play the game, no matter how adroit he had been in an operating theater.

In November of 2006, after the Democrats won back control of the Senate, Frist limited himself to the occasional Washington social event as he and his wife prepared to return to Nashville. He said he was building a new home there. In a sad, unself-conscious parody, the new edifice resembled a downsized White House, with pillars, portico, and all. He could take shelter there from the argument that had overwhelmed him.

The land we live on was claimed in God's name, but the world's first officially secular government sits on it. We invoked God in making our Declaration of Independence, but not in our governing authority, the Constitution. Only one clergyman signed the former; none the latter. Yet we are among the world's most devout people; most of us see the Bible as literal truth, the Word of God. We base our nationhood on the unalienable rights the Creator bestowed upon all of mankind. So what role should He play in our public life?

Faith and its traditions and institutions can strengthen society's social fabric, and amplify its commitment to family and justice. But if the Word rules all, the faithful are duty bound to spread—yea, even enforce—it. The result: sectarian crusades in secular realms. Some are noble (abolition or the bioethics movement), but some foment intolerance (the anti-Catholic Know-Nothings, the ravings of Louis Farrakhan), or warp scientific inquiry, public education, and foreign policy. We are one country, yet forever torn between two methods of understanding, Revelation and Reason, and two sacred texts, the Bible and the Constitution. Of all the arguments that define us none is more vexing—alternately troubling and inspiring—than the one we had for four centuries over the role of faith.

America, the late Jerry Falwell proclaimed, was a "faith nation." His political foes disputed the specific term, but they cannot gainsay the basic point. The polling figures are as familiar as they are immutable: 90 percent of us say we believe in God; 85 percent believe in the personal power of prayer; 70 percent are affiliated with an organized religion; 42 percent say they attend religious services regularly; and 38 percent refer to themselves as "committed Christians." Senator Barack Obama summarized these numbers in his tart fashion. "Substantially more people in America," he said, "believe in angels than they do in evolution."

Looking back, it is clear that it is our destiny to argue about faith in public life. History makes us do it.

One reason is the centrality of the Bible—not just what it contains, but the fact of its new, wide availability at the time of our founding. Our earliest seventeenth-century settlers arrived with Reformation ideas. They came bearing new ways of thinking and guiding their lives created by post-Gutenberg technology (the movable-type printing press) and individualistic, post–Martin Luther theology. To these early Protestants, and for those who came here over the next two centuries, the Bible—not popes, prelates, or princes—was the arbiter of morality and the road map to heaven. What's more, it was within the power and the ken of any mortal to read it and interpret it for himself. He could and did go forth into the New World to seek its riches and master its dangers with a rifle, an ax, and a Bible. "Those who believe that knowledge of God comes direct to them through the study of the Holy Writ," observes historian Paul Johnson, "read the Bible for themselves, assiduously, daily. The authority lay in the Bible, not the minister."

The result was a uniquely American invention: a lively, supply-side marketplace of religion. "The direct apprehension of the word of God," writes Johnson, was a formula for dissent—"for a Babel of conflicting voices." Diverse faith was, and is, like the energy from splitting the atom. "Nowhere else in Christendom was religion so fragmented," writes colonial historian Gordon S. Wood. "Yet nowhere was it so vital." It was all the more vital because, in a New Eden of America, there was more urgency in finding the right biblical path away from sin. The place was pure; the temptations of freedom were great.

As with other parts of our heritage, this marketplace was so fervent because it was based on freedom of the individual. As with other market-places, it was buffeted by crowd psychology, the dynamics of salesman-ship, and the laws of supply and demand. Without the clerical structure of an official church, preachers rose to power on the strength of eloquence and marketing skill, convincing the layman of the wisdom of their inter-pretation. Popular preachers were early fruits of our democratic think-ing—"in a sense, the first elected officials," says Johnson, "of the New American society."

Philadelphia, birthplace of our Republic, was known through most of the eighteenth century as the ultimate faith-based bazaar—site of the leg-endary, building-packing sermons of George Whitefield, American's first revival evangelist. The Founders who convened there in 1787 to draft a Constitution knew the history of the city. They were not hostile to reli-gion; indeed, they were not all firmly against some version of an official church, if it could be democratically selected.

Just two years earlier, a committee of the Continental Congress had come within a single vote of moving in that direction. Drafting rules for selling land in the Northwest Territory, the committee voted to allot for "the maintenance of public schools" one section within each square of surveyed squares. Then they voted to devote "the section immediately ad-joining the same to the northward for the support of religion. Profits aris-ing therefrom in both instances to be applied forever according to the will of the majority of male residents of full age within the same." In other words, the public would pay to "support religion," presumably by con-structing the church the locals wanted.

To James Madison's great relief, the "support of religion" clause was voted down in the end. "How a regulation so unjust in itself, foreign to the authority of Congress . . . smelling so strongly of an antiquated Big-otry, could have received the countenance of a committee is a matter of as-tonishment," he wrote to James Monroe. Presbyterian clergy, Madison reported, "were in general friends of the scheme," but they had tempered their "tone, either compelled by the laity of that sect, or alarmed at the probability of further interferences of the Legislature, if they once begin to dictate in matters of religion."

In writing a Constitution, Madison and the other Founders took an-other step back from the approach the Continental Congress had consid-ered. The idea of a state-supported church—even one democratically chosen by local elders—would not even be considered. When it came time to draft a Bill of Rights four years later, they hammered home the point. "Congress shall make no law," the First Amendment says, "re-specting the establishment of religion, or prohibiting the free exercise thereof." The framers were not banishing faith from the public square— but they were banishing the possibility of state monopoly in the market of creeds. They made the point in 1796 in another, but significant, context. In the Treaty of Tripoli, they tried to soothe the Muslim ruler there by as-serting that "the United States is not, in any sense, founded on the Chris-tian religion." That wasn't quite right, of course. We *were* set in motion by Christians in the name of Christian kings. But after 1776, the kings did not govern us, and neither did their faith. No one faith could. You could believe in any you chose—or in none at all.

The fact is that the focus of the Founders—what they thought the country indeed was "founded on"—was not Christianity per se, or the Bible, or at least the Bible alone. The focus of their intellectual, political, and moral ambition was the world, history as it was lived, and the En-lightenment spirit of inquiry and science. Many were Deists, skeptical of Christian dogma about the divinity of Jesus. They studied Athens and Rome—not Jerusalem—for most of their clues to the nature of govern-ment. Their holy trinity was Hume, Locke, and Montesquieu. The deci-sion of the committee of the Continental Congress is a footnote in history, but a crucial one, reflecting and foreshadowing an argument for the ages: They concluded that the only kind of education that government should pay for is the kind that takes place in a secular classroom.

But, as was the case in 1785, it was always a close question. In 1801, Baptists, a minority in Connecticut, wrote to President Jefferson to com-plain that their state viewed religious liberty not as an immutable right but as a privilege granted by the legislature—as "favors granted." In his famous and carefully considered reply, Jefferson said nothing about Con-necticut, but noted that it was an "act of the whole American people" (the Bill of Rights) "which declared that *their* legislature should make no law respecting an establishment of religion, or prohibiting the free exercise thereof, thus building a wall of separation between church and state."

Perhaps no single "thus" has generated so much controversy. To be sure, Jefferson's "wall" means there can be no state-sponsored church. But must it mean no role for faith in public life?

Probably not. Even in his letter, Jefferson seemed to make the point. He closed his "wall of separation letter" to the Danbury Baptists this way: "I reciprocate your kind prayers for the protection and blessing of the common Father and creator of man." However guarded his words, he was reciprocating *something*. Faith and public life are not a unity, but Jefferson understood that here they are virtually inseparable in many ways.

The idea of "revival" is one example of how faith and politics in America are intertwined. Indeed, it is, arguably, our most important political metaphor. We are a nation that operates by continual revival. Without an established church, with each of us free to read the Word for himself, we compete with each other to win souls, and revivals are our unique method for doing so. The religious Great Awakenings were mirrored in our politics, and vice versa. In a nation that prays for the advent of Good News, every deal is New, every political campaign is a crusade, and every crusade is a campaign. The mechanics of a Billy Graham event (he no longer calls them "crusades") and those of a candidate rally are indistinguishable. Much of the language is the same, sign-up tables are the same, prayer counselors and precinct workers are the same. Only the objective is different: souls versus votes.

What we think of as civic life would not exist without the religious impulse to lead, to educate, and to convince. That impulse fostered the founding of our great universities and colleges, from Harvard to Notre Dame to Brigham Young to Brandeis. It encouraged us to be the most charitable of people, with faith-based institutions leading the way from the time of the Puritans through Dorothy Day and her Catholic Worker mission to the mainline Protestant and Jewish settlement-house movement, which in turn gave rise to the modern science of social work. The abolitionists sprang from the churches of New England and Upstate New York; the civil rights movement from the Baptist and African Methodist Episcopal churches of New York City and the Southern Bible and Cotton belts. The Reverend Jesse Jackson used his preacher's status and rapper's gifts to launch successful voter-registration drives throughout the South during the 1980s.

Mixing faith and politics—souls and votes—can be uplifting, but it can be toxic, too. In the South, religion was a bulwark of slaveholding society, with elders interpreting the Old Testament view of chattel, including human chattel, literally. In the North, the captains of industry mixed in their Union League Clubs a lethal cocktail of Calvinism, Darwinism, and profit. They made their workers drink it in the mines and on the factory floors. Literal readings of Scripture retarded the advance of equal rights for women and, in more recent years, for gays and lesbians. Churches have protested the moral blindness of science—of the eugenics movement, for example—but also have stood in the way of worthy experimentation. The Women's Christian Temperance Union launched itself with good intentions, aiming to achieve a sober, God-fearing society, but wound up fostering criminality and linking arms with anti-Catholic bigots.

Intolerance was and is a risk. In colonial times, the emotion of religious conflict could be drained away by distance. This was a vast, open country, and those with a different or controversial view of the Bible could simply leave, or be banished, to a place where they could practice their faith relatively undisturbed. (The Mormons were literally hunted as they moved, until they found peace beside the Great Salt Lake.) By the mid-nineteenth century, however, the flood of Irish Catholics was too overpowering, too visible, and too economically vital, to be out of view. The result: sectarian riots and faith-based discrimination.

Appropriately, the ballot box was and is an antidote to religious discrimination. The Catholic example is instructive. In 1884, a clergyman speaking to the Religious Bureau of the Republican National Committee famously blasted the Democratic candidate, Grover Cleveland, as an agent of "rum, Romanism, and rebellion." The GOP candidate, James G. Blaine, did not immediately repudiate the remark, and he lost New York City (and the election)—in large part due to Irish Catholic voters.

Protestants took to establishing their own secret societies, dedicated to rooting out Catholic influence. In 1893, a group called the American Protective Association promulgated a new secret oath for its members. Among other things, they swore to "do all in my power to retard and break down the power of the Pope" and "not vote for, or counsel others to vote for, any Roman Catholic, but [to] vote only for a Protestant . . ." The Catholic response was to plunge into politics that much more deeply; the first fruit of their labors was the 1928 presidential candidacy of New York governor Al Smith.

It took another generation, and the advent of the charismatic John F. Kennedy, for the United States to elect a Roman Catholic president. That, too, was a crusade, melding our fundamental metaphors for renewal and hope—a Great Awakening, a move to the West—into the phrase "New Frontier."

In domestic politics, the biggest story of the last generation is plain to see in retrospect. In summary form, here it is: Dismayed by what they saw as the loss of respect for biblical values, evangelical Christians abandoned their aversion to electoral politics and joined with anti-abortion, culturally traditional Catholics to build a new, faith-centered Republican Party that elected Ronald Reagan, Newt Gingrich, Tom DeLay, and two generations of Bushes.

It took a biblical generation—forty years in Old Testament reckoning—for the trend to reach its apogee, in Bush's reelection campaign of 2004. Its influence began to wane thereafter (the unpopularity of the Iraq War, sold in part by and for religious fundamentalists, hastened the process), but the rise of the Religious Right remains a big turn in the road of American history, and one of the most consequential developments of our time. Like a coda on a symphony, the 2004 presidential campaign produced the fast-rising candidacy of Arkansas governor Mike Huckabee in 2008. He had spent much of his career in the pulpit, as a Southern Baptist preacher. He had led one congregation. Now he was proposing to lead another: the GOP.

This cycle of conservative Christian political awakening began at a time of new beginnings in America, the 1960s, and it began, appropriately enough, with the issue of Bible prayer. The proximate cause, ironically, was not electoral politics per se, but six decisions of the U.S. Supreme Court.

In New York, as in most other states, public school students began the day reciting the Pledge of Allegiance and either the Lord's Prayer from the Gospel of Matthew or the Twenty-third Psalm from the Old Testament. Facing a challenge to that practice, New York State Regents prepared a "non-denominational" substitute. It said: "Almighty God, we acknowledge our dependence upon Thee, and we beg Thy blessings upon us, our teachers and our Country." But even that was too much for the Supreme Court. In the 1962 case of *Engel v. Vitale,* it ruled that requiring a prayer of *any* kind in the schools was a violation of the First Amendment. In a Pennsylvania case the next year, the justices ruled that the practice was unconstitutional even if students could get permission not to take part in the public praying.

Although civil libertarians and their Democratic allies saw the cases as a victory, an emerging cadre of conservative Republicans immediately saw it as a cause—and an opportunity. History tends to regard Arizona senator Barry Goldwater as a libertarian who cared little about religious matters and who, in later years, expressed alarm at the rise of the Religious Right. But in his 1964 presidential campaign, Goldwater stressed his strong belief in the need for a swift "return of prayer to the public schools of the nation."

Cases that followed over the next few years stoked the anger of religious conservatives. In 1965, the Court struck down a Connecticut law that barred the dispensing of contraceptives—at a time when Catholic teaching still held the use of such devices to be immoral. In 1968 the Court struck down a ban on the teaching of evolution. In 1973 the Court substantially loosened rules governing the national distribution of pornography, holding that it was up to localities to decide what was or was not obscene by applying their "local community standards." Finally, most famously, the Court ruled in 1973 that women had a qualified, constitutionally protected right to an abortion, most clearly at early points in pregnancy.

Taken together, the cases ignited a political supernova, the light from which took years to reach the consciousness of the political establishment. I caught a glimpse of its power in the mid-'70s as a reporter in Louisville, in Bible Belt Kentucky, in the audience of an ad hoc group called the Jefferson County Commission on Obscenity and Community Standards.

The city of Louisville itself was not a fundamentalist hotbed, but the surrounding blue-collar county suburbs were, populated for the most part by rural folks who were drawn to the metro area to work at the industrial plants of GE and Ford. The chief executive of the county, the county judge, was up for reelection, and he saw a way to appeal to that crowd by establishing the commission. The idea would be to set—in advance of any court case, should there be one—the county's very own "community standards." It was a political stunt: The commission never did establish the standards, if for no other reason than that no one was eager to be seen examining evidence.

But it was the citizens who came to testify who mattered. Politically, I came to realize, they were harbingers of the new era, in which "cultural politics" would be, or would seem, as important as the economics-based politics that traced its roots to the New Deal. One by one, voters trooped to the microphone in a school gymnasium to describe what they saw as the decay of society's moral and religious signposts. They saw their families as under siege, assaulted by an evil laxity. To them, the rapid spread of pornography was just one example. There was no prayer in the schools. No one respected the Bible.

This was the time of "Deep Throat" in two versions. In New York and Washington, the Nixon administration was under attack, hounded by leaks from an FBI man who had been given the porno-flick nickname "Deep Throat" by editors of *The Washington Post*. The journalists were out to expose the political evil of unconstitutional authoritarianism. In Louisville, at least in that gym, they fretted more about the movie of the same name, which they thought posed a greater danger than Nixon.

The disgust at the two "Deep Throats" sparked a reawakening of overtly biblical language in mainstream—that is, white middle-class—politics. The church-based civil rights movement was suffused with biblical vision and verve; now the same faith-based emotion spread to the suburbs in a different context.

The first to say so explicitly was Jimmy Carter, the governor of Georgia who rose from obscurity to the presidency in 1976. He did so by promising a post-Watergate moral housecleaning in Washington, and sold himself as a truth-telling man of the soil and proud "born-again Christian." Carter was the first major candidate to declare his born-again bona fides—and the first to directly appeal for the votes of fellow evangelicals. Carter's sister testified to her brother's spiritual quest for "total commitment to Christ." In a speech to the Democratic National Committee that year, Martin Luther King Sr. declared: "Surely the Lord sent Jimmy Carter to come on out and bring America back to where it belongs." In an interview in *Playboy,* Carter himself confessed to a lustful heart. The metropolitan wise guys laughed, but his confessional, revival-tent moment played well in the countryside.

The electoral-map results were astonishing: Carter, the born-again Bible Belt avatar, *swept* the South—the first time a Democrat had done so since 1960, and, it turned out, the last time since. The meaning was clear: Even though millions of white voters in the South had migrated to the Republican Party because of its "states'-rights" stand on race, Democrats could win the region if they could maintain, and build on, the new faith-based activism of the evangelicals. Republicans and conservatives, led by new RNC chairman Bill Brock of Tennessee, recognized the threat immediately, and went to work countering it.

So began a new political war, this one based not on race but on religion. It was actually a two-front war: one among conservative, anti-abortion Catholics in the North; the other among evangelical Christians in the South. The former, based initially in Connecticut, was led by acolytes of William F. Buckley's. The second was led by Brock and counseled by Richard Nixon's "Southern Strategy" guru, Harry Dent of South Carolina, and by a new breed of preacher awakened to the call of politics—ironically—by Jimmy Carter himself.

This new alliance had four goals: to undercut Carter with his evangelical base; unite conservative Catholics and fundamentalist evangelicals (who had feared and despised each other on theological and social grounds throughout American history); build a new national grassroots machine to turn out faith-based voters; and find an inspiring candidate around whom to unite for the 1980 election.

Undoing Carter was the easy part, since he was perched uneasily atop a national party that was, on most issues, at odds with evangelicals and conservative Catholics. Baptists had expected him, as president, to champion their causes—such as a return to prayer in public schools—and to abandon other positions he had been forced to adopt during the 1976 campaign. Carter did not do either. He continued to support *Roe v. Wade* and its progeny, continued to back the Equal Rights Amendment, which evangelicals viewed as an attack on the "traditional" family—and continued to allow alcohol to be served at White House functions, even if drinks were no longer available in the White House Mess. "I hope you give up your secular humanism and return back to Christianity," a prominent Baptist preacher told Carter.

Here was the opening the Republicans needed, and it was immediately spotted by a group of religious conservatives that met regularly in Washington to plot the counterrevolution among the faithful. Catholics in the North had been stirred to action by *Roe;* the National Right to Life Committee was gaining power. In the South they needed grassroots groups with whom they could link arms over abortion and other issues such as school prayer, gay rights, and "secular" science. All they lacked was a public leader and motivator to gather the reins.

And that is how Jerry Falwell barged into the picture. New Right activists in Virginia knew about him and were impressed. He was boisterous and literally from the wrong side of the tracks in his hometown, home base of Lynchburg. He was a born huckster who spoke in the deep, hickory-smoked accent of Southside Virginia. His televised sermons filled the pews of his Thomas Road Baptist Church to the acoustically contoured rafters, and he had turned his local broadcasts into a nationally syndicated powerhouse called the "Old Time Gospel Hour."

As Falwell told the story years later, a delegation led by strategist Paul Weyrich came down from Washington to see him and propose that he launch a group to engage evangelicals in politics from a conservative Republican angle. "They approached me and I agreed that it was a good idea," Falwell recalled. "The idea was to take the country back." (In fact, Falwell had been selling himself to the Beltway powers.) The name, Falwell and the others decided, would be "the Moral Majority," an echo of Nixon's "Silent Majority" from Dent's 1970 "Southern Strategy" election campaign for the GOP.

From the start, the goal was not only to register and inspire conservative evangelicals, but also to win the presidential election, which meant agreeing on a figure to lead the crusade. "We needed a candidate to rally around," said Falwell, "and we set about finding one." Falwell, Weyrich, and the rest of the group met with most of the Republicans who were thinking of running for president in 1980. It did not take them long to find the one they could agree on: former California governor Ronald Reagan. His California record was not perfect. As governor in the 1960s, he had not opposed state funding for abortions, and his professional roots were in the Hollywood movie industry, a font of secularism and moral corruption in the eyes of most evangelicals. But he had worked hard to win their support in recent years, decrying the absence of prayer in schools and backing, when he ran for the GOP nomination in 1976, a "human life amendment" to the U.S. Constitution.

With a candidate to sell and a constituency to reach—the one that Carter had identified—Falwell and his Washington-based media and direct-mail advisers compiled lists and opened Moral Majority chapters at the new suburban megachurches and old-fashioned rural outposts alike. Adapting a technique used by labor and business lobby groups, Falwell & Co. compiled "scorecard" ratings of candidates on moral issues. The Moral Majority staged rallies across the South and Midwest to support candidates, all of them Republicans.

The rallies were a powerful mix of rock concert, revival meeting, and political rally. At one in Alabama, huge screens in the darkened auditorium presented slide shows of examples of evil in the world of 1980, especially what Reagan would come to call "the evil empire," the Soviet Union: shark-toothed rows of missiles aimed at the United States, Khrushchev banging his shoe on the tabletop at the United Nations, Soviet tanks rolling into Prague. Falwell took the stage to thunder a warning against "godless communism" and—though he didn't say it in so many words—its allies in America: the godless, heathen liberals who supported abortion, gay rights, and secular science, and who opposed school prayer, the family, and tax breaks for religious schools.

After the ominous music and scary pictures, after the speech about the danger of liberals, Falwell talked about answers: God, of course, but also right-thinking candidates. Lo and behold, two of them happened to be in the audience: Jeremiah Denton, a former admiral and Vietnam War hero who was running for the U.S. Senate, and Albert Lee Smith, local congressional candidate. They stood at their places, the spotlights beaming down on them as they were showered with applause. Reagan was not there, but the Gipper was cheered, too.

The overall theme of the rally: God will rain down his wrath on us if we do not elect these people!

On election day, Denton and Smith swept to victory in Alabama, and Reagan swept the country, including the entire South except for Carter's home state of Georgia.

The pattern and the alliances were set. Only the names, candidates, and technical expertise changed in the intervening years. The Moral Majority faded but begat the more technologically sophisticated Christian Coalition, which promoted the presidential candidate Pat Robertson in 1988. Falwell (who had no love for Robertson), supported George H. W. Bush that year, the first step toward becoming what amounted to a family retainer. The third and last iteration of this line was Dr. James Dobson, who was not a preacher per se but a family counselor (better for the soft sell) and a radio host who deployed the latest computer technology to service his listeners and build his national following.

When it came time to build George W. Bush's political career from the ground up, Karl Rove began by introducing his charge to the Bible Belt of Texas: the small towns in the west and the new megachurches of Dallas and Houston and San Antonio. And it was Bush, not Carter, who became the ultimate in born-again presidents. He favored the teaching of "intelligent design" as an alternative to evolutionary theory. He opposed the creation and use of human embryos for stem-cell research. He supported a Human Life Amendment to the Constitution. He opposed a gay-rights constitutional amendment, and supported efforts in the states to define marriage as a union of one man and one woman. He supported the use of government money by churches to do social-welfare work. He opposed a court decision to take the words "under God" out of the Pledge of Allegiance. He nominated two justices to the Supreme Court whom right-to-lifers trust and admire, even if those justices, now that they are confirmed, are likely to tread carefully as they dismantle *Roe*.

Bush was the ultimate faith candidate in 2000. There was an even more perfect iteration in 2008, however—a Southern Baptist preacher turned politician named Mike Huckabee. The former governor of Arkansas (from the town of Hope, no less) campaigned among evangelicals in the Iowa Republican caucuses as a "Christian Leader." Since he was an ordained minister (he had pastored two congregations), that was literally true. And he won the caucuses.

Though Bush had become a pariah to much of the nation by the time of the 2008 campaign, the voters who got him elected remained as important as ever—especially to Republicans eager to succeed him. One of them was Senator John McCain, who in the 2000 campaign had denounced Falwell, Robertson, and others as "agents of intolerance" and division. Now McCain wanted their support. Some rethinking on matters of science was required. In the very earliest stages of the '08 campaign, when the bidding wars already were well under way among evangelical activists, McCain gave a speech at the Discovery Institute, the world's leading proponent of intelligent design. Seeking to run on the base that Bush and Rove had built, McCain at times depicted himself as a proponent of teaching the theory in public schools. "I think there is nothing wrong with teaching different schools of thought," he said in 2005. But a year later, he qualified his support for intelligent design. "Should it be taught in science class?" he said in a conference in Aspen, Colorado. "Probably not."

A few months later, McCain issued what he hoped would be his definitive statement on the matter. He did it in a book he cowrote with his longtime aide, Mark Salter. McCain praised Charles Darwin's work, and argued that the "only undeniable challenge the theory of evolution poses to Christian beliefs is its obvious contradiction of the idea that God created the world as it is in less than a week."

As far as McCain was concerned, the Bible in that case was metaphor, not literal truth. "Nature does not threaten our faith," he wrote. "On the contrary, when we contemplate its beauty and mysteries we cannot quiet in our hearts the insistent impulse of belief that, for all its variations and inevitable change, before its creation, in a time before time, God let it be so, and thus its many splendors and purposes abide in His purpose."

If that was a little too murky, McCain was back in the fall of 2007 with a clearer declaration—not on intelligent design, but on the design of America. "The Constitution established the United States as a Christian nation," he told the website Beliefnet.com in an interview. Surveys showed that a majority of Americans tended to agree. That would be news to the Founders, Christians all.

McCain's bid to secure the allegiance of evangelicals fell short. Two other 2008 candidates worked hard to woo them. One, ironically, was a Mormon—Mitt Romney of Massachusetts. As earnest, devout, and clean-cut as he was, Romney had a hard time keeping up with Huckabee, who had spent ten years pastoring churches as a Southern Baptist preacher. He ran an ad in Iowa proclaiming himself a "Christian Leader." Not surprisingly, the ad started an argument.

Four

WHAT CAN WE KNOW
AND SAY?

Who did Jill Abramson think she was? Well, she was a tough cookie, one of the toughest in journalism. The managing editor of *The New York Times,* she epitomized a certain kind of New Yorker, a bred-to-success blend of intellect, ironic self-awareness, and street smarts. In the early twenty-first century, she needed all the nerve she possessed, for the fault line of an age-old American conflict between free speech and national security ran through the newsroom outside her office in Manhattan. In the famous Pentagon Papers of 1971, the U.S. Supreme Court found a "heavy presumption" in favor of the press's freedom to publish classified information. As brainy and brave as she was, however, many voters had begun to worry that editors such as Abramson enjoyed too much freedom to settle this fateful American Argument on their own in a post-9/11 world.

There was a time when Abramson did not have to worry about government reaching into her notebooks, or those of the journalists with whom she worked. As a reporter for *The Wall Street Journal* during the 1980s, she had broken stories from the Senate Ethics Committee, which was investigating a financial scandal that involved several senators. Later, she and a colleague, Jane Mayer, unearthed the inside saga of the Senate Judiciary Committee's hearings on Clarence Thomas's nomination to the Supreme Court. In both cases, congressional authorities launched "leak investigations." In both cases, she and her newspaper's lawyers were able to brush off the inquisitors with relatively little trouble. "In those days," she says, "you simply told them you weren't going to play ball—and they would go away. There wasn't this extremely aggressive set of tactics used to compel reporters to reveal confidential information. In those days, the lawyers would just say 'we're not cooperating.' "

"Those days" ended with the 9/11 attacks. Suddenly, journalists faced newly aggressive federal prosecutors backed by less sympathetic judges. "Our lawyers sensed a change in the courts," Abramson said. "The presumption of certain press protections was no longer on our side." By the winter of 2007, *The New York Times* was bogged down in fighting an array of investigators who were demanding reporters' notes, records, or testimony—or all three. By far the most important, and controversial, was a Department of Justice investigation into the question of who furnished information to the *Times* for a December 2005 story that revealed the existence of a secret government wiretap surveillance program run by the National Security Agency. The paper's reporters had come across the story more than a year earlier, but Abramson and the other top editors had agreed, after urgent appeals from administration officials, to hold it and try to develop the story more fully in the interim.

Abramson was no antigovernment rebel. She took seriously her duty to weigh the equities carefully. She reminded anyone who asked that she was a citizen, too, with the same concerns about the dangers of terrorism that other Americans have. "I was in Washington for 9/11, and I now live just a few blocks from Ground Zero," she told me. "I lost a great friend and colleague from the *Journal,* Danny Pearl, to the very forces of terrorism that are clearly a tremendous ongoing worry to our country. I have a stake in national security, too. We don't take national security concerns casually. We *do* go through a careful balancing test with each of these stories. When the government asks us to withhold publication, we pause and give a very respectful hearing to those concerns."

In the case of the NSA story, she noted, the pause was long—more than a year. Eventually, she and the other editors decided to publish because of mounting concern within the government itself about the program's legality. It was that, rather than the details of the program itself (which, she says, the paper knew more about than it ever published), that deserved to be aired, says Abramson. "We certainly couldn't be accused of being cavalier."

But the paper could be, and was, accused of making on its own a decision in which the government also had a legitimate interest: the release of classified national-security information. After the *Times* story broke, a furious President Bush ordered a leak investigation, and Attorney General Alberto Gonzales hinted at the possibility that he might prosecute the newspapers' reporters. One possible weapon: the rarely deployed Espionage Act of 1917, which makes it a crime to knowingly receive classified information. Gonzales later "ratcheted down the rhetoric," Abramson observed, and she said she was never worried. "It's a pretty radical route that had rarely if ever been used against journalists." Much more likely, she said, the government could subpoena the reporters to testify in the investigation of the officials charged with leaking the story in the first place.

The Justice Department, charged with finding the source of the leak, moved with careful circumspection at first, focusing more on the bureaucrats than the reporters. At the start of 2008, the case was still ongoing. Abramson insisted that she did not feel intimidated. "I feel all the more determined to make sure, as managing editor of the *Times,* that the newspaper fulfills exactly the role that the Founders had in mind for the press, which is to hold the government accountable," she said. It is very easy to forget how afraid they were of extremely concentrated executive power, and the potential for abuse, and the press was seen as a very important check on that. "What *does* have a chilling effect," she said, "is that it's made our sources much more worried about talking to us," and "leak investigators" are interviewing "everyone inside the government who might be the journalists' sources" for the NSA and other stories. "It's complicated the process of talking to people who want to disclose things going on in Washington that trouble them."

If a weather map could depict the flow of global communication, America would be the big red storm system. We were reared with little or no reverence for the medieval idea that information flows from the top, controlled by king, church, or government. We rejected the presumption that government had an inherent right to keep its actions secret, even as we suggested or inferred a right of individual privacy to keep government away from *our* free flow of information and ideas. The resulting turbulence is essential to self-government, and to the dizzying velocity of information that generates twenty-first-century prosperity. Still, we are not and cannot be absolutists. A perfect market in public knowledge can be dangerous, especially in an age of terror. We tolerate limits on speech and inquiry—for libel, sedition, treason, national security—and may have to accede to more. Beyond the law is conformist social pressure, the flip side of democratic individuality, not to be different or difficult. Even (Tocqueville thought especially) a democracy such as ours is capable of imposing groupthink by means of a suffocating, speech-silencing, vigilante zeal. Where is the balance? That is our Argument.

We were born in speech, and born to speak. A quick glance at the global statistics shows the stunning impact of our habit and history. With less than 5 percent of the world's population, the United States nevertheless accounts for more than 20 percent of worldwide Internet traffic and 30 percent of all the Internet protocol (IP) addresses. In January of 2008, nine of the world's top-ten most heavily trafficked websites were American. More than half of all satellite transmissions are routed through the United States. The intensity—the information density, if you will—exists even though we lag behind Europe and Asia in cell phone and broadband connectivity. And that density is just as evident in the old media, including the oldest. Not only is the Library of Congress the world's largest, but five of the next ten largest are located in America, too. We have more television stations, radio stations, newspapers, and magazines than any other country—measured on a per capita or absolute basis.

If you consider travel a form of speech—and in America we do—we are the most talkative people on Earth. The average American travels more than 17,000 miles a year in his or her own country, commuting to and from a job for the most part. More important, more characteristic, are the *permanent* moves. Americans change residence an average of once every five years, "more often," notes historian James M. Jasper in *Restless Nation: Starting Over in America,* "than any other culture except nomadic tribes, although in line with our ancestors." In many countries and cultures, it is not only impractical to change residence or travel widely, it is illegal, a political statement of rebellion against local or national authority. The opposite is true here.

The intensity of our chatter is matched by its creativity. Americans did not invent the technical basis of the World Wide Web (Britain's Tim Berners-Lee did), but it took amped-up Americans to bring it to life. The *Financial Times* of London conducted a survey of influential, pattern-setting websites in the world in 2006 and found that seven of the top ten were American: *Google, eBay, Wikipedia, Amazon, Yahoo, MySpace,* and *YouTube.* Our media methods and tropes—from the very idea of "cable news" to the argumentative political theater of *Hardball* to the online jousting of the blogs—are mimicked worldwide. Everyone wants to talk in the American idiom, even if what they want to say is: Death to (or pity) America.

This New Eden of information is thrilling and powerful, but also potentially dangerous. To turn Nietzsche's epigram upside down, what made us stronger could also kill us—or so the government and its officials began to argue at the dawn of the twenty-first century. In doing so, they launched the latest round in a profound and essential American Argument.

Because free speech is the foundation of our way of life, our fitful urge to suppress it is all the more troubling. In the name of national security, officials throughout our history have tried to choke off our three rivers of information: free speech, open government, and personal privacy, a necessary adjunct to the ability to think and to speak without fear. In the past, we have emerged stronger after these spasms of suppression. Will that always be the case? We have to hope that the answer is yes, for if the answer is no, we will not be free enough to answer at all. Still, is there a limit to how much speech we can stand?

Only one planet in a billion, they say, has the atmosphere, mass, and temperature to support carbon-based life. The odds for creating a country such as ours out of the material of the Middle Ages were not quite as long, but our story does contain hints of the miraculous—or the skeptic's equivalent: fortunate timing. A perfect alignment of history, geography, ideology, and luck created the storm of American speech.

The British insistence on royal control of public speech was crumbling at the time of our founding. It had been undermined by Cromwell's revolution, the post-Reformation spread of religious diversity, and the post-Gutenberg rise of printed literacy and scientific thinking. Instead of one autocratic source of Truth dictated from above, educated people had come to believe in the idea—propounded by Milton and Bacon, amplified by philosophers such as John Locke and David Hume (and later John Stuart Mill)—that Truth could only be ascertained by the contention of theory and fact. Freedom to think and to speak was indispensable not only to science, philosophy, and faith, but, logically, to the proper administration of government.

The Founders were constructing a new government at precisely the time when the idea of free speech had gained currency as the New Answer.

They applied it, moreover, to a vast and soon to be continental country, the very size of which created demand for innovations in, and dependence on, communication technology. Over time, Americans did not always (or even usually) discover the pure-science fundamentals of new communications modes, but we were almost always the first to apply them commercially, if for no other reason than that the giant, rapidly growing country desperately required it. It was that way with the telegraph, the radio, and the Internet. We made the market. Size mattered.

The campaign to ratify—or oppose—the new constitution was arguably the world's first experiment in mass-media free speech. It engaged a whole nation as no media-driven conversation ever had. Since the authority of the new government would come from "We the People," meeting in special conventions of the thirteen states, the combatants in the contest needed to influence not only the elites of each state, but a wider circle—at a minimum, all adult-male property holders. In a new nation of some 3 million souls (including slaves), that meant reaching perhaps 500,000 voters. It sounds like a tiny number, but by the standards of the day—and the need for informed argument—it was a colossal undertaking. Scores of newspapers and pamphleteers took part. The collection of newspaper essays known as *The Federalist Papers* was the most famous.

Accustomed to the cacophony, Americans were not about to form a new government in silence. To win ratification in enough states to form the union, the Federalists had to promise that the new Congress would immediately submit to the states a Bill of Rights—and it is worth noting that the First Amendment was Congress's first order of business. Ratified with nine other amendments in 1791, the amendment prohibited the federal government from making any law "abridging the freedom of speech, or of the press, or the right of the people peaceably to assemble, and to petition the Government for a redress of grievances."

At the same time, the Bill of Rights enshrined protection against "unreasonable searches and seizures." A man who felt safe in his home, the Founders knew from personal experience, was free to think and speak without fear of literal invasion. The Fourth Amendment assured Americans the right to be "secure in their persons, houses, papers and effects," and to be shielded from intrusion except on a showing of "probable cause, upon Oath or affirmation, and only with a particular description of the place to be searched and the persons or things to be seized." Key words: "papers and effects." Modern translation: phone calls, e-mails, and Web searches.

Personal privacy could and would amplify the flow of speech and information, the Founders knew. The most influential pamphleteer of them all, Thomas Paine, wrote *Common Sense* anonymously. "Who the Author of this Production is," he wrote in his high-minded introduction, "is wholly unnecessary to the Public, as the Object for Attention is the Doctrine itself, not the Man." He was right. It was the most influential pamphlet of the time, and perhaps even in world history.

Governmental secrecy was another matter. The Founders knew that secrecy could be useful, even crucial, especially in war. George Washington's guerrilla strategy during the Revolution often had depended on it. They also knew it could be crucial in diplomatic talks. The Founders were both realistic and elitist enough to think that if they opened the proceedings of the Constitutional Convention to the public, they would never get anything done. As they gathered in the State House, therefore, their first organizational vote was to deliberate in private. They locked the doors, papered the windows, and swore each other to secrecy until their work was done. Neither the Constitution nor the Bill of Rights contains a demand for what we now regard as "open government." Indeed, both chambers of Congress in the early years often met behind closed doors; publication of official proceedings was spotty at best in the new republic's first decade.

Nevertheless, the Founders' worldview, and that of the Constitution itself, was basically skeptical of secrecy. Article I requires each chamber to keep a journal "and from time to time publish same, excepting such parts as in their Judgment require Secrecy." Crucially, all votes had to be recorded in that journal. The votes—the essence, after all, of congressional business—could not be kept secret under *any* circumstances. Article II requires the president to "from time to time give to the Congress Information of the State of the Union"—with no provision for that information to be kept secret. While Article III is remarkably silent on how the U.S. Supreme Court should conduct its business, the Bill of Rights speaks loudly about the public nature of all criminal trials in the country, which must be not only "speedy," but also "public."

"Sunlight," Justice Louis Brandeis wrote many years later, "is the best disinfectant," and even though they covered the windows, the Founders would have agreed.

War is the complication, and the excuse. As law professor Geoffrey R. Stone explains in his authoritative book *Perilous Times,* the tightest restrictions on the flow of American speech have come during times of war—or during what the powers that be *claimed* to be times of war.

Only a decade after the United States of America was born, it was nearly torn to pieces by this Argument. The year was 1798, the cause another revolution in the name of freedom—this one in France. We were not supposed to have political parties at all, but it did not take long for the political world of the new country to break in two, in a clash between speech and war. The issue, simply put, was whether France was to be feared or admired—and your freedom to speak came to depend on which view you espoused.

It was, ironically, the Federalists who chose to make an issue of the dangers of speech. They had used their right to free speech brilliantly to argue for the ratification of the Constitution they devised, but no sooner had they succeeded than they had second thoughts about its deployment by others in an atmosphere of war or near-war.

The Federalists saw in Paris in 1789 the rule of the Mob: a massacre of the ruling class in the name of the People, a Reign of Terror in which the word and will of the street was the only power. They saw a new society of levelers whose aim was not to protect individual (and property) rights, but to control all of the resources of the nation for the supposed benefit of the People. They saw such despotism as more evil than what it replaced.

The Jeffersonians, by contrast, saw a painful but glorious and inevitable birth of freedom on the Continent. The Jeffersonians agreed that a main aim of government was to protect property and individual freedom, but they distrusted the Federalists as the city-based financial class. They feared their eagerness to establish the mechanisms of national credit, since they saw credit as a form of enslavement. They saw the Federalists as elitists, and saw themselves as the genuine tribunes of the People. Simply put, Thomas Jefferson loved France and all things French. He remained supportive of the French Revolution even after its deadly lunacy became plain. He loved not only France, but also the idea that freedom's spread was inevitable and just. America, and its brother France, had unleashed an irresistible force. "This ball of liberty, I most piously believe, is now so well in motion that it will roll round the globe, at least the enlightened part of it, for light & liberty go together," he wrote. "It is our glory that we first put it into motion."

The new France that had been put "into motion" was an aggressive and bloody machine, however. After the execution of Louis XVI in 1793, and military moves by France into neighboring countries, war broke out between France and its enemy, Britain. The United States was officially neutral, but the Federalist administration, led by Washington and Hamilton, signed a friendly treaty with London the next year. They viewed it as a commercial cleanup exercise; the Jeffersonians saw it as an act of betrayal and treason. The streets of Philadelphia teemed with anti-Washington demonstrations.

The conflict on the Continent crossed the ocean. By the summer of 1798, the Federalists and their allies elsewhere in the English-speaking world were alarmed by the rise of the Jeffersonian "Democratic-Republicans," of course, but also by what was widely seen as France's renewed attempt to throw its weight around in the New World. American independence, the Federalists charged, was being undermined by French military spies and sympathizers.

Every American was now a traitor in the eyes of his political enemies, or at least could be all too easily labeled as such. It was a grim time of anger and fear about foreign influence. Presiding over it was a party that feared losing an election, and that saw its own looming loss, self-righteously, as a threat to the very existence of the country.

And so it was that the government sought to render the First Amendment meaningless only seven years after its ratification. Congress enacted the Sedition Act in 1798. President John Adams signed it into law insisting it was a "war measure," even though the United States was not at war. Anyone could figure out the true aim of the statute by reading the expiration date: March 3, 1801, the day the next administration would assume power.

The statute's language was startling, even frightening. It prescribed fines and jail terms of up to two years for any speech or writing that was "false, scandalous and malicious" and "against" the government, the Congress, or the president; or had the "intent to defame" them or bring any of them "into contempt or disrepute; or to excite against them, or any of them, the hatred of the good people of the United States, or excite any unlawful combination therein for opposing or resisting any law of the United States or any act of the president done in pursuance of any such law." Only one elected federal official was left unprotected: the vice president, who, at the time, was . . . Thomas Jefferson.

The Federalists told themselves that they were honoring American values—as distinguished from British ones—by criminalizing only seditious statements that were "false, scandalous and malicious." In practice, judges ignored that nicety in presiding over twenty-five arrests and ten successful prosecutions.

The Federalists got *theirs* two years later, in the election of 1800. They lost the presidency to a figure many of them viewed as the antichrist himself, Jefferson. The partisan Federalist judges were swept from the bench. In later years Congress apologized to and voted compensation for those convicted under the act. It expired before it could be reviewed, but the verdict was immediate and clear. "Although the Sedition Act was never tested in court," Supreme Court Justice William Brennan wrote in the landmark case of *New York Times v. Sullivan,* "the attack upon its validity has carried the day in the court of history."

The Sedition Act was only the first act in the history of "wartime" attacks on free speech. The other main episodes are as troubling, though in each of the latter cases a *real* war, or something close to a war, was in progress at the time. When the South seceded in 1861, President Abraham Lincoln suspended the common-law writ of habeas corpus in what was left of the United States, in effect making secret and beyond review the process of apprehending and imprisoning dissenters. Lincoln's action brought a rebuke from the Supreme Court, which ruled that only Congress had such power, but Lincoln ignored the ruling. (Congress voted two years later to approve the policy Lincoln had pursued on his own.)

Lincoln limited speech through the use of technology as well as by wielding presidential power. From the onset of the Civil War—the First Battle of Bull Run, or Manassas in Southern parlance—he ordered government officials to monitor and censor all traffic passing through the country's then-new telegraph system. The censorship had immediate political uses: the government cut the lines to prevent early word from getting out about the unexpected disaster at Bull Run, which was a blow not only to the Army but to the president.

During World War I, President Woodrow Wilson authorized officials to prosecute conscientious objectors and others who criticized the government, and he backed the passage of a new Sedition Act that was a carbon copy of the discredited one of a century earlier.

The new law, passed in 1918 as an amendment to the Espionage Act of 1917, was the culmination of a generation of private-sector hysteria, stemming originally from the proto-Socialist Paris Commune in 1873 and extending to the rise of labor-union activism here. While the Espionage Act was supposed to be limited to cases in which an American actually aided an enemy in wartime, the Sedition Act made it a crime to "utter, print, or publish any disloyal, profane, scurrilous or abusive language" about the government itself. It was the time of the paranoid Federalists all over again, only worse.

We tend to forget how sweeping—shocking—this law was. Some 1,500 domestic opponents of America's involvement in World War I were indicted under the Sedition Act, including many pacifists and socialists who ultimately went to jail. Justice Department officials conducted the infamous "Palmer Raids" that jailed such figures as socialist Eugene Debs and even a sitting member of Congress, a socialist named Victor Berger of Wisconsin. Antiwar "radical" newspapers and magazines were suppressed as federal postal authorities suspended their mailing privileges. The law was repealed in 1921—one of the few good things you can say about the Warren G. Harding years—but the Espionage Act remains very much on the books.

And we tend to forget that these statutes were upheld by the Supreme Court. Oliver Wendell Holmes is famous for his dissent in a case that (unsuccessfully) challenged the Sedition Act, but it was Holmes who wrote the majority opinion supporting the Espionage Act. He defended it with his famous statement that "free speech would not protect a man falsely shouting fire in a theater and causing a panic." The question in every case, Holmes said, is "whether the words used are used in such circumstances and are of such a nature as to create a clear and present danger that they will bring about the substantive evils that Congress has a right to prevent." In the case at hand, which dealt with activists who tried to appeal to prospective military recruits, the answer was yes, there was danger.

The attitude resurfaced during World War II. President Franklin D. Roosevelt authorized FBI director J. Edgar Hoover to wiretap at will anyone he deemed to be a pro-Nazi sympathizer—not to mention other, more routine political enemies. As the Vietnam War dragged on and domestic dissent rose, President Richard Nixon, citing as precedent the actions of FDR and LBJ, authorized bugging and wiretapping of what he called domestic "subversives."

In each case, the ship of state righted itself eventually, writes Professor Stone in *Perilous Times*. The Nixon era and Vietnam, for example, produced the Pentagon Papers case—a high-water mark in the history of press freedom to publish what it knows. Stone summarizes the hard-won and oft-delayed victories for free speech: "Lincoln's suspensions of habeas corpus were declared unconstitutional ... the [Supreme] Court's own decisions upholding the World War I prosecutions were all later effectively overruled, and the internment of Japanese Americans during World War II has been the subject of repeated government apologies and reparations. Likewise, the Court's [Cold War–era] decision ... upholding the convictions of the leaders of the Communist Party has been discredited, the loyalty programs and legislative investigations of that era have all been condemned, and the [Nixon administration's] efforts to 'expose, disrupt and otherwise neutralize' antiwar activities during the Vietnam War have been denounced by Congress and the Department of Justice."

We have survived such episodes, says Stone, and "the nation's commitment to free speech rebounded, usually rather quickly, sometimes more robustly than before." As long as "wars are of reasonably limited duration," he concludes, "the dangers of suppression of speech seem to be something we can withstand." His book was published in 2004, however, and things have hardly improved in the meantime. Vice President Dick Cheney has said that the nation faces a "long war" against implacable and hard-to-find enemies. It is a war that could last decades. Will we still be free to talk about it by the time it comes to an end?

In the twenty-first century, the front line of the argument between speech and war is not on a printing press or a street corner, but on an Internet connection, cell phone network, or webpage. Within days of the 9/11 attacks, President Bush secretly authorized the National Security Agency to tap—without first obtaining warrants—telephone calls to and from foreign numbers the agency deemed to be linked to possible terrorists and related suspects. He did so even though Congress, in 1978, had specifically declared that the NSA could not tap the calls of American citizens in the United States without special authorization from a secret court established specifically for that purpose. Bush (or, more particularly, his legal advisers) felt the need to issue the secret order even though the special court had rejected NSA requests in only a handful of cases among thousands. To be specific, between 1995 and 2004, the Court approved 10,613 out of 10,617, meaning that it had rejected four.

The new NSA surveillance effort was erected on top of other secret systems long since in place. One was ECHELON, a cooperative effort among major English-speaking countries—including the United States, the United Kingdom, Canada, Australia, and New Zealand—to monitor much of the planet's civilian telephone, fax, and data traffic. An initiative of the Clinton administration, ECHELON did not zero in on specific individuals, but rather "data mined" the world of communications for terrorist patterns in the chatter.

Those were some of the *secret* measures, unknown to all but the smallest circle of government officials. But there were many others openly approved by Congress in the weeks after 9/11, and they were equally controversial. The Patriot Act, initially passed with little controversy, eased FBI access to Internet records, gave the FBI broader powers to conduct domestic surveillance, and authorized the Treasury Department to create a financial-intelligence gathering system for use by the CIA. It allowed evidence gathered by the CIA to be used by federal grand juries and in seeking permission for criminal wiretaps, expanding the CIA's reach into domestic law-enforcement for the first time. "Frankly, there are so many collection programs out there, even I may not know them all," said Democratic representative Jane Harman of California. She should have known. At the time I talked to her about it, she was the ranking Democrat on the House Intelligence Committee.

If there were programs she did not know about, and there might have been, President Bush would not have been the least bit sorry about that fact. He was never one to care for legal niceties to begin with, even if they were rooted in the Constitution. Rather, Bush did not think he had to confide in Congress, let alone get its permission to operate in this sphere. His administration argued that his independent, unreviewable authority stemmed from two sources. One was the Joint Resolution passed by Congress three days after the 9/11 attacks, authorizing Bush to use "all necessary and appropriate force against those nations, organizations, or persons he determines planned, authorized, committed, or aided the terrorist attacks . . . or harbored such organizations, or persons, in order to prevent any future acts of international terrorism against the United States by such nations, organizations or persons." The Congress framed the call in terms of "military force," administration officials conceded. But Congress also broadly charged the president with preventing another attack and gave him the sole job to go after the persons "he determines" launched or aided in perpetrating the mayhem of 9/11. How else is he supposed to "determine" that than by expanding surveillance? That alone is enough authority for the NSA program, officials argued.

The White House's other justification was even more breathtaking: that the president's power as commander in chief allowed him—and him alone—to authorize the NSA to tap citizens' calls without a warrant. The need for wartime speed and flexibility was something that only the Boss could address.

The administration evidently did not think it would ever have to make this case to the public, let alone in court. Then, in December 2005, *The New York Times* dropped its bombshell, a detailed, front-page story about the NSA warrantless wiretap program. The president not only vigorously defended the program, but refused to tell the public virtually anything about it, except to say that "if Al Qaeda is calling into the United States, I sure as heck want to know about it." His loyal attorney general, Alberto Gonzales, issued a stout defense, and threatened to haul the *Times* into court for violating the Espionage Act of 1917.

History has a way of repeating itself. A group of journalists and scholars—specialists in terrorism policy and the Middle East—filed suit to stop the NSA program. Represented by the American Civil Liberties Union, they argued that their ability to function had been hampered by an unconstitutional invasion of their free speech and privacy rights. The plaintiffs cleverly picked a friendly forum: a federal district court in Detroit, a city that is home to the nation's largest concentration of Arab and Muslim Americans—men and women likely, fairly or not, to be "persons of interest" to the government.

The plaintiffs also got lucky. They got a judge, Anna Diggs Taylor, who had been married to a Democratic congressional representative from Detroit. More important, she had a rich history of dedication to civil rights, stretching back to dangerous volunteer work in Mississippi in hot summers of the early 1960s. A Yale Law School graduate and appointee of President Jimmy Carter's, Taylor was the first black woman to serve on the federal bench in Michigan, and had been there for more than a quarter century when the NSA case arrived.

She put the wood to the president. The commander in chief's powers were defined and limited by the Constitution—not by the creative imagination of the president and his attorney general, she ruled. "There are no hereditary Kings in America and no powers not created by the Constitution," she wrote.

The president appealed. He sent his press secretary forth to say that the NSA surveillance "has helped stop terrorist attacks and saved American lives." Precisely how the program had done that was, of course, a national-security secret. The following year Taylor's fiercely worded opinion was overturned. The NSA program grinds on, whatever it is—its true extent still enveloped in the deepest secrecy, its barest outlines known only to a handful of elected leaders. In the fall of 2007, the president and the now-Democratic Congress were still arguing about how to bring the program under the proper supervision of the courts.

Whether that would help Jill Abramson and *The New York Times* to get the real story was at best unclear.

In the meantime, yet another front opened in the never-ending argument between speech and security in wartime. This one involved a symbolically important satellite dish in Staten Island, not far from where the Twin Towers once stood. It pitted the almost unlimited power of the federal government in the post-9/11 world against a forty-three-year-old Pakistani American who was merely trying, he said, to make a buck selling access to a cable channel.

The man in question was named Javed Iqbal. He ran a company called HDTV Ltd., which downloaded satellite feeds from the Middle East (hence the dish in Staten Island) and piped them to homes in the metropolitan New York area. Federal investigators evidently had had Iqbal under surveillance for some time. They arrested him after he offered to install the channel Al-Manar for an informant posing as a Lebanese citizen. Nothing wrong with *that,* except that the channel was the televised publicity branch of Hezbollah, which the U.S. State Department officially designated as a "foreign terrorist organization" in 1997. In March 2006, the U.S. Treasury Department designated the network itself as a "global terrorist entity." That legal label in turn allowed the government to freeze Al-Manar's assets in the United States and prohibit any and all transactions between American citizens and the network.

The weapon of choice used to go after Iqbal was a decades-old trading-with-the-enemy statute that had been updated after 9/11 to reach anyone who dealt with a designated terrorist group. That, allegedly, meant Iqbal, who was charged with supporting terrorism. "He isn't being charged for operating a training camp," wrote *The Arab American News,* "gunrunning, stockpiling weapons, plotting a terrorist attack or even being a member of a terrorist group." All he was doing was trying to sell someone some TV access, the paper argued. "Vibrant democracy is supposed to uphold freedom of speech, regardless of content, in order to facilitate the exchange of ideas so they can be better decision makers. That's the idea, anyway."

Not quite, but it fell to Anthony Romero, the son of a Puerto Rican immigrant, to make the case anyway. With degrees from Princeton and Stanford, he still navigates with an eye on his late father's struggles to make do. "My worldview is about dignity and my father's dignity came from within," says his son. "You treat everyone with the dignity that they deserve." An openly gay Latino, Romero is executive director of the American Civil Liberties Union. As such, he runs the nation's oldest, largest—and most controversial—organization dedicated to defending free speech and privacy rights. "I have the best job in the world," Romero said. "I read the newspapers, get angry, and come to work to do something about it."

The Iqbal case tested his patience. The authorities slapped Iqbal with violating Treasury regulations, but prosecutors hinted there was more. "The charge lurking in the background is material support for terrorism," said an assistant U.S. attorney who appeared at Iqbal's arraignment. His attorney called the charges "completely ridiculous." Romero's office expressed "serious First Amendment concerns" and noted that the Treasury law—the one under which Iqbal was arrested—has an exception for news outlets. "The fact that the government is proceeding with the prosecution in spite of " the exception, said New York ACLU lawyer Donna Lieberman, "raises serious questions about how free our marketplace of ideas is."

Did Al-Manar traffic in "news"? Did it deserve to be considered part of the "marketplace of ideas"? Are calls to murderous jihad "ideas"? Much of the Al-Manar broadcasting menu, government affidavits said, celebrated suicide bombings and violent jihad against the United States, Great Britain, Israel, and the West as a whole. The stream of heated talk in Arabic was both inspiring (if you were a terrorist) and savage, calling for the "destruction of the infidels" wherever they may be. If there is no constitutional protection for "shouting fire in a crowded theater," as Justice Oliver Wendell Holmes said, wasn't this a conflagration in the making?

The ACLU was preparing to defend Iqbal and Al-Manar, however. "This is about what rules and values will guide an American system of justice that we can hold up to Americans and to the entire world," said Romero. "We're fighting for tolerance, equality, for due process. We're fighting for American values. At some point, history will judge us by what we believe in and what we stand for. Are we going to be on the right side of history or the wrong side?"

It's a question we need to debate, but we can only do so if we feel free to speak.

Five

THE LIMITS OF
INDIVIDUALISM

It was a frigid January day in New Hampshire, but despite the temperature the line of voters snaked through the high school cafeteria and out the front door. Everyone wanted to meet Bill Clinton and shake his hand. The candidate was just as eager to meet them. He wanted to administer—needed to administer—what I thought of as "the tractor beam of empathy": the uplifting, soulful look of concern that made him what he was, and that eventually made him president.

The Tractor Beam was Clinton's survival tool in the days before the New Hampshire primary in 1992, when his campaign was foundering on controversy and scandal over sex and the draft. He would give a speech in a high school gym on a school day, guaranteeing a large, captive crowd (though most of them couldn't vote, at least they didn't know much about the Vietnam War). After a speech—the theme was always essentially the same: "community, opportunity, responsibility"—Clinton and his entourage would move to the cafeteria. He would set himself up in front of the empty steam tables and prepare to greet the world.

One by one, the locals would move in front of him as though in an assembly line. They would give their names (if he didn't already know them, which he often did). He would look down in a brotherly way (for he was tall enough, at 6′3″, to look down on almost anyone). He would place a spidery, E.T.-like hand on their elbow and gaze at them sympathetically, narrowing his gray eyes to concentrate his attention. The voters would unburden themselves: fast-moving streams of confessional chatter about their families, dreams, schemes, and agendas. And for the minute or so that each voter stood before him, it was as though there was no one else in the universe (or at least New Hampshire) and no concerns but theirs.

It could seem hokey, even preposterous, but it worked and the voters cherished those moments. By primary day, thousands had been uplifted, if not transported, and they told their spouses, children, parents, and friends about the experience. When the votes were counted, Clinton had rescued himself, finishing a salvageable, spin-able second. He was "the Comeback Kid," and the Tractor Beam, I always thought, was what won him the nomination and, six months later, the presidency.

When he came to Washington, Bill Clinton resolved to be the empathy president. In his campaign slogan, "community, opportunity and responsibility," the word closest to his heart was "community." In college at Georgetown, he recited Martin Luther King speeches from memory, glorying in their message of shared mission. Clinton's wife, Hillary Rodham, felt the same way, even though she had arrived at Wellesley as a freshman with a copy of *The Conscience of a Conservative* by Barry Goldwater. At Yale Law School, she had helped found the new field of "children's rights," which sought to use the courts to ensure that society cared for abused and neglected kids. Sometimes in life, she would later famously say, it takes a village—a village in which people cared for, and were asked to care for, each other.

Politically, the Clintons came of age together at Yale, during the academic ascendancy of Harvard philosopher John Rawls, who published his famous and influential *A Theory of Justice* in 1971. It was required reading on elite campuses and informally required elsewhere. For activist students who chose to stay within the bounds of traditional politics—for students like Bill and Hillary—Rawls provided a powerful argument for, and description of, an ideal modern welfare state. The essence of his vision was simple enough: that the best government was one that distributed liberty and wealth equally with greatest efficiency, providing "fair equality of opportunity" for all, especially for the disadvantaged. It was okay, in other words, to distribute benefits unequally if the poorest and weakest benefited disproportionately. Any society could best be judged—should only be judged—by how well it treated the most vulnerable of its members.

By that standard, America was failing in the early seventies. The richest and most powerful country in the world still had tens of millions mired in poverty. Drugs and crime were imprisoning what the Reverend Jesse Jackson later called "the least of these"—most, but by no means all, of them African Americans—in what social scientists were concluding was a permanent "underclass." The New Frontier had come and gone; so had the Great Society, both with mixed results. But for Bill and Hillary Clinton, and for other young students of their time and place and ambition, Rawls charted a decent, responsible way forward.

Years later, as they arrived in Washington in the winter of 1993 to occupy the White House, the Clintons still felt that their presidency needed to mean something grand in that Rawlsian way. What action, what crusade for community, would they propose that was worthy of the 1960s? The answer: She, not he, at least initially, would take on the monumental (and, for a First Lady, unprecedented) task of guaranteeing affordable health care for all Americans.

This was not a new idea, especially abroad. The Germans had designed and built the first modern welfare state in the nineteenth century, including a rudimentary national health-care system. After World War II, the British had committed themselves to "cradle to grave" health care; in one way or another, most modern European countries already had or would soon do the same.

Glimmers of this communitarian idea were scattered across the American landscape and American history. Indeed, self-starting utopias of shared endeavor were everywhere in the nineteenth century, from the Oneida community in Upstate New York to the Shaker villages of New England and Kentucky to the Amana colonies of Iowa. Using a fee levied on coal operators as part of their national contract, the United Mine Workers established their own hospitals throughout Appalachia, where private care of any kind—and at any price—had always been difficult to come by. After World War II, President Harry Truman had suggested that the country adopt a national health-care system similar to the one the British were establishing. The idea went nowhere.

Why? The specific reasons were complex, but the core explanation was simple: Health care was never considered something we owed each other. The system, if it could be called that, consisted primarily of individuals and families seeking care, and individual doctors and hospitals dispensing it. It was not the government's job. The first hospitals were charity and/or church related (many of the most important ones remained so) or were connected to universities. Cities and states were pioneers and leaders in public-health programs, but those had more to do with epidemiology and mass-inoculation preventative care than individual care. Cities might provide indigent care, but most of us were supposed to fend for ourselves, and to pay for it.

And for that care you would pay (or, as things developed, your employer's insurance might pay) a hospital and a doctor. It was person-to-person, and the person on the other end was a doctor making decisions on his own (or so the patients thought). This was part of the American way: the hero doctor, dating back to Dr. Benjamin Rush in Philadelphia. The spirit was captured by another Philadelphian, Thomas Eakins, in his famous painting *The Gross Clinic,* and, later, by Norman Rockwell on the cover of *The Saturday Evening Post.* To burnish that image, the American Medical Association turned itself from an academic enclave into one of Washington's first modern lobbying powerhouses.

By the time the Clintons arrived, the quaint, painterly world of health care had all but vanished from real life. In its place stood a colossal, mind-bogglingly complicated $2-trillion-a-year system (if it could be dignified by that term). The federal government controlled part of it through the two Great Society programs (Medicare and Medicaid) championed by President Lyndon Johnson in the 1960s, during the last full flowering of communitarian thinking in Washington. Health-insurance companies controlled much of the rest, servicing, and profiting from, the promise of corporate America to provide coverage for its employees. In bureaucratic parlance, there were dozens of other "stakeholders," from the major drug companies to for-profit and not-for-profit hospitals, to universities, to the military—which, along with the prison system, was the only part of the federal government to provide direct care to patients. It was, and remains, literally impossible for anyone to comprehend it all, or envision the detailed architecture of it.

But Hillary Clinton, she of the Village, would try not only to comprehend it, but to redesign the whole thing, and to do so in secret. On the first day of the new administration, her coterie of advisers literally bounded out of their cars on Lafayette Square as they made their way to their temporary headquarters. The plan that she and they eventually came up with was both daring and cautious.

Hillary Care proposed to take one giant step for American mankind. Henceforth, her plan said, Americans would consider affordable, decent health care a right of citizenship: an *entitlement*. But rather than create a new federal bureaucracy to deliver it directly (even the postal service wasn't really a government agency anymore) she proposed an array of new regulatory oversight of hospitals, HMOs, drug companies, insurance companies, and the rest. Employers would be required to provide health care for their employees (many, but by no means all, did so voluntarily in 1993). Employers who did not or could not offer their own plan would be required to pay into regional funds. Each region would set up its own purchasing co-op, and each co-op would ask for bids from the health-care providers, as federal employee unions already did. And then there would be an agency that would evaluate the claims and track records of each would-be provider. Thus, the health-care industry—one-seventh of the nation's gross domestic product—would be made to work for all.

Fashioned without committee hearings, the gargantuan piece of legislation weighed in at 1,342 pages when it hit the mahogany desks of members of the U.S. Senate. Anyone looking down from the gallery that day, as I did, had a pretty sure sense that the bill was going nowhere: It was the size of two Manhattan phone books. It was too heavy to carry, too long to read—and too easy to characterize (not quite fairly, since it did try to use market mechanisms) as the kind of government-knows-best thinking that the conservative movement had spent nearly forty years trying to discredit. A broad coalition of business interests, inside and outside of the health-care industry, killed the bill, but in reality it wasn't too hard. The thing killed itself, and its mere existence was one reason, though not the main one, that the GOP took control of the House in 1994. Hillary Care was simply too heavy a lift, even for the Tractor Beam of Empathy.

Hillary learned a profound political lesson, one she could have taken from *The Conscience of a Conservative*. From Goldwater's time forward, the country had been bombarded with decades' worth of corrosively skeptical, antigovernment rhetoric—much of it, especially after the Vietnam War and Watergate, justified. A leader had to be careful trying to sell government as the answer even to such a basic, glaring problem as health care.

By the time she launched her campaign for president in 2007, the terrain had changed. Corporate America had come to see that bloated, out-of-control health-care costs were killing its ability to compete in world markets. Now the issue was not just a matter of human decency, but trade; now business had a rooting interest in favor of government involvement, at least to the extent of controlling the prices for drugs and treatment provided by hospitals, doctors, drug companies, and HMOs. Several states, including Arnold Schwarzenegger's California, had enacted "play or pay" laws, requiring employers either to pay for health insurance for their workers or pay into a state fund for insurance. Spending by that fund would be carefully controlled by government, with tight regulation of what the providers could charge.

Other leading candidates—first John Edwards, then Senator Barack Obama—came forth with comprehensive proposals. Edwards's mandated that every American get health insurance if he or she could afford it, or through a government program if not. Obama's plan relied on tax incentives to accomplish almost the same thing—close to universal coverage at a time when 47 million Americans had no coverage at all.

At first, Hillary approached health care with hot-stove caution. She was aware that Republican governors, if for no other reason than to control their indigent health-care costs, were now talking about covering everybody in some way. When I saw her in the summer of 2007 I mentioned Arnold and the others. "I think you're winning the argument after all these years," I offered. As I recited this, Hillary arched her back in statue-on-a-pedestal fashion and nodded with an "I told you so" smile. "It's pretty ironic, isn't it?" she said. "I think maybe we ought to let the states do it one at a time, until the whole country is covered," she told me with a wry tinge of bitterness. "It might be a lot less trouble."

But campaign politics was campaign politics—and it was driving her back to the future. In the run-up to the Iowa caucuses, she found that she needed to match Edwards and to try to outflank Obama, whose plan did not require that everyone be covered. Suddenly, Hillary jettisoned her hard-won caution. She was for mandates, too, though she remained wary of speaking in the language of entitlement. That declaration was left to another Democrat who, with a new Nobel Prize to call his own, had taken on the status of oracle and moral scold. Health care, former vice president Al Gore said in a video he recorded for his own cable channel, "ought to be a matter of right." The government ought to pay for and administer a direct "universal" system itself. But Gore could say that. He wasn't running.

The Founders' vision and the continent's riches led us to think (or to dream) that we could prosper primarily as individuals and fami-

lies, largely unburdened by what we saw as instruments of colonial oppression: taxes and economic regulation. "Taxes" and "tariffs" were fighting words and concepts; it took a constitutional amendment, no less, to
permanently institute an income tax 126 years after the founding document itself was written. Nevertheless, even pioneer life required government, however rudimentary. Settlers needed roads upon which to roll
westward, land deeds enforced by courts and judges, couriers to deliver
mail, and an army to fight the tribes.

Besides, the dream of self-sufficiency, of venturing into the woods
alone, was not the only one that animated our early years. In some ways, it
was the exception. As seen from the coasts, the continent could be as forbidding as it was inviting. In New England, settlers preferred the town
common and the Mayflower Compact as cooperative ideals; in the Middle
Colonies, a gracious town life was the beau ideal; even the frontier habit of
"barn raising"—building new barns, or replacing ones that had burned
down—bespoke a commitment to common action. Early on, public education came to be seen as a necessary community task. From there, many
other tasks followed, at first handled by charities and private corporations,
and later, in many cases, by government—first local, then national in a
kind of upward capillary action of government and bureaucracy. The
New Deal, our democracy's answer to socialism and fascism, was the
apogee of this arc. If we assumed the God-given worth of every individual—our central creed—how could we countenance a nation in which, as
FDR put it, one-third of us was "ill-clothed, ill-housed, and ill-nourished"?

A country founded on the principle of individual freedom—"life,
liberty and the pursuit of happiness"—has both a gift and a problem. "No man is an island," the English poet John Donne wrote in the
seventeenth century, but in the late eighteenth century, at least in America, you very nearly could be, at least physically. The continent was so im-
mense, the forests so thick, and the land so fertile, that a man could
literally live alone. Strictly speaking, if survival was all that mattered, he
did not even need a market to sell to. He had everything he needed in the
woods, streams, and fields.

This was how Americans saw themselves, or claimed to see themselves. In his first Farewell Address—the one in 1783, when he resigned
his commission as commander in chief of the continental army—General
George Washington envisioned his disbanded troops heading out to the

"extensive and fertile Regions of the West," which would "yield a most happy Asylum to those, who, fond of domestic enjoyment are seeking for personal independence."

This independence was not only geographical, it was psychological, spiritual, political—and legal. With the colonial grants wiped away by revolution, new American landowners could buy and hold land in "fee simple," just the way the highest-ranking feudal lords had done at the top of Old World society. Every man was his own lord and vassal. He could make whatever money he could, and keep most of it as his own. There would be taxes in the New World, but they were not "direct." Indeed, for the first century of its existence, Washington derived the bulk of its revenue from global trade—from import tariffs and duties—and from sales of federal land.

The spirit of economic individualism was always with us, and by the middle of the nineteenth century it had become a kind of secular religion in the world of business, even when the aim of *big* business was to snuff out the very entrepreneurialism that nurtured commerce to begin with. In 1886, at the height of the first Gilded Age, the U.S. Supreme Court declared that the Southern Pacific Railroad—and, by extension, all profit-making corporations—were entitled to be viewed as individual persons in the eyes of the law. We were the first country in the world to view them that way, but it made sense: Individualism was Us, even if Us was a corporate leviathan. Americans have never fully accepted the idea that tax tables should be designed, and revenues disbursed, in a way that makes government the redistributor of wealth and guarantor of income. "Fairness" is one thing, redistribution another.

There was another view—a counterpoint—and much of our history is about the struggle of communal thinking to gain sway in the economic life of America. The question has never been whether Americans would pitch in to help each other—but rather the extent to which government could require them to do so. Observers from Tocqueville onward have commented on our willingness, even eagerness, to join voluntary associations, from civic groups to teaching circles. Americans give more to charity per capita than citizens of any other country. Bill Gates and Warren Buffett established the wealthiest charitable foundation in history. We may "bowl alone" more often these days, as author Robert Putnam gloomily puts it in his metaphor for anomie, but we also worry about the fact that we do so. Walt Whitman, our bard of brotherhood, saw no conflict between his own credo of the individual and his love of all mankind. "[W]hoever walks a furlong without sympathy," he wrote in "Song of Myself," "walks to his own funeral drest in a shroud."

But what is the government's role in reconciling two age-old American concepts: "There's no such thing as a free lunch" and "united we stand"?

What the sociologist Amitai Etzioni calls the "communitarian idea" came with the earliest settlers, at least to New England. In the Mayflower Compact in 1620, Pilgrims aboard that ship pledged to establish an inspirational, one-for-all and all-for-one Christian polity when they landed. Colonial founders in places such as Philadelphia and Savannah had their architects lay out plans for idealized cities that embodied, at least on the land plats, a yearning for an equitable community life and shared labor. In the first half of the nineteenth century, Henry Clay's "National System" of roads and other improvements helped thicken the idea of a continental community. At the end of that century, President Theodore Roosevelt turned chest-beating nationalism into the engine of direct social uplift. His Progressives installed—over fierce objection—limits on the exploitation of cheap labor and resources. In the name of fighting the Depression, FDR erected the real monument to the communal ethos, the New Deal, although he was careful (and not quite honest) to call the centerpiece of the era, Social Security, an "insurance plan."

It was not, and is not. Social Security is a pay-as-you-go transfer of tax money from one generation to the next. It has accomplished its original objective—protecting the elderly from destitution—and then some. It is not self-insurance, however.

World War II produced in America the biggest cooperative economic enterprise in the history of the planet: the construction of a war machine and a new, more centralized society to operate it. That, in turn, made us a nation much more accepting of federal government programs, taxes, and regulation. Even in the hills and hollers of the southern Appalachians, the very heart of frontier thinking, most voters accepted that the hated federal government had done a good thing when its Tennessee Valley Authority began transmitting electric power to illuminate and heat their homes. Whatever chance Senator Barry Goldwater had in 1964 of defeating President Lyndon Johnson—and it was not much—he lost the moment he questioned the value of Social Security and, for that matter, the TVA.

Indeed, 1964 was a fateful year in the American Argument about the limits of individuality and the role of government. At the zenith of communal thinking, a revolt against it was brewing among a younger generation of Goldwater acolytes. After LBJ's massive victory, he was determined to build his Great Society. His goal was not only to complete the mission of FDR, but to go beyond it in an unprecedented effort to root out the causes of violence, poverty, and racism. Determined to show his intellectual bona fides, one-up the Kennedys—and also perform good works—LBJ, and Richard Nixon after him, recruited heavily in academia, bringing social scientists to Washington to apply their theorems.

But at the very moment the Great Society was coming to life, the other side of the argument was beginning to gather strength, or at least hope. The founding fathers were Ayn Rand, William F. Buckley, and Milton Friedman. The foot soldiers were kids—the other side of the Baby Boom.

That Other Side had a face: the owlish, bearded, yet boyish face of Grover Norquist. If the Clintons presented themselves as embodiments of village thinking, Norquist saw himself as the antidote. In his view, that meant unleashing the power of profit, untrammeled by government taxes and rules. If Norquist had had a slogan, it would have been the one emblazoned on the green and white license plates of the state of New Hampshire: "Live Free or Die."

Appropriately, New Hampshire was the place in which Norquist, at the age of thirty-one and only a few years out of Harvard College and Harvard Business School, first made his anti-tax mark on politics. Even more appropriate, he did so at the rickety old Highway Hotel in Concord, at a gathering of the core of the "Live Free or Die" crowd: the 1988 annual session of the Gun Owners of New Hampshire.

Filing into the ballroom, the Gun Owners were a scruffy but dignified lot, decked out in well-worn flannel shirts, suspenders, and jeans. More than a few members sported Jeremiah Johnson "mountain man" beards. They tended to live in rural areas; they shot deer and other game for their own freezers and liked the wild, lake-dotted terrain of the north, or the scruffy timbering country to the west.

What they didn't like, above all, was government. Even the mildest possible form of gun-control legislation was anathema to them—but that was only the beginning of their list of dislikes and pet peeves, especially when it came to the federal government. They didn't like taxes. They didn't like government spending. They applauded Big Government only when it fought against even Bigger Government: communism. Of course,

New England's own form of communism existed to the south of New Hampshire, in their view. It was called "Taxachusetts." They tended to forget that they cashed veterans' checks, drove their pickups on federally funded interstate highways, and hunted on land protected by the government, and benefitted from Social Security and Medicare.

The Gun Owners preferred to live in a state that, unlike Massachusetts, had *no* state income tax and *no* state sales tax. Nor was it merely the "mountain men" who loathed the idea of taxation. So did all the new refugees flooding across the state line into the suddenly mushrooming towns of the southern tier of New Hampshire. The Gun Owners were the colorful old-timers, but they represented a much larger, and growing, constituency.

Which is why, in that winter long ago, both Lee Atwater and Grover Norquist cared about the proceedings in the Highway Hotel. Atwater was the already-infamous tyro who was managing Vice President George H. W. Bush for the Republican nomination. He was preparing the ground for a visit later that day and had devised a piece of theater the Gun Owners would love. Bush would arrive accompanied by none other than Chuck Yeager, the famous test pilot (and gun-rights advocate) who had flown higher and faster than any man alive had ever done.

Norquist, meanwhile, had aides working conference tables in the lobby, trolling the anti-tax crowd. He had been reared as a Nixon Republican in the comfortable Massachusetts town of Weston, near Boston, but had recoiled in college at what he regarded as the excesses of big-government thinking—something that Richard Nixon, in many ways, not only tolerated but imitated. Instead, Norquist went for the harder stuff, finding inspiration not only in anticommunist pamphleteers but, later, in avatars of enlightened self-interest such as Rand and Friedman. He was from a different quadrant of his generation than the one everyone saw on television—Woodstock, communes, and all of that. And yet he and his fellow activists shared the hippies' distrust of the System.

To Norquist, the "state" was the source of tyranny. Like many such kids (the Reagan and Bush administrations would later be peopled with them), he was a boyhood anticommunist, inspired, as other kids were, by games of cowboys and Indians, by the hunt for Reds. Confined to the home front in the Cold War, these junior Cold Warriors saw taxes, regulation, and ivory tower social engineers (Governor George Wallace of Alabama called them "pointy-headed intellectuals") as the equivalent of totalitarian commissars. In Rand's monumental bestsellers, *The Fountain-head* and *Atlas Shrugged,* the Russian refugee preached that defiantly individualistic striving was the only power that moved civilization forward. For many GIs returning from World War II, and many of their children, Rand was a guide, if not a hero. Parents and children alike were eager to strike out on their own after an era of shared sacrifice. They also responded to the message of economist Friedman, who taught that the motive power of markets, and the "freedom to choose" that they provided, was the sole guarantor of political liberty and the best hope of social justice. Another hero was William F. Buckley, who taught, among other things, that faith and the soul were gloriously impervious to social engineering, whether it was applied by Soviet socialist utopias or officials of the welfare office in Washington.

Tactically, Norquist plotted with the cold-blooded, agitprop verve of the New Left radicals he despised. The most effective ploy in politics, in the view of campus activists at Harvard, Columbia, and elsewhere, was to issue a list of "nonnegotiable demands." That was how you put the dean and the trustees on the defensive. Either they agreed, or you went on strike, or occupied a building. Norquist liked the idea of holding up the Man.

He thought of his own unique way of doing it: Make politicians sign a pledge. He copied the essence of his maneuver from Meldrim Thomson Jr., the anti-tax skinflint who ran for governor of New Hampshire in 1972. Thomson ran on the then-novel idea of a "tax pledge." Never, never, never, he vowed, would he propose or permit the state government to impose *either* an income tax or a sales tax. Thomson won on the strength of the "pledge," Norquist told me in New Hampshire. Most successors, Republican and Democrat alike, did the same.

So, Norquist thought, why not force candidates for Congress and the presidential nominations to take the pledge, too? In 1986, while Congress was busy reorganizing the tax code, Norquist launched a national version of the "pledge"—a demand for a sweeping promise to oppose *any* tax increase of any kind. Most GOP candidates signed it. By that winter of 1987–88, his Americans for Tax Reform were a force that no Republican was eager to antagonize.

Least of all George H. W. Bush, who faced a challenge from one of the fathers of tax-cut politics, Jack Kemp. So in one of his first campaign-trail acts, the vice president signed the pledge, as Atwater had urged him to do. Now it was time for Bush to show off his credentials.

Bush entered the packed ballroom to rousing cheers, the volume growing as the crowd saw Yeager at his side. In a short speech, Bush promised to be a champion for the "constitutional right to bear arms." He declared his opposition to tax increases but didn't have to say much. The Bush campaign had flyers to show that he'd taken "the pledge." So, it turned out, had every other Republican candidate in the race save one, Senator Bob Dole of Kansas, a legislator of the old school who cared more about balancing the budget than merely cutting taxes, and who always wanted to keep his options open.

Norquist and his allies in the Bush campaign set a trap for Dole. They would spring it a few weeks later, at a pivotal televised debate in New Hampshire. By prearrangement, Bush sat innocently in his seat as one of his minor competitors, former governor Pierre "Pete" du Pont of Delaware, handed a copy of Norquist's "Pledge" to Dole and demanded that he sign it. Dole looked like a man who had just been handed a court summons. Dole "literally recoiled, like a vampire," Norquist recalled with a cackle. The senator refused to sign.

Maybe that was not the only reason, or even the main reason, why Dole lost the New Hampshire primary the next week. Others put it down to a last-minute attack ad aired by Atwater and Bush media adviser (and now Fox News president) Roger Ailes.

But I think the mountain men did it.

The Argument over the limits of individualism ranges far afield. We endlessly debate what government can *prevent* us from doing, for example, because we tend to assume we can do anything government does not specifically prohibit. The very word "regulation" seems to chafe on the American mind (except in Washington). And yet we do need it, for public safety, for public health, for fair dealing.

The best way to sell regulation and taxes to the voters, successful politicians learn, is by packaging it as a route to *enhancing* individual freedom. The classic old-fashioned example is transportation. In a continental country, planes, trains, and automobiles are literally routes to freedom. But roads, to take the earliest transportation case, could not exist without communal effort. The first great highway, the National Road—built between 1811 and 1839 and stretching from Cumberland, Maryland, to Vandalia, Illinois—was the product of one of the first great regulatory efforts in the nation's history. Federal authorities not only specified the diameter of the roadbed gravel down to the last inch, they required those living along the route to maintain the right-of-way if they wanted the privilege of living along it. It was government-mandated community in the name of freedom and opportunity—and a model for much that came later in, say, railroad regulation in the West.

The same pitch—government that empowers individuals—has been made over and over. It has justified everything from education programs to agricultural subsidies to the Securities and Exchange Commission.

Our ultimate debate over regulation—one that makes little or no sense to the rest of the world—is about guns. That there are far too many millions of them floating dangerously around the country is impossible to gainsay. In major cities, any teen in search of drugs has an all too easy time obtaining a Glock to call his own. But whatever your view of the right to bear arms—and most Americans favor stricter gun-control laws—the Second Amendment is too deeply embedded in memory, myth, and United States Supreme Court decisions to be easily overridden. In the early years of the new millennium, proponents of gun rights expanded their base state-by-state, pushing "concealed carry" laws and "castle" laws to protect anyone who shoots an intruder who invades a residence. It is an old common-law right that courts had whittled away, and that the gun lobby expanded by legislation.

Gun-control advocates such as Marc Morial, the shrewd mayor of New Orleans from 1994 to 2002, tried to limit the spread of handguns in cities by suing the manufacturers. Many Democrats supported the legal crusade, but by 2007 they had backed away from making much of an issue of it. Why? The party needed to attract male voters, especially whites, who had been abandoning the Democrats in droves for decades. So the party piped down about the dangers of guns. Indeed, in the frantic closing days of the 2004 presidential campaign, Senator John Kerry made a point of being photographed in camouflage, tramping through an Ohio farm field on a hunting trip, a shotgun draped carefully over his arm. He lost the state anyway. In the closing days of the 2008 campaign in Iowa, former Arkansas governor Mike Huckabee took to the fields with a shotgun and bagged three pheasants.

After a decade of learning to swim upstream in the Reagan rhetorical tide, Bill Clinton was an expert at juggling the rhetoric of individualism and community. In his campaign slogan, "community" was balanced with the words "opportunity" (read: Business will be okay, too) and "responsibility" (read: We will not give money away to welfare cheats).

In 1993, in what amounted to the second half of a budget deal that President Bush had initiated in 1991, Clinton pushed through a tax increase—without a single Republican vote in the House of Representatives. He balanced that with a "welfare reform" package that he sent to the Congress in 1995. The idea was twofold: to improve the program and, once and for all, end the abuses that had sent generations of antigovernment commentators into a frenzy.

Bruce Reed, Clinton's policy director, assembled a welfare-reform plan that would still provide decent benefits to unwed mothers and would offer a wide array of educational and health services. But it also, and for the first time, would impose tough work requirements on those mothers. Reed and other aides gathered in the appropriately named Roosevelt Room to hash out what to do. Political aide Harold Ickes Jr., the son and namesake of FDR's famous curmudgeonly interior secretary, insisted that the work requirement was unfair and punitive. "You just can't do that," he said, pounding on the large mahogany table. "We're not supposed to be punishing people we want to help."

With a smile, Reed noted that precisely sixty years earlier, in 1935, FDR's brain trust had debated the same question when they were designing what would come to be called the Aid to Families with Dependent Children program. The chief opponent of the work requirement, Reed said, was Harold Ickes Sr.

In 1935, the senior Ickes had won the argument. But times had changed. In 1995, the junior Ickes lost.

Senator John McCain was an Arizonan, which was appropriate, since sometimes you could almost see the geological forces of American politics wearing him down like a desert mesa. A great individualist himself, but also a navy man and an engaging spirit, he seemed to embody the contradictions and crosscurrents of the American Argument over the role of community in government. He was a Goldwater man—he was, after all, a Republican from Arizona—and if you saw McCain at his ranch in Sedona, as I did one spring weekend, you saw a fellow who thought of himself in the Western tradition of ornery leave-me-alone-ism. And yet as a third-generation navy man—the son and grandson of admirals—and as a former prisoner of war who had had literally years to think about the meaning of his country, McCain was obsessed with trying to solve big governmental problems with big governmental solutions, whether it was new military weaponry or a balanced federal budget through measured tax hikes.

Though he hailed from Goldwater country, he was not reflexively antigovernment, or anti-tax. In his first run for the presidency, in 2000, he had been a critic of the Friedman-Reagan-Bush "supply-side" theory of the world. In that go-round, he was proud to be what Jack Kemp and other Reaganites derisively called a "green eyeshade Republican." He worried about debt, and championed fiscal responsibility. He was for reforming government's role in economic life, not reflexively downsizing it. And he was for *raising* taxes in certain cases, not cutting them, and for reducing the role of "big money" in politics, not expanding it. If there were going to be tax cuts at all, he said, they should go only to those who needed them most—not to the wealthy.

After Bush won the presidency, McCain remained a skeptic and voted against some of Bush's tax cuts. But by the fall of 2006, as he was gearing up for his second run for the White House, he underwent a conversion: He voted to make permanent a series of Bush tax cuts he had initially voted against. The New Hampshire mountain men would have approved, or so McCain hoped.

But New Hampshire was changing, and so was the country. In 2000, for the first time in decades, the state had elected a governor, Democrat Jeanne Shaheen, who had not taken the Pledge during the campaign. John Lynch, her successor, paid homage to the idea but raised other forms of taxation. Indeed, his constituents were as worried about health-care costs as folks in any other part of the country—and two generational waves of immigrants from Massachusetts had perhaps dulled the ardor of the old "Live Free or Die" go-it-alone thinking.

Former senator John Edwards was out to test the impact of these changes in New Hampshire. His health-care plan was molded on a template that any disciple of John Rawls's (or Martin Luther King Jr.'s) could applaud. "Who are you willing to leave behind without the care he needs?" Edwards asked at an event in Manchester. "Which child? We need a truly universal solution, and we need it now."

Maybe even the mountain men would agree.

Six

WHO JUDGES THE LAW?

The brass elevator doors in the Capitol opened and there, smiling sheepishly, stood John G. Roberts Jr., Esq., accompanied by the man whose job it was at the time to introduce Roberts to members of the U.S. Senate. President George W. Bush had just nominated Roberts to the high court. Roberts needed to meet the senators who would soon vote on his confirmation. For this largely social and ceremonial task, the White House had chosen former senator Fred Thompson of Tennessee, a man so soaked in stagy bonhomie that he played a politician on TV as well as in real life. At 6´6˝, he towered over Roberts. The two were alone in the elevator when I entered. "Don't say a word to this guy," said Thompson, kidding on the square. Roberts wasn't there to make news, but to avoid it.

The whole idea was that he didn't really need to speak, that his credentials and biography were tailor-made to speak for him: Harvard College, Phi Beta Kappa; Harvard Law, magna cum laude; Supreme Court clerkship; high-level legal jobs in and out of government; two kids; lovely wife; pillar of a local (Catholic) church in a suburb known for fine but understated homes. Nothing trendy, showy, or pushy: the man on the wedding cake of the Bush presidency, hair neatly combed, unobtrusive suit well fitted, above reproach and, seemingly, politics.

Of course, appearances can be deceiving. If you looked at Roberts's record, and talked to people who knew him, you understood immediately that he was political in every sense except "elected." He had long been a made man in the Bush family, operating one of the less nakedly rough-and-tumble, but nevertheless crucially important, precincts of the enterprise, the federal judiciary. Now he was part of a project, guided by Vice President Dick Cheney and White House counselor Karl Rove, to remake the federal judiciary from top to bottom in the image of the Bush worldview: pro-business, pro-life, tough on terrorism, secretive, dismissive to the point of being contemptuous of the prerogatives of Congress and public (world) opinion, aggressively bullish on the prerogatives of presidential power.

Roberts's political pedigree was long. He debuted on the radar screen in 1980, as a clerk to Chief Justice William Rehnquist, and again in 1981, when he was hired by the Reagan-Bush administration to work for Attorney General William French Smith. For six years after that, Roberts worked for White House counsel Fred Fielding. After Bush I was elected president in 1988, he chose Roberts to be a key deputy to Solicitor General Kenneth Starr (himself no stranger to politics). Seeking to reward Roberts, in 1992 Bush the Elder nominated him for a federal judgeship. Unfortunately for Roberts, Bush lost the election to Bill Clinton before the nomination could be voted on. But he remained in the family Rolodex.

Roberts waited his turn in private practice, and then, shrewdly, offered his help to the Bush family at a moment of crisis: the disputed 2000 presidential election and recount in Florida. Respected for his expertise in constitutional law, he flew to Tallahassee in December 2000 to brief Governor Jeb Bush on procedures for "certifying" his brother's controversial victory in the state.

Reward was swift in coming. Early in 2001, Bush the Younger nominated Roberts to a federal judgeship, though it was scuttled by a Senate temporarily in the control of the Democrats. Two years later, when the GOP had regained Senate control, Bush nominated Roberts again. He was confirmed to a seat on the prestigious U.S. Court of Appeals for the D.C. Circuit.

In 2005, when it came time to find a replacement for Justice Sandra Day O'Connor, Roberts easily made the short list. He had the right philosophical pedigree: He had a well-documented reluctance to use the power of the courts to make policy. Still, it could not hurt to prove his loyalty if he wanted the job. Terrorism cases were the way to do it, especially if you wanted the backing of the vice president.

The *Hamdan* case gave Roberts the opportunity he needed. At the time, the most pressing legal matter in the eyes of Bush and Cheney was the case of Salim Ahmed Hamdan, a Yemeni who had been Osama bin Laden's bodyguard and driver when he was captured during the 2001 Afghanistan war. Shortly before that war, Bush had ordered the creation of secret "military commissions" with the power to try "unlawful enemy combatants." Hamdan, who had been kept incommunicado at Guantánamo Bay, Cuba, was one. He seemed the perfect candidate to be dealt with by such a commission, which would operate out of public view and without even the minimal due-process rights afforded by the Geneva convention. Hamdan had never worn a uniform or fought for a recognized nation—meaning, in the eyes of the Bush-Cheney White House, that he was fair game.

But Hamdan had managed to get a lawyer and, in November 2004, he got a U.S. District Court in D.C. to rule that Bush's commission had no right to try him, which is where Roberts came in. On July 17, 2005, he joined another judge on the U.S. Court of Appeals in ruling that Hamdan *could* in fact be tried in secret by the Bush tribunal. As a member of Al Qaeda, the court ruled, Hamdan was not entitled to any protection under the Geneva convention. Aware that he was on the Bush Supreme Court short list (Cheney had already interviewed him in depth) and knowing that the ruling would generate public controversy, Roberts deferred to a colleague when it came time to decide who would write the opinion. Roberts did so even though, as a former White House deputy counsel, he was much better versed in the topic at hand: the reach of a president's commander-in-chief powers. Roberts also knew that he didn't have to write the opinion. Cheney, Rove, and, ultimately, the president would know who the real author of the decision was.

Two days later, Bush nominated Roberts to fill the O'Connor vacancy on the Supreme Court.

Now Roberts was making the rounds of the Senate, moving from Senate office to Senate office on a social mission with profoundly serious purpose. In spite of Thompson's warning, he was game to chat—briefly. "People have been very gracious," he said, as Thompson scowled. "On the other hand, I guess this is the easy part." He rolled his eyes in mock dismay, as if to say "I think I can manage." In fact, it seemed that he already had.

We were designed to be governed by words. Reverence for them is in our blood, instilled by reverence for the Bible and by Founders steeped in letters, libraries, and law. Every nation needs a sovereign; ours is the Constitution. Each president swears at inauguration to "preserve, protect, and defend" not people, government, or democracy, but the very words that are our national Holy Writ. The result is a paradox. Because the law is our exalted sovereign, it is, in theory, above politics; but because law governs our lives, law necessarily *is* politics.

The paradox produces an American Argument, not only about the law and the Constitution themselves, but about the judges who apply them. Whom should we choose (and how) to tell us what law means? What rules for interpreting law should judges employ? How much deference do we owe these arbiters? Our attitude toward them is contradictory. In their black robes and hushed chambers, judges are our temple priests. We bestow upon federal judges, including Supreme Court justices, lifetime appointments. Yet most state and local judges are elected—a greater percentage of the bench here than in any other country. Many are elected for brief terms. Running for the bench has become big business. If you don't "run" your campaign, someone else does it for you by proxy. Senate confirmations have become as contentious as presidential elections. After all, the law itself is harder to change than the guardians of it. The rules of interpretation that those guardians apply are technical, opaque, and apolitical; the motives behind invoking them often are not.

When the Founders launched the Revolution, they were not just casting off the British imperial yoke. They were abandoning sources of authority that had held societies together for millennia. But if the individual states were to remain "sovereign"—a key objective of the men who met in Philadelphia—how could there be a central source of authority to assure order and liberty?

The answer: the law, as written by the People. Historians, among them Gordon Wood and Akhil Reed Amar, have begun taking special note of the Preamble to the Constitution, long ignored as a mere piece of political throat-clearing. The phrase "We the People," Wood and Amar say, is the key to understanding what the Founders were up to. To weld thirteen colonies together without robbing them of their individual sovereignty, the Founders' idea was to claim that authority to draft a constitution came from the People themselves.

Once Madison & Co. said *that,* then the Constitution they were drafting—assuming that it was approved by "the People" in special conventions and elections set up for the purpose—would have not only the force of law but the force of a moral power far greater than that of kings, prelates, and tribal rulers combined. "Only by believing that sovereignty was held by the people outside government," Wood writes, "could Americans make theoretical sense of their remarkable political inventions." The most remarkable invention was the idea of a written constitution akin to a sacred text: not God-given, but People-given.

Here is the nub of the American Argument in law: We were the first nation in the world to declare that we would be ruled by words—the words of the Constitution. Yet it is precisely *because* the law is so crucial in our scheme that we refuse to set judges and courts above politics. Not only do we elect many of our judges. On many topics, the Congress—not the courts themselves—sets the rules for what kinds of cases can be brought before the federal bench, and even the rules for *where* the judges can sit. It is the Congress, and therefore politics, that has the power to decide who can even *be* a federal judge in the first place.

And yet the Constitution is more than "fundamental," as Alexander Hamilton put it. It is akin to sacred. Our attitude, if not always our behavior, is one of worship. The words are more than words. They are alive.

But how can words be given power? Hamilton's preference was for a certain British institution—the hereditary monarchy. As a man of the world, the product of harsh experiences, he worried about the "ill humors" lurking in the human soul and society, and he saw the monarchy as an anchor of permanence and bulwark against public passion. This was sentiment he could express in the drawing rooms of Manhattan, but almost nowhere else. In the aftermath of a Revolution, only a few years distant from the Declaration of Independence and the war, the idea of monarchy was a nonstarter in debates over ratification of a new Constitution.

As he saw it, a high court was the next best thing. One of New York's leading lawyers, Hamilton fixed his faith on a new "supreme" court with justices appointed for life. Only such a court would be independent and mature enough to provide a balance wheel. Writing in *The Federalist No.*

78, he famously declared that the new federal judiciary, topped by a Supreme Court, would be "the weakest of the three departments of power." But, in the same essay, he frankly admitted the opposite. Though the Court has "no influence over the sword or the purse," it, paradoxically, would be the final arbiter of the "will of the People."

How could a Supreme Court populated by unelected, lifetime judges be trusted with the ultimate democratic task? Logically, if you follow Hamilton's bouncing ball of delegation. After the war ended in 1783, the People (not the state governments) held all—every ounce—of the legitimate American political authority. In special elections and state conventions, the People selected representatives who traveled to Philadelphia. The constitution they drafted there proposed delegating *some* of the People's authority—not to a government, but to the Constitution itself. That document would be the vessel into which the People's authority was to be poured. Since this was a "limited" delegation—Hamilton's word— somebody had to ensure that the new government did not overstep the bounds of authority delegated to it. Neither the Congress nor the president could be trusted to do so. How could they? They were, by design, susceptible to the passing passions of public opinion. No, only an independent judiciary, its eyes fixed on the Constitution itself, could do that, and only the judiciary had the *right* to, since the first delegation of authority was to the Constitution itself, not directly to the Congress, or the president, or anyone else.

Hamilton states this startling idea blandly enough as he explains how the judges would operate. "There is no position which depends on clearer principles," he wrote, "than that every act of a delegated authority, contrary to the tenor of the commission under which it was exercised, is void." Since the Constitution was the primary delegation, and the legislative and presidential ones incidental to that, the Constitution takes precedence. "No legislative act, therefore, contrary to the Constitution, can be valid." It is the Court, not the legislature or the president, that ultimately represents the People.

Still, Hamilton's famous essay skirts, and certainly does not satisfactorily answer, the two questions that it raises. How and why can we trust judges to decide fairly what is "contrary to the Constitution"? And by what principles should the judges—must the judges—decide a particular case that comes to them?

As to the first, no one, Hamilton concedes, is immune to "ill humors."

"[M]aking the proper deductions for the ordinary depravity of human nature," he admits, it won't be easy to find judges who "unite the requisite integrity with the requisite knowledge." But even if we find good and true men and women, how do we ensure that they do their jobs correctly? Here, even the practical, cold-eyed Hamilton rushes off into the mists of jurisprudence. "To avoid an arbitrary discretion in the courts," he says, "it is indispensable that they should be bound down by strict rules and precedents, which serve to define and point out their duty in every particular case that comes before them."

Hey, no problem. All the judge has to do is locate the relevant precedent and follow "strict rules," and she will know what is constitutional—what is an expression (or violation) of the People's Will. A brilliant and accomplished lawyer, Hamilton, of course, knew better: Would that it were that easy.

How do the priests interpret the Oracle? Are they supposed to look only at the plain meaning of the words as commonly understood today? Or as the words were understood in 1787? Or in accordance with what we think the Founding Fathers intended to be the result in a particular case? If the goal is to apply their intent, do you do so by looking at the document as a whole, or only at a specific passage? Or do you examine the society they were seeing around them (and the problems they wanted to solve) in the American colonies in the late eighteenth century?

The questions do not end there. Besides the document itself, should the justices be free to consider anything else—any other document, any other set of laws? What about the English common law, "natural" law, or *international* law? And how much deference should current interpreters of the Oracle give to past interpreters and interpretations? We claim to follow the common-law principle of "stare decisis"—literally, "let the decision stand"—which means that a principle applied in one case to one set of facts shall apply to other similar situations: There is a precedent. This is "judge-made" law: a supposedly rock-solid coral reef of accumulated decisions and wisdom of judges down the ages. But who is to say whether the situations are similar enough to invoke what is called "controlling" precedent? More judges. So what they "make" they can unmake, a process that, if overdone, risks not being "law" at all.

Of course, a judge can unmake what others have made. There are two simple ways to do so: He can either assert that the facts are different in the case at hand, so the controlling case does not really control the new one, or he can simply say that "public policy" requires the change. He can also claim to find changes in society, or discover new "rights" implied in the Constitution.

A judge's favorite theory for interpreting the Constitution is not, in and of itself, *any* indication of his politics. Some of the most "conservative" are in fact the *most* willing to ignore precedent; the most eager to look for creative interpretations. It is worth remembering that our founding documents (the Declaration of Independence and the Constitution) were written primarily by lawyers. Lawyers knew then, and know now, how to use supposedly neutral principles of jurisprudence to achieve the ends and aims they seek.

Modern "conservative" analysts wring their hands over examples of what they regard as "judicial activism." Yet, ironically, the power of even the most reticent and conservative justice rests on a founding act of breathtaking judicial activism.

In *Marbury v. Madison,* Chief Justice John Marshall in 1803 established the fullest authority of the Supreme Court, its power to rule acts of Congress unconstitutional, by finding something in the Constitution that wasn't clearly there. Article III, the briefest of major sections, says the "Judicial Power shall extend to all cases . . . arising under . . . the Laws and the United States." That could have been interpreted to mean that the court could only assess whether those laws had in fact been violated, not whether they were constitutional to begin with. Marshall proclaimed the sweeping latter power, which we now take for granted, but which was not automatically assumed to exist by our ancestors.

Here is the paradox—the American Argument in law—as it first manifested itself: To give life to the sacred words of a Constitution, we could not read them literally. Yet once the power of the words *was* made clear, Marshall interpreted them *literally* to strike down the federal statute at issue in the case! The Constitution, he said, specifically set out the kind of cases the Supreme Court could hear—and that list did not include the kind Marbury had in mind, even though a federal law said otherwise. The Constitution (and the Court) reigned supreme. Marshall's maneuver was the first to demonstrate that the power of law is the power of judges to interpret it.

The case launched another tradition: using the Constitution to deal with political conflict that the other branches of government could not handle. Marshall saw an urgent need to broker a peace between nascent political parties at a time when warfare was threatening to rip the young republic apart. The Federalists who had lost the election in 1800 were suing to take possession of judgeships they had been awarded in the last hours before the Jeffersonians had taken over. Under a law passed in 1789, they should have been able to do so. The Court said no, the statute was unconstitutional. Stability was the victor.

Any tool of interpretation can be used—or misused—in the search for a particular result. No proponent of "strict construction" or "originalism" today defends the ultimate example of both: Chief Justice Roger B. Taney's infamous, morally bankrupt opinion in the *Dred Scott* case of 1857. In "strict" terms, he was correct. The Framers, and the Constitution they drafted, did not consider African American slaves "persons" entitled to *any* civil rights protection. And no passionate foe of "activism" dares decry the ambitious sweep and moral force of *Brown v. Board of Education,* the 1954 decision that ignored the principle of stare decisis to overturn the Jim Crow idea of "separate but equal" treatment of the races.

I n America, judges are not above politics, but they sometimes come close to drowning in it. The idea that they maintain Olympian distance from everyday affairs—something to be striven for, at least—can seem naive, or worse. In the run-up to the *Dred Scott* decision, President-elect James Buchanan secretly got briefings from members of the Court and begged them to issue a ruling before he took office, on the pathetically mistaken notion that this would take the issue off his presidential dinner plate. Justice Taney, a slave-state judge with slaveholding family roots, became a political hero in the South—and a judicial devil incarnate in the North. President Franklin Delano Roosevelt trained his political fire on the Supreme Court, which, under Chief Justice Charles Evans Hughes, had struck down much of FDR's ambitious economic legislation. The result was the infamous "court-packing" plan of 1937; he proposed to add new slots for justices and replace those who were older than seventy. The plan failed, and it enhanced FDR's reputation for arrogant power grabbing. It turned the public against him, but he never apologized for treating the Court as a branch of politics.

Inf you want to pinpoint ground zero of the Big Bang in modern judi-cial politics, Ted Kennedy's desk was it. There, on July 1, 1987, he mounted his lookout and fired his cannon at Judge Robert Bork, whom President Ronald Reagan, just minutes earlier, had nominated to be a jus-tice of the Supreme Court. After six years in the wilderness, the Democrats had returned to power in the Senate, and Kennedy, now in the majority again on Senator Joe Biden's Judiciary Committee, aimed a half decade of pent-up anti-Reagan anger at the judge. "Robert Bork's America," the sen-ator thundered, "is a land in which women would be forced into back-alley abortions, blacks would sit at segregated lunch counters, rogue police could break down citizens' doors in midnight raids, schoolchildren could not be taught about evolution, writers and artists could be censored at the whim of government." It was one of the most famous one-sentence demo-litions in history: Bork eventually was voted down 42–58. Everything since has been a "post-Bork tit-for-tat," said Ron Klain, a former Judiciary Committee chief counsel and Clinton administration attorney.

Four years later, when President George H. W. Bush nominated Clarence Thomas to the Court, nominations had metastasized into polit-ical *campaigns*. Thomas, only the second African American nominated to the Court (and the first to be chosen by a Republican president), was a controversial figure. He was black, but was a bitter foe of the long-prevailing (dating from the Civil War) orthodoxy in the black commu-nity, which stated that strong federal action was the indispensable key to black freedom and prosperity.

How would they get Thomas "elected"? Ken Duberstein, his "Sherpa," knew something about campaigns; he had worked for Ronald Reagan and been his last chief of staff in the White House. He quickly saw that Thomas needed to build a shield against attacks from within the African American community. In private conversations, Thomas always insisted to Duberstein that the black folks who knew him best—those from his boyhood home of Pin Point, Georgia—accepted him as one of their own, and even agreed with him that self-help was the key. "I said, 'Clarence, if they are always saying that, why don't we bring them up here to Washing-ton to say that?' " The idea came none too soon: The NAACP, Duberstein heard, would announce its opposition to Thomas's confirmation the next day—a potentially devastating blow to his chances. "We didn't have much time," Duberstein recalled. "We rented the buses, Clarence called the people, and the next day we had something to blunt the NAACP."

Today, said Duberstein, nomination fights are "Pin Point, Georgia, times one hundred. The difference now is that it is a *nonstop* campaign. You need something every day, every news cycle."

W hen oilman William Clements was elected governor of Texas in 1978—the first Republican to win since Reconstruction—the tectonic plates of Texas politics began to shift. The result was the War of the Trial Lawyers, which rages to this day, and which taught George W. Bush and his crowd that the courts, and the judges who serve in them, are politicians by other means. That was the reigning view when I began going to Austin to report on Bush in the 1990s. It was the view that he, Karl Rove, and the rest of the inner circle brought with them to Washington after the 2000 presidential election. Ironically, but perhaps appropriately, nothing proved the point more than the way in which Bush won the White House—by way of a 5–4 decision of the U.S. Supreme Court.

Texas was an extreme example of a classic American conflict between "the law" as an idea of almost sacred inviolability, and the hard fact that the law is often all about who gets what. The Founding Fathers preferred that judges be appointed, and appointed for life. That was the way it generally worked in jurisdictions of the United States that existed before the federal government came into being, and for a generation thereafter. But when Andrew Jackson swept in from the West—that is, from west of the Appalachian Mountains—he brought with him the idea that state judges (and perhaps federal ones) should be elected, and for limited terms. That is the way the newer states did it, which eventually influenced things back East. Federal judges are still appointed (subject to congressional confirmation, of course), but Jacksonian Democracy survives. According to the Carnegie Corporation, twenty-eight states, including Texas, employ forms of popular election for judges. Most of those judges have limited terms, which means they have to run not only once but over and over again.

Texas is one of the most raucously political of these. But until Clements arrived in Austin, the judicial elections were generally sleepy affairs. Things were handled in an insider fashion. It worked this way: The governor had the power to appoint—with no legislative review— judges to fill unexpired court terms. Those appointed judges tended to be routinely elected to full terms, often unopposed. When they retired, they tended to do so midterm, so that the governor could quickly appoint a successor.

In Clements's time, the insiders' procession turned into rough-and-tumble electoral politics. Hailing from the oil business, he chose as chief judge of the state Supreme Court one William Garwood, a corporate lawyer with close ties to Exxon. Democrats saw the selection as a poke in the eye—and a challenge. Clements (for whom Rove worked as a consultant) had his reasons: He wanted to lure the business community, which had been used to dealing with Democrats for a hundred years, into the GOP fold. Democrats form a united front of labor unions, minorities, and—fatefully—trial lawyers, who had been accustomed to receptively antibusiness judges on the bench. The lawyers preferred judges who would listen to the little guy, especially little guys represented by them in lawsuits, where generous fees were possible. Garwood was not their kind of judge.

When he ran for a full term in 1980, the Democrats were ready. They had read the campaign rules, and discovered that there essentially were none: no contribution limits in judicial races, no spending caps, no limits on spending by third parties. They attacked Garwood with an onslaught of ads accusing him of conflicts of interest, flooded the field with organizers, and, shockingly, beat him on Election Day. "That was the first example of a really controversial judicial election," recalled William Chapman of the Texas Trial Lawyers. The other side—and Rove was on the other side—was impressed. "It was a wake-up call," said business lobbyist Kim Ross.

Rove was one of those awakened. Soon enough, he had made the trial lawyers the GOP's enemy number one. Rove also had realized that there was consultant money to be made in the judicial races. In 1988, Republicans assembled a "Clean Slate '88" of seven candidates for the Supreme Court, with Rove handling the race of Tom Phillips, the candidate for the chief judge's seat. It was a big money maker. But it also was an object lesson in the explosive mixture of public opinion and the courts. The issue was money: how to protect corporations and professionals, such as doctors, from massive jury awards.

By the time they got to Austin in 1994, the team of Bush, Rove & Co. knew what they wanted in judicial appointees and candidates: solid citizens who were not minions of the Religious Right (Bush had other, less visible avenues through which to reach them), who were loyal to Bush, and who would give a wide berth to business. "It wasn't ideological but it *was* political," said Ross. Names would filter up to the governor's office, where they would be vetted by Bush's innermost circle; Rove would come by to talk to the potential candidate and, perhaps, acquire the candidate as a client for the election. Fealty was the key: "If you had taken a shot at Bush or Rove in any way, forget it," said Ross. Only team players needed apply. "They wanted decent people who were, shall we say, malleable," said Austin Democrat George Shipley.

As a result, the Texas business community generally liked George W. Bush. In fact, that is an understatement. They formed the core of a funding network that filled a $100 million war chest for him before he launched his 2000 campaign.

Even with that money, Bush might not have gotten to Washington at all had it not been for what many—and not just partisan Democrats—regard as perhaps the most audacious act of "judicial activism" in modern times: the Supreme Court decision to hear and decide *Bush v. Gore* in December 2000, in the aftermath of the disputed presidential election.

If the Supreme Court had wanted to be conservative and cautious, it would not have agreed to hear the case at all. The justices could have left the matter to the states—or at least not intervened when they did. At the time, Florida was in the midst of a recount of "under votes"—ballots in which no vote for president had been clearly registered—ordered by the highest court in the state. In the normal course of things, the Supremes would have waited for that recount to be completed. Or, if the Supremes had wanted to be *really* conservative and cautious, they would have allowed the dispute to go to the forum in which the Constitution specified that it belonged: the Congress of the United States, which had dealt with similar presidential-election disputes in 1824 and 1876, when the Electoral College results were similarly murky.

Instead, the Court plunged in, not only agreeing to review the matter, but, in effect, deciding the election in Bush's favor, even though he was officially ahead in Florida by only 537 votes (out of nearly 6 million cast) and thousands of "under vote" ballots remained to be reexamined and recounted. And on what basis did the Court do this? In a brief "per curiam" opinion—the kind that no one signs as author—the Court pulled a wild theory out of thin air, and then, knowing what they had done, declared that no one could ever cite the case as precedent. They had taken and decided the matter in mere hours—so quickly that some briefs were never filed, and others not fully circulated among the justices.

Here is how the Supreme Court reached its goal. The Florida high court, the Supremes noted, had told the lower court to use for guidance a state statute that calls for officials to seek a "clear indication of the intent of the voter" when examining ballots. But that statute, the U.S. Supreme Court said, was so vague that it violated civil rights guarantees embedded in the Constitution and extended to the states by the Fourteenth Amendment. But whose rights were being violated? Not Al Gore's or George Bush's—even though they were the parties to the case. No, the high court was looking out for the civil rights of the men and women who cast those "under vote" ballots, who could not possibly be treated fairly because the standard for judging their intentions was too vague. Except that they were not the ones seeking redress in the Court.

Even conservative judicial observers ridiculed this reasoning, which was the controlling one in the case. More astonishing and, to some, troubling, was the rhetorical question some commentators asked: So what? In *Bush v. Gore,* wrote Judge Richard Posner of the U.S. Court of Appeals for the Seventh Circuit, the Supreme Court was wisely, patriotically, following a "pragmatic approach to the law." The "pragmatist," Posner wrote, "regards adjudication, especially constitutional adjudication, as a practical tool of social ordering . . . ," not as an "algorithm intended to lead judges by a logical or otherwise formal process to the One Correct Decision."

But Posner had a point. Sometimes the correct decision is not the right one in terms of strict jurisprudence. John Hart Ely, a revered legal philosopher, argued that the Supreme Court was sometimes justified in ignoring Hamilton's iron discipline of "precedents and strict rules," when the aim was the expansion of civic participation and democracy. Examples include the abolition of slavery, the advancement of voting rights and educational opportunity. Justice Stephen Breyer argues the same in his 2007 book, *Active Liberty: Interpreting Our Democratic Constitution.* In Posner's view, the Court was right to act to avoid the "chaos" stemming from more days and weeks—perhaps even months—of doubt about the identity of the forty-third president. There was a potential, Posner wrote, for "political and constitutional crisis."

Good thing we avoided all *that.*

I t didn't look like a campaign headquarters, but it was. It didn't look like a political campaign—but it was. For a powerhouse of public life, Dr. James Dobson operated out of a surprisingly nondescript base camp. His view of the Rocky Mountains was spectacular, but the nerve center of his Focus on the Family operation was a bland campus of the kind that might house a software company or electronics store. Still, the forgettable architecture belied the intensity of what went on inside. Dobson, a medical doctor and evangelical Christian, had turned a family-counseling practice into a media empire of religious outreach and political influence. He was on more radio stations than Rush Limbaugh, reached more direct mail and webpage readers than most for-profit businesses on the Internet, and had made himself a force to be reckoned with—and even feared—in the White House and Republican Party.

When I flew out to see him in the spring of 2005, Dobson was at the zenith of his influence. He was using it to give himself a seat at the table of one of the government's most sacred secular rituals: the selection of judges for federal courts. An ardent foe of abortion and an equally ardent supporter of measures to outlaw gay marriage, Dobson had long since concluded that his mission required him to play hardball with the judiciary, and with the U.S. senators who controlled key roles in the process of picking judges. He had trained his hottest fire on Republican senator Arlen Specter, the ardently pro-choice chairman of the Senate Judiciary Committee, a Philadelphian of moderate views who also supported federal funding for stem-cell research, a sin in Dobson's eyes. To keep his job—meaning, to calm down the White House—Specter had been forced to promise Dobson and other evangelicals that he would not let his personal views (more liberal than theirs) stand in the way of up-or-down votes on the conservative nominees that the Bush administration would put forward. "We made it clear to him and the others that we're watching them," Dobson said, his sunny visage clouded by a cold, clinical menace. "We expect them to respond."

Which explains why, one morning a few months later, Dan Coats, a former U.S. senator from Indiana, got a call from Karl Rove. The president's political mastermind never called with easy tasks. "My first thought was 'Oh, oh, this can't be good,' " Coats recalled.

Known for earnest religiosity and a calm, equable manner, Coats was a graduate of Wheaton College in Illinois, the famed "Harvard of the

Evangelicals." Wheatonians thought of themselves as peaceable lamp-lighters, not flamethrowers. During his ten years in the Senate (followed by five as Bush II's ambassador to Germany), Coats had for the most part tried to be a man of goodwill. His cause was not building hegemony, but rather encouraging "faith-based" charities to tackle social problems such as poverty and crime.

Now Rove wanted to dispatch him to the front lines of partisan warfare in Washington. The president, Rove told him, was going to nominate his good friend and lawyer, Harriet Miers. A few months earlier, Rove had called on Fred Thompson for John Roberts, but that had not been so hard a sell. He had been a known quantity.

Miers was a different story. She had never been a judge, and therefore had no track record of opinions. She belonged to a suburban Dallas megachurch, but she had never married and had no family to trot out before the cameras. She wore an oversize crucifix at her debut press conference as Bush's choice, but some evangelicals wondered aloud how devout she was, or how recently she had become devout.

Coats did what he could, repeatedly talking up Miers to Dobson and others. He worked the phones. He held meetings. He tapped the Wheaton evangelical network, and the Prayer Breakfast crowd in Congress. As it turned out, he *was* perfect, but she was too deeply flawed. Her sole qualification was her loyalty to Bush. It wasn't enough, and the president withdrew her nomination.

Taking no chances with Dobson and his allies, the White House sent up a replacement nomination sure to please them. Federal Judge Samuel Alito's education and training were sterling: Princeton, Harvard Law. He had a list of cases they could examine. (Indeed, he had been annoyed that Miers had been chosen ahead of him on the first pass.) His only flaw was that Specter actually liked him, since Alito had served on the federal bench in Philly. Dobson & Co. were assured—by Coats, among others—that the judge in fact was One of Them, a religious conservative (a devout Catholic) who would be receptive to their views.

Now the *other* side was inflamed. In the Senate itself, Coats's "Sherpa" tour became a phony pageant. Alito had been presold to the Republican members and pre-denounced by interest groups that were Dobson's mirror image among Democrats. The meetings with senators were largely a waste of time. In private, Coats later said, most Democrats were polite and respectful, some even rather supportive. "Then, the same senators

who would say nice things behind closed doors would walk out and denounce him," said Coats. "Some of them would even say to him, 'I wish I
didn't have to go out and do this, but . . .' "

Alito was confirmed by an almost straight party-line vote: 58–42, with
only one Republican voting nay and only three Democrats voting aye. It
was the closest confirmation vote since Clarence Thomas fifteen years
earlier. The whole process left Coats angry and depressed. "It's all politics
now," he said. Kenneth Duberstein, the former White House chief of
staff who had been the "Sherpa" for Thomas, agreed. "It's completely out
of hand."

I n June of 2007, Chief Justice John G. Roberts Jr. handed down his
first major opinion in a free-speech case—indeed, one of his first
major pronouncements of any kind. In it, he led a 5–4 majority in striking down federal limits on what advocacy groups could spend on television, radio, and Internet advertising in the days and weeks before a
federal election. Among those who cheered the loudest when they heard
the ruling were the anti-abortion activists who were plaintiffs in the case.
Dr. James Dobson wasn't one of them, but he cheered, too.

Seven

DEBT AND THE DOLLAR

"Approachable" is not a word one uses to describe Alan Greenspan. Behind the sleepy-looking eyes lies a brilliant mind, which tends not to suffer fools gladly, if at all. Never loquacious, he had, as chairman of the Board of Governors of the Federal Reserve, learned to guard his already guarded utterances even more jealously. To try to engage him in a substantive conversation in a social or casual setting—that was Not Done.

And yet he would sit still, like a patient professor, if someone dared to ask a question, and he got one at a dinner party in the fall of 2006, just after his term was up. Given that the country had a colossal publicly held debt ($5 trillion at the time), and a vast trade deficit (about $400 billion in 2005); given that the world (especially China) was awash in dollars and U.S. Treasury Bonds, and perhaps growing tired of holding our paper; and given the fact that some oil-producing countries had begun making noises about denominating sales of petroleum in euros; given all of *that,* did he not perhaps think that the dollar—our sacred, almighty dollar—might be relieved of its role as the globe's reserve currency? And, if *that* happened, did it not then mean that we would no longer be able to borrow from the rest of the world with impunity by simply printing more currency? And would not *that,* in turn, cause the value of the dollar to plummet, along with the American standard of living and our role as leader of the free world? In other words, had we reached the limits of imperial debt?

Greenspan emitted a slightly impatient sigh. He had heard each and every doomsday scenario; indeed, he had been reared on them growing up in New York City in the aftermath of the Great Depression. "It doesn't matter if those sales contracts are written in euros," he said. "The important thing is how the accounts ultimately are settled. At the end of the day, that is and will be in dollars." But how do we know that our currency will remain preeminent, given the colossal debts that we are carrying on our national balance sheet? "We don't," he said. "But that is like British people in the nineteenth century worrying about the pound."

The point, Greenspan implied, was that Britain and the pound ruled until World War I brought their dominance to an end. Further exhausted by World War II, essentially broke with the added expense of maintaining an empire upon which "the sun never set," Britain grudgingly, finally yielded to the United States and to the newly preeminent dollar.

For nearly two decades it had been Greenspan's job to balance growth and order, to make sure that Americans had enough credit to build for their future while ensuring that money—that is, credit—was not so easy to obtain as to lead to ruinous inflation. (The Fed did that by the interest rates it set for the money it loaned to member banks.) And while Greenspan had no direct control over how much money the Congress could borrow through deficit spending, he had the moral authority of his chairmanship to try to browbeat the politicians into being at least somewhat responsible. If they weren't—if they cut taxes too radically or spent too much—he had one ultimate weapon: He could raise interest rates and cause the kind of recession that might cost them their jobs.

Greenspan was born and trained for the job. He was a musically inclined economist (a former clarinet student at Juilliard) whose early intellectual hero was Ayn Rand, with whom he shared a deep distaste for the then-reigning political orthodoxy of the twentieth century, which was that the redistributive social welfare state could actively guide mankind to permanent prosperity. Greenspan believed that markets could do the job, if only they could be certain of the value of money. His personal answer: Permanently tie the value of the currency to the price of something precious and of limited supply—gold.

By the time he got to the Fed in 1987, he had abandoned his obsession with gold and replaced it with a belief that controlling the supply of money was the key to economic stability. This was the theory of his monetarist Jedi master, economist Milton Friedman, who taught that inflation was the single greatest threat to democracy and prosperity. The way to control it, he taught, was to limit the supply of money. With inflation tamed, the "supply side" of the economy—manufacturers, lenders, marketers, the service sector—would be willing to risk new investment. Creditors would benefit, but so, eventually, would everyone.

If Congress wasn't willing to control inflation by limiting government borrowing (and printing of money), then the Fed, through its control of the nation's banks, would do so by raising interest rates on the money it loaned to federally chartered banks. It seemed contradictory: Wouldn't raising the "cost" of money—of loans—*add* to inflation? No, Friedman answered, because the high cost of money would throttle down economic activity, limiting demand and therefore inflation as it did so. It was like a vaccine: Use the disease to kill the disease.

The monetarist theory fit neatly into the conservative movement's agenda for power in America in the 1980s. If John Maynard Keynes had made the case for more government in the 1930s in the Western democracies (which were fighting Nazism and communism, and inoculating themselves against statism by partaking of it), Friedman made the case for less government. The key to prosperity, he taught, was not the direct manipulation of the market by government (through government-funded jobs programs, regulation, and the tax code) but rather through the potent, but less micromanagerial, control of the money supply.

To monetarists, balancing government budgets was less important than reducing the footprint of government overall; and balancing the budget by raising taxes, in their view, was worse than government borrowing. Nor did they think that the strength of the dollar was directly tied to the national balance sheet. America's leading role in the world, its rock-solid political stability, the creativity and fluidity of its financial markets—all of these would keep the dollar as the reserve currency for the foreseeable future, as long as we did not destroy the currency's underlying value by reckless inflation.

But just as war is too important to be left to the generals, the economy is too important to be left to the economists. By late 2007, our national debt was as large, in relation to our overall economy, as it had been since the last years of the Truman administration, when we were still working off the colossal expense of World War II. The term "balance of trade" had been rendered meaningless by the reality that we were importing goods and services at four times the rate we were exporting them. In the old days—twenty years earlier—most of what we "owed" in terms of national debt we owed to ourselves, or our children, in the form of Treasury bonds. Now more than half of those bonds were held by foreigners. We had to bet that they still believed in us—and in the dollar.

Every country argues about money, but only Americans have made it a staple of democracy from the time of our origins. We bicker over the value of our poker chips even as we stack them. No Argument sounds more abstract, yet none is of greater real-life consequence. Currency and credit are our lifeblood. If the blood pressure is too low (too little money and credit in circulation), we risk depression; if it is too high, we risk runaway inflation. In its many guises, the argument always pits economic order against economic growth.

But who should control the flow? Hamilton feared giving that power to the People—that is, to politicians who would rather print money than raise taxes to pay the cost of government. And yet, we ask, who has the right to deny us the freedom to bet on our own future? We are the sum of this dispute: between hard money and cheap, creditors and debtors, gold bugs and buyout artists, sober bankers and drunken pols (and greedy lenders).

One of the very first questions Americans asked each other (even before we thought of ourselves as "Americans") was, What is our money and what is it worth? They talked about it in the earliest sessions of the first legislative assembly on this continent, in July 1619 in Jamestown, Virginia. The tiny settlement had no Temple of Juno, of course (where coins were struck in ancient Rome), and no Royal Mint. The adventurers had brought trinkets with them to trade with Indians, but not a lot of coins with which to do business with each other. They realized that the simplest item they could use for currency was the crop that they had begun to produce, and that was bringing good prices in England: tobacco. The unit of currency would be a bound tobacco sheaf—a "hand."

That was the easy part of the discussion. The tougher question, of course, was, How many hands to a pound? And here, in chrysalis, was one form of an American Argument that remains with us to this day, between farmers and laborers on the one hand, and merchants and creditors on the other. The planters naturally wanted to set the value of a hand as high as they could push it (even as they were dedicated to putting more and more of it in "circulation"); the buyers and shippers wanted to keep the value of a hand as low as possible. The legislature reached a compromise—five hands to the pound—for the year. Ever since, in one way or another, we have debated whether money should be "easy" or "hard," paper or metals-backed, silver or gold, local or national.

Why do we argue about this? The answer is simple enough: because, from the start, we had the need and the freedom and considered it our right to do so. Our main colonizing nation, England, operated on a theory that a great country's duty was to hoard its cash and currency. The distances from home were so great—as were, soon enough, the distances from new areas of settlement to the cities and towns of the East Coast—that the locals had to take the lubrication of finance into their own hands.

As the world's first modern "republican democracy," we were the first society to allow its citizens a role (if not the primary role) in deciding the value, circulation, and amount of our currency and the principles and rules of borrowing from ourselves and the world to support it. Can the ongoing act of defining money really be democratized? We're trying to find out.

In America, these disputes actually pose two even more fundamental and less directly economic questions: How can we trust the People, who tend to be debtors rather than creditors, to run their own affairs? And do we trust the Future? Those who trust both tend to believe that the more money there is in circulation, the better, and if the government has to go deeper in hock to make that happen, well, so be it. The other view—the creditors' view, the view of the already-haves—has less trust in the People, if not the Future. In this view, democracy is singularly incapable of avoiding the temptation to borrow more money than it can afford, which means more money than its balance sheet and economic vitality can support.

Optimism, or at least the rhetoric of optimism, generally triumphs. The answers we tend to give in America are that we trust *both* the People and the Future—sort of. That trust has not ruined us just yet, but the experts I have listened to for years (you cannot avoid them if you cover politics in Washington) tell us that the future is not what it used to be, at least for our country. They fear that we may lose a key to our freedom: the ability to decide what our money is worth by setting our own interest rates. Here's the problem. To stimulate the economy, the Fed needs to keep rates low. But to sell Treasury notes (loans) to an increasingly dollar-wary world, the Fed may have to offer an attractive (high) rate of return. We still have control. Can we keep it?

As a country, we were never poor, but in the beginning we never had enough money. Our colonial masters wanted it that way. They wanted to keep us "barefoot and pregnant" in the monetary sense: an agricultural backwater with no way to finance our own growth. In the British colonies, the military hand of royal government rested lightly for most of the nearly two centuries between Jamestown in 1607 and Philadelphia in 1787. But the neglect wasn't benign. The British kept control with few troops (which were busy elsewhere), but with a tight, sometimes suffocating, administration of taxes and trade.

They preferred for us to be a docile place, and one way to ensure that was to send as little hard money as possible here, and take back to London as much as they could. The British knew that whoever defined what money was and how much of it was in circulation literally controlled the future, for it was through investment that the economy of our vast, fertile continent would grow. London had no interest in amplifying the possibilities of America; the aim was to accumulate and keep as much hard currency as possible in the mother country. That was the "mercantilist" theory, and the colonial political strategy.

So we were money-starved, which soon enough became an issue. Heavy taxes and duties sent ships laden with "specie"—gold or silver coins—to London, leaving the locals to concoct what we came to call "country money" for our own affairs when English (or just as often Spanish) coins were rare. Printed or handwritten claims to everything from shipments of rice to hogsheads of tobacco took the place of "real" money. That, plus other forms of local scrip, worked well enough—so well, in fact, that the British banned the use of paper money altogether in 1764. It was an economic provocation as serious as the later onerous, and much more famous, taxes on tea and newspapers.

Americans were the first people to be trained from the start in the relationship between a nation's economic strength and the value of its currency. The object lesson was administered during the years between the Revolutionary War and the convening of the Founders in Philadelphia. The bonds we had floated to pay for the war were of uncertain value at best; a cacophony of currencies, issued by state and local banks and individual lenders, circulated everywhere but viewed as suspect even by their own sponsors.

By the time the Founders met, the twin economic powers of government—borrowing and coinage of money—had become both symbol and substance of the debate over the role of a new federal government. Alexander Hamilton, the man of money and markets, understood that to have a future, the American people would have to be able to borrow against their own destiny—and would need a central government to do it for them by establishing the rules of valuing and lending money. At the same time, he feared allowing Congress to be the instrument of that borrowing. Rather, he favored a federally chartered, but privately run, independent national bank.

So he and the Virginians worked out a trade: the Capitol for capital. Thomas Jefferson and the other gentleman farmers of Virginia got what they wanted, a national capital in what was to become Washington, D.C.; Hamilton got what he wanted, a new government with sweeping power to assume state debts and borrow money against the "credit of the United States" (however much credence that had to a skeptical world), and the sole power to define and circulate currency.

These provisions weren't crucial just to Hamilton, but to the new nation as a whole. As if to prove the point, the measures were spelled out by the Founders in the first substantive passages of Article I of their new Constitution. Under it, we chose for the nomenclature of our money not the British system (except for the penny). We chose the Spanish—the dollar—for our own.

Arguments over the value and distribution of money and credit have been at the heart of the federal conversation ever since. As a trans-Appalachian frontier opened up in the early nineteenth century—and with it, new waves of democratic thinking—Americans clamored to wrest control of the system of money and credit from the bankers to whom the Federalist Founders had entrusted it.

"Jacksonian Democracy" was in good measure about what economists call the "velocity of money." In the New West, pioneers and speculators alike were demanding the expansion of credit and the circulation of money. Land was opportunity—literally the future—and they needed cash and credit to buy it. The result was a new version of the colonial tug-of-war between London and the Philadelphia–New York axis; now it was between the East Coast and the New American West. Jackson "broke" the Bank of the United States because he wanted to send its deposits—the specie and the lending it could support—west, which is what he did. The specie went west with the pioneers.

But even that was not enough to meet the demand, which drove newly empowered state banks to float loans with paper money. And Jackson, who had literally broken the National Bank so that he could send the hard currency west, resisted that. Rampant speculation led to a colossal bust, and Jackson clamped down on the state banks' ability to issue paper money.

Thus began a new iteration of the Argument. Now it was not merely between the East and the Frontier, but between existing creditors, who held "hard" gold specie—and everybody else. Over the decades, that has translated into debates over the role of money "backed" by gold deposits, by silver (more plentiful than gold), by the federal government's power to raise revenue through taxes and tariffs, or by the nation's role as a global superpower.

The definition of money has expanded with the role and reach of the federal government. As the Civil War began, "hard money" men in Congress insisted, as one of them put it, that "gold and silver are the only measure of value. These metals were prepared by the Almighty for this very purpose." But President Abraham Lincoln ordered the Treasury to stop redeeming short-term notes in gold, and Congress voted to issue as "legal tender" paper money—the infamous "greenbacks"—that could not be redeemed by gold.

It took the country fourteen years after Appomattox to return to the gold standard. The new and victorious industrial powers of the North and East dominated politics—and the definition of money. As creditors and, increasingly, importers of raw materials, they wanted a "strong," gold-backed dollar. So did Britain, which essentially ran international finance on the gold standard. But in the rural areas and small towns beyond the reach of America's great cities, and among those new immigrants there who were struggling to grab a lower rung of the American ladder to success, agitation grew for a cheaper, more plentiful money supply.

The answer, or so the agitators thought, was silver, which was in comparatively plentiful supply. The tourniquet of gold produced periodic depressions—in 1873 and 1893. To keep the government liquid and calm the latter panic, J. P. Morgan himself organized a syndicate that loaned the government $100 million and shored up the gold-based system. The other side was busy, too. Jacob Coxey, a theosophist from Ohio (who had named his son Legal Tender), led an "army" of unemployed men to Washington on behalf of "democratic silver." The argument came to a head in the election of 1896, when Republican William McKinley stood for gold, Democrat William Jennings Bryan for silver.

Gold won.

But the growth of government, especially in wartime, created irresistible pressure to expand the definition. After yet another financial panic in 1907, the powers that be realized that they needed somebody—some *thing*—besides J. P. Morgan to keep the circulatory system going. Meeting on Sapelo Island, Georgia, in 1910, where they stayed in the world's first luxury condominium resort (complete with a tennis court sheltered by a barnlike roof), the captains of commerce and politics designed the Federal Reserve System, which Congress enacted in 1913. The gold standard remained—and would remain for another twenty years—but the key to the new system was that the Fed would have the power to lend newly created money to federally chartered banks, and could adjust the rates at which they could borrow. The members would be nominated and confirmed, and would serve for long terms. The Fed was supposed to prevent bank panics (it failed miserably during the Great Depression) and smooth boom-and-bust business cycles by influencing interest rates.

The architects of the new system thought they were ending this American Argument once and for all. But since early in the twentieth century it has taken a new form: the relationship between the government's "fiscal" decisions—regarding how much the Congress raises and spends—and the "monetary" ones the Fed imposes. The key to protecting and managing the currency isn't the rather quaint question of how much gold we have in Fort Knox (147.3 million ounces), but how stable and credit-worthy we are in the eyes of the rest of the world.

We want the Fed to have as much leeway as possible to raise or lower the interest rates it charges. But keeping that latitude as wide as possible requires that Congress and the American people act as responsible borrowers themselves. As the world's lone "superpower"—and the biggest national economy on the planet with plenty of assets—the government can borrow money at reasonably low interest rates from its own citizens and from investors around the world. The idea is that they will *want* to be repaid in dollars. But what if other countries offer higher interest rates for their bonds, and what if the currency they pay interest in is "stronger" than the American dollar?

Washington loves gurus, and in the 1960s and 1970s, the reigning one in economics was a long-dead Englishman named John Maynard Keynes. Starting in the Kennedy years, the government operated on the Keynesian premise that it could stimulate the economy by spending cash on public works, education, health care, and the like. Deficits mattered, but they could be tolerated—and even temporarily encouraged—as a way to prime the pump of prosperity. You could raise taxes later.

It worked well enough—until it didn't. Deficits grew, but so did unemployment and inflation. When Ronald Reagan came to town in 1981, he brought with him a new theory—"supply-side economics"—that had the same effect, at least in one sense: big deficits.

Reagan promised a new math. According to it, you could goose the economy *and balance the budget at the same time*. You could do it, he said, in a counterintuitive way: by slashing tax rates. That would put more cash in the pockets of consumers, which, in turn, would stimulate work and investment. All of that, in turn, would eventually stimulate *more* tax revenue than if you had not cut tax rates in the first place. It was the *Stone Soup* of macroeconomics.

With the Senate in Republican hands for the first time in nearly thirty years, Reagan got most of the tax cuts he asked for—and then some, as business lobbyists cajoled Congress into a famous "feeding frenzy" of special-interest provisions. Meanwhile, Reagan and the GOP could not deliver on the third part of the original equation: sweeping cuts in spending. These were all the more necessary because the president insisted on the need to bury the "evil empire" of the Soviet Union with a defense buildup—and the Democrats defended their traditional programs with a zeal unseen since the days of LBJ.

At first, the tax cuts stimulated only anguish. A recession that had originated during Jimmy Carter's term deepened; Democrats, led by their own smiling Irishman, Speaker Tip O'Neill, won back thirty seats in the House in 1982. Revenues dropped; spending rose. The dismal result was a government getting deeper in debt and an economy that was not recovering.

Republicans and Democrats sounded the alarm, for different reasons.

Most Republicans in Congress had come of age in the years of Democratic dominion. They had learned to plead for balanced budgets even if that meant tolerating high tax rates. A new theory that said you could balance the budget by cutting taxes made no sense, and they regarded it as bad policy, especially since Democrats would never agree (and were not agreeing) to eliminate programs that they had erected and protected for a generation.

Democrats were suspicious—"apoplectic" is probably a better word—for another reason. If "supply side" failed, deficits would soar, and the New Deal–Great Society would be in jeopardy, which is precisely what they saw happening. To Senator Daniel Patrick Moynihan of New York, supply side wasn't an economic theory at all; it was a plot by neolithic conservatives to deliberately starve the government of funds and move the decision-making action in society back to the market.

Caught in the middle of these conflicting pressures was the beleaguered but game treasury secretary, Donald T. Regan. He was a former CEO of Merrill Lynch, but his more important training was in the Marine Corps. He was one of a long string of modern Republican treasury secretaries who liked tax cuts, but remained somewhat dubious about supply-side theology. His job was to assure "the markets" that everything would remain on the level in Washington: that numbers would be reliable; that the entire enterprise, as they say in the finance world, would "pencil." He once explained precisely what his job was all about. "Gentlemen," he said. "Here is what I do. I go to Wall Street just about every day and stand there with a tin cup in my hand and say 'More, please.' " He did not seem happy about it.

Fritz Hollings was not afraid of the market. He knew that New York City was where the lenders were, and, as the thirty-six-year-old governor of South Carolina, he needed money for his impoverished state. This was during the fifties, when Dixie was struggling to awaken, finally, from the economic slumber that had overtaken it after the Civil War. As a corporate lawyer and lieutenant governor, Hollings knew that there was no EZ Credit—for individuals or states—in New York in 1958. You had to show you were credit-worthy. South Carolina, when Hollings took office, could not do that. "We were flat broke," he recalled nearly fifty years later. "Wall Street wasn't going to listen to little ol' me. I had to do something. We had to go raise taxes, and get the spending in shape, and eventually we got ourselves a 'triple A' credit rating from Standard and Moody's."

That is how Hollings, a Democrat and dedicated "Kennedy Man," began bringing South Carolina into the twentieth century. It is also how he came to be obsessed with public debt—and a fierce advocate for handling it carefully. When Hollings arrived in the Senate in 1966, he gravitated to the spending committees, and then became a founding member of the Budget Committee. There, during five presidencies—from Reagan to Bush II—he was a key figure in the ongoing debate over how much we dare borrow from ourselves and from others. At what point do we risk jeopardizing our children's future, especially if our only collateral is the productivity of our own future generations?

At eighty-four years of age and back home in Charleston, Hollings said that, for the first time, he worried that we might reach the point of no return as a debt-ridden country. Checking a "National Debt Clock" on his computer, he read aloud the number on the screen at that instant: more than $5 *trillion,* roughly half of which we owe to ourselves (in the form of loans against future tax revenue, much of it money supposedly destined for Social Security). The other half was owned by foreigners, the largest such share since the nineteenth century: individuals and governments from Tokyo, Shanghai, Riyadh, London, Moscow, and elsewhere. The sanguine view is that we have been in hock like this before, and that our economy—and our bonds—remain the surest investment on the planet. Now Hollings was not so sure. His best evidence: His friend Warren Buffett told him in 2004 that he had begun pouring money into foreign currencies. "We're writing hot checks against our own future," said Hollings. "It doesn't affect me," he said in the exaggerated, cornpone drawl he uses to emphasize a point. "I'm gonna be dead and gone up there with ol' Strom Thurmond. But we're risking the lives and liberty of our children. We're in the kind of situation I spent all those years trying to avoid."

I n 2007, no one in Washington had a broader view of the global economy than Rodrigo de Rato y Figaredo. As managing director of the International Monetary Fund, his job was to help keep the world economy moving ahead and, within limits, he had the power to do so. Each year, IMF teams assayed the balance sheets and financial health of dozens of nations. The IMF could extend loans (and forgive existing loans) to struggling countries, as long as they were trying to improve their finances. The IMF also looked at the world as a whole, monitoring currency and credit on the planetary economic weather map.

The IMF (and its companion organization, the World Bank, which dealt mostly with individual development projects in "developing" countries) were basically American creations. In 1944, leaders of the Allies gathered at a hotel in the White Mountains of New Hampshire to establish the rules of postwar capitalism. We were going to be the victors, but only if the prostrate free economies of the world were able to stand on their own two feet again.

Vivid in the minds of the delegates was the Depression of the 1930s. In 1944, the standard—Keynesian—explanation for the catastrophe was that governments had not intervened enough with the public spending to "prime the pump." In the decades since, another explanation has come to be accepted: that American monetary policy, which was to keep a tight control on the supply of money and credit, caused a cascade of defaults among rural banks that led to the Crash and the Depression that followed it. In post–World War I Germany there was too much money—money printed at a furious rate to pay back onerous war debts. In the United States, there was not enough.

In the orthodoxy of the IMF—an orthodoxy that de Rato embodied in his years as Spain's economic minister—nations got themselves in trouble by borrowing too much, by running large deficits on their national balance sheets. When they did, they rendered themselves suspect in the eyes of investors, who feared (as Hamilton did) that out-of-control printing presses would wreck the value of the local currency and lead to social and economic upheaval. The IMF's reporting teams regularly scolded countries for their fiscal indiscipline. Spain had been one of those countries. In part because of de Rato's leadership in the Aznar center-right government, which ran the country from 1996 to 2004, Spain had cut welfare spending, balanced its budget, and set off on a spurt of investment and enthusiasm that had made it the fastest-growing economy in Europe.

What would de Rato say about us? He answered questions one day over lunch in the dining room of the IMF world headquarters on Pennsylvania Avenue. He answered essentially the same question Alan Greenspan had been asked: Is America borrowing and spending itself into oblivion? And, might not the world abandon the dollar, and move toward the euro or Japanese yen as the reserve currency, leaving ours vulnerable not only to speculation but to sudden devaluation? In other words, did the phrase "sound as a dollar" still have any meaning?

It was true, de Rato answered, that nations had begun holding some of their reserves in euros as the European Community gained credibility as an economic unit larger, as a whole, than the United States. He estimated that perhaps 30 percent of the world's reserve holdings were now in euros. The dollar would remain the primary reserve currency, he said—especially since most of the oil-producing states preferred to denominate their sales and investments in dollars. Whether that would remain true forever, who knew?

America, he said, was a different case from that of other countries, in which the value of the local currency was rather directly tied to the national balance sheets of borrowing and trade. True, we were running colossal trade deficits—sucking in goods (and now services) from the rest of the world, especially China, at a prodigious rate. True, our publicly held "national debt," the amount we had borrowed from ourselves and others to finance our budget shortfalls, was more than $5 trillion. True, the Baby Boomers were soon to begin retiring, adding trillions of dollars in retirement and health-care costs to the responsibilities of government. Our willingness to raise taxes to pay for all of this was, to say the least, suspect.

Could the dollar take it? In other words, could we manage to preserve our ability to define, with more latitude than any other nation enjoys, what our money was?

The IMF had officially—and somewhat gingerly—raised precisely these concerns, treating the United States, for the first time, like one of the wobbly nations that needed guidance. But de Rato himself was more sanguine. The fiscal and trade deficits weren't the only things that mattered in the case of the United States, he said. No country was more open to investment, he said, or had a wider array of investment instruments to offer the world. "You are an unrivaled financial supermarket," he said. And leaving aside military might—in and of itself impressive—there was no nation on the planet more likely to remain politically stable, and thus more attractive to long-term investors. "In many countries," he said, "it matters very much to investors who is in charge of the government. There can be wide swings, and that scares people. Here it doesn't matter who is president, who controls the Congress. Things move along."

Or so we have to hope. In one of the more infamous home videos of the early twenty-first century, Osama bin Laden bragged to his friends over dinner that his aim in attacking the World Trade Center had been to cripple the American economy. It had not worked—though the attack had led the Bush administration to launch a war in Iraq that could cost us trillions by the time all the spending is accounted for.

In a world threatened by terrorism, de Rato asked rhetorically, is there a better place to invest than here? "If the world goes haywire, I'd rather be here than in Cairo," he said. But how about, say, London?

By the end of of 2007, it was ever harder to justify optimism about the self-sustaining, self-correcting ecology of the dollar. Its value had continued to fall against other currencies, especially the now-regnant euro; the annual deficits on the balance sheet of the United States, while still not large, given the enormous size of the American economy, sapped confidence. The price of a barrel of oil kept rising, partly prompted by the decline of the dollar. Investors in the Middle East, who kept most of their assets in dollars, were slowly but surely rethinking that commitment and denominating sales and making investments in euros.

Meanwhile, a speculative boom in American housing and real estate had burst. The Federal Reserve, now under the leadership of Princeton economist Ben Bernanke, lowered interest rates to keep the merry-go-round in motion—further depressing the value of the dollar. True, the cheap dollar made it easier to sell American-made goods abroad (and American manufacturers' order books were full), but we were never going to win a race to the bottom against the Chinese, who, by the way, had to decide whether there was any way to dump the trillion dollars' worth of Treasuries they held.

Critics on all sides lamented our fiscal state, made worse, in the eyes of many, by a post-9/11 defense budget that, by 2006, had surpassed $500 billion a year—more than the combined defense spending of the rest of the planet. The Cold War had been expensive, but, as Greenspan had pointed out in a 2007 book, the collapse of communism had opened vast new markets to us in Eastern Europe for investing the trillions of dollars we had printed. Still, this new endless war—what the administration called a "Long War"—offered the prospect of spending with no end point, no fallen wall, no treaty ceremony on an aircraft carrier. Robert Hormats, a respected economist at Goldman Sachs, argued in his own book that we were on the road to ruin unless we raised the revenues, and cut wasteful spending, to put some semblance of discipline and confidence behind the loans we were continuing to secure. "No nation has been able to have guns and butter forever," he said.

No one doubted the vitality and fecundity of the American marketplace, but we seemed destined to live in an era of working harder for less real money—and another round of selling off the natural resources and other real property assets that were our inheritance to begin with. In the Mesabi Iron Range, the Chinese were buying up and reopening old taconite mines. In the coalfields, new strip and deep mines were opening to feed China's electricity grid. They would pay us back in dollars, but would we still have the freedom to argue about how much those dollars were worth? Would the future bring growth and order, or neither?

Eight

LOCAL V. NATIONAL AUTHORITY

Brian Williams had covered his share of disasters as a reporter, but he could not believe what he was seeing and hearing as he prepared to anchor the NBC *Nightly News* from New Orleans. Hurricane Katrina was lashing the city, generating a gargantuan, deadly surge of water in the streets. Whole neighborhoods were inundated. Looters were out; dead bodies floated in the fetid water. The calamity had been predicted for days. Officials from the president of the United States to the local police had been warned, and had even issued public alarms. The governor of Louisiana had preemptively declared a state of emergency. Yet there was no clear line of command—indeed, no command at all. "It seemed that every public official was in charge—and none," Williams said later. At the Louisiana Superdome, a National Guard officer explained to Williams that a federal agency had the con. "This is a Department of Homeland Security Show!" the officer declared. Except that it was not: At the time, the Guard was under state command.

In late August and early September of 2005, Hurricane Katrina exposed a deep fault line in the landscape of American politics and history and, in achingly vivid fashion, the ever-present, uniquely vehement American Argument over the relative roles of local and national power. The country's freedom and prosperity are due, in good measure, to the subtle and complex division of authority called federalism: the inherently contradictory notion of the joint sovereignty of the states and the United

States. But here, in the midst of Katrina, Williams was witnessing a narrative of federalism gone scandalously awry.

From his perch at the Superdome, the vast concrete football arena that served as an emergency shelter, Williams could see the chaotic results of clashing authority and tradition. Local officials anywhere are proud and covetous of their authority. "Above the door of every mayor's or governor's office is a sign—or the idea of a sign—that says 'we can handle this,' " said Williams.

Louisiana, with its gumbo of ethnicities and unique history of French and Spanish jurisdiction, is perhaps our most colorful example of local pride and power. When the Feds show up, it often is for no good reason, in local eyes. "I found that people in Louisiana didn't jump for joy when someone would say to them, 'I'm from the federal government and I'm here to help you,' " Williams recalled.

Yet a stark failure of federal power was at the center of the Katrina story: It was the national government's duty (delegated in the nineteenth century to the U.S. Army Corps of Engineers) to build and maintain the dams, locks, and levees on the country's "navigable waterways." "That was the essential thing to understand about the Katrina situation," said Williams. "This was the Feds' job and it was the Feds who failed the city and its people, especially those people in poor neighborhoods who were of course the most vulnerable."

For generations, Louisianans had pressed Congress to spend more money on the levees, but the results never approached being state-of-the-art. Once the storm hit, the desultory and confused response of other pieces of the federal bureaucracy made matters worse by adding more confusion than actual aid. The then-new Department of Homeland Security had no direct experience in disaster recovery; the agency that did, the Federal Emergency Management Agency (FEMA), had been depleted by bureaucratic shuffling and budget cuts.

The deployment and control of the Louisiana National Guard came to symbolize the mess. By law and tradition, state governors command Guard units. Indeed, in the oldest American states, the units have been in existence longer than the federal government itself. In times of war or insurrection, the president can "nationalize" the Guard on his own; at other times, a governor has to agree to allow him to do so. In New Orleans, the Feds and Governor Kathleen Blanco argued over who was in charge—and never really settled the dispute.

Williams saw the results. In the early days of the disaster, he said, the Guardsmen at the Superdome were "performing aggressive body searches" of victims seeking shelter there. If they were getting any sensible guidance from state officials, it was not obvious. "I asked what they were searching for and they said they had been told to take away cigarette lighters." Williams then pointed out to them that the army rations that were being doled out—"meals ready to eat" (MREs)—each contained a pack of matches. In Washington, administration lawyers argued for days about the president's power—or lack of power—to nationalize Guard troops without the governor's permission. It seemed to some, in retrospect, that officials were looking for excuses not to act.

After three days, the Feds dispatched Lieutenant General Russell Honoré to New Orleans for the ostensible purpose of taking charge of the Gulf Coast situation. Officials of the Department of Homeland Security denied that President Bush ever had asked the governors of Louisiana and Mississippi if Honoré could do so. But take charge he did—at least for the cameras. When Honoré arrived at the Superdome, "it was like a scene out of a movie," said Williams. "Honoré was shouting at the Guardsmen, 'Put your weapons down! Put your weapons down!' " They did so, though technically—constitutionally—he was not their commander.

Clashing personalities—and ineptitude and pettiness—further tangled the lines of authority. "Federal, state, and local officials were in over their heads all the way up and down the line," Williams said. The president and New Orleans mayor Ray Nagin grew to loathe each other as a result of what came to be known as the Shower Incident. When Bush arrived on Air Force One to inspect the city and deliver a speech, he invited Nagin and other officials to come on board. He also allowed Nagin, who hadn't been able to use a fully functioning bathroom for nearly a week, to use all of the facilities on the plane. Two hours later, Nagin was still in the shower, infuriating the president. The mayor, for his part, was equally upset that the president had grown impatient.

The essential problem was structural, however, and it was likely to remain so. "We can't reverse the patterns of history," said Williams, who spent as much time on the ground in New Orleans as any American journalist. "The local-state-federal balance is woven into the DNA of the country." But Katrina and 9/11 together exposed the need to rethink who does what and why, at least in terms of disasters. And that process is a federal responsibility.

We love our country, our "nation," not so much. It took the Civil War to give "nation," a Latin word with foreign hints of iron and tribe, dramatic resonance. Lincoln spoke of our nation at Gettysburg, Roosevelt at his first inauguration, George W. Bush at the National Cathedral after 9/11. Still, we remain reluctant nationalists. Even as the Founders assembled a "more perfect Union," they feared the kind of central authority against which they had just rebelled. They were men of local mind and means, representing states with close to two centuries of history. As a result, we have dual citizenship: in a place and in an idea of a place. We orient ourselves by land more than by "the land." These days, localism is less about territory than about jobs and culture, but the dynamic is the same. We are a fabric of sub-federal strife—East v. West, North v. South, Tidewater v. Upland, Consumers v. Marketers, Employees v. Hedge Funds, and Red v. Blue. The sundering force of "faction"— Madison's nightmare—gave us our bloodiest war and now gives us a slow-motion civil war of religious, sexual, and social accusation. But the grass roots also generate new ideas, adaptability, and an indispensable skepticism toward Washington. "States' rights" remains a force despite the homogenization of corporate commerce and the pull of political centralization in an Age of Terror. We are still, in many ways, a bottom-up country, producing new forms of localness, from immigrant lobbies to Facebook networkers. The Web is our newest West, talk radio our digital Dixie. The Argument rages: Are we pyramid or wagon wheel? Does mainframe government make us stronger, or too slow and heavy to move?

At every turn the question is the same: Who controls the levers of national power, and how much leeway does that leave—should that leave— for the rest of us?

The American people had accumulated nearly two centuries of local and state history before their representatives gathered in Philadelphia to "form a more perfect union." The phrase, in the Preamble to the U.S. Constitution, was perhaps our first official effort at spin, for at the time there was no union at all.

Though the colonies shared an English heritage, they nurtured unique identities. Royal charters decreed varied theories of governance; the proprietors and settlers had disparate views of how to apply them.

Commerce reinforced local identity, within states and between them. The tidewater and coastal river towns looked east, across the Atlantic, for trade in goods and in ideas, while "upcountry" rarely looked beyond the port towns—if it looked that far at all. The larger colonies, such as Virginia, Massachusetts, and New York, aggressively protected their commercial prerogatives.

At the time of the Revolution there were three colonial subcultures— each more distinctive than we now tend to remember.

The Puritans of New England were launched as a community commanded by the clergy, dedicated to salvation in their City on a Hill. Jeremy Belknap, an eighteenth-century historian, quoted a sermon on this topic that had been given by an earlier cleric in the Bay Colony: "It concerneth New England always to remember, said the pastor, that they are originally a plantation of religion, not a plantation of trade. The profession of purity of doctrine, worship and discipline is written upon her forehead. Worldly gain is not the end and the design of the people of New England—but religion."

Virginia, at the southern end of the early colonial chain, was a "plantation of trade." By the 1630s, men were making serious fortunes on tobacco. But, in the main, Virginia at first was not so much about the money as about a different enterprise: replicating the equable ease, and lighthanded rule, of the English countryside. For the adventurous younger sons of prominent families, Virginia was a fresh start on rich land in pitch-dark forests. The goal was to become a gentleman. George Washington wrote a guide to manners for men of good character in a New World. Deep religious piety was not part of the instruction.

Between New England and Virginia spread the unabashedly commercial Middle Colony enclaves of New York and Philadelphia. Here, the Market reigned from the start. The Dutch, who ruled New York for its first crucial decades, were traders above all and were for the most part blithe about, if not hostile to, questions of faith or Old World gentlemanly hierarchies. They were in it for the business, pure and simple: fur pelts, for example, the richer and thicker of which could be woven into felt hats for the wealthy heads of Europe. As historian Russell Shorto explained in his book *The Island at the Center of the World,* the British later tried to paper over this Dutch history with English laws and Anglican dogma, but the hardheaded Dutch outlook remained. Later, William Penn opened his Pennsylvania greensward with a clarion call to freedom of religion. It was a noble idea, and Penn meant it, but his chief objective was commercial: to attract industrious German farmers.

The alliance formed at the time of the Declaration of Independence in 1776 was just that—an alliance, and a shaky one at that. Scholars have long noted a small but significant typographical indication of its tentative nature. The title reads "The Unanimous Declaration of the thirteen united States of America." After signing the document, Benjamin Franklin warned, "We must hang together or, most assuredly, we will hang separately." Franklin's fear was well grounded. The confederation formed after the Revolution was less than powerless: the form of a national government without the substance, unable to carry out the most elementary tasks, such as securing borders and quelling unrest. So how could we create a country and yet preserve two centuries of regional identity? The novel answer was dual sovereignty, in which states would retain considerable power and their own constitutions even as "the People"—through special votes and conventions in the states—would bestow sovereignty upon a national government with a new constitution.

The Federalist Founders knew that they were kick-starting an engine of perpetual controversy, and they shrewdly made a virtue of that fact as they touted their new vehicle. The most famous sales document is James Madison's *The Federalist No. 10*. A strong, territorially extensive national government would be the best check against tyranny, he said, because it—and only it—could embrace a variety of factional and regional interests. The states would check the central government; the central government would ensure that a multiplicity of voices was free to check the power of any one state or faction—or the central government itself. This was a complex piece of Newtonian clock-making. It was built on Montesquieu's theory of "checks and balances." The Frenchman insisted that his theory would only work in "small republics." It was Madison's idea—his contention—that it would work better in a continental nation.

The Madisonian clockwork was not an easy sell. Anti-Federalists—there were lots of them—saw his fear of tyrannical states as a red herring, a cover for the aggrandizements of a new central power backed by big-city money interests. "The United States are to be melted down," wrote one anti-Federalist in Philadelphia, into a despotic empire dominated by "well-born aristocrats." In Massachusetts, a delegate to the commonwealth's convention declared, "These lawyers, and men of learning, and moneyed men . . . will swallow up all us little folks like the great Leviathan; yes, just as the whale swallowed up Jonah!"

To achieve ratification of the Constitution, the Federalists had to promise that they would propose and support a Bill of Rights. They delivered on the promise in 1791, including a provision—the Tenth Amendment, which "reserved" to the states or the people powers not specifically "delegated" to the new federal government. The aim was to reassure leaders of the states that the federal government would not trample on the freedoms of their citizens. Ironically, however, most of the controversy since then has been from the other direction: to make sure that the *states* do not trample on the freedoms of *American* citizens.

The noble aim of the Preamble notwithstanding, we have never been a perfect union. In fact, centuries before the advent of "Red v. Blue," citizens and states were threatening to leave it altogether—even during the early years of the Republic.

The first Americans to propose breaking the new union apart were New Englanders. The Federalists loathed President Thomas Jefferson almost on more grounds than they could count: his preachy agrarianism, Deist thinking, and hypocritical usurpations of federal power. In the run-up to the election of 1804, Federalists in New York and New England convened a group they called the "Essex Junto," and entertained the idea of withdrawing from the Union to create a "northeastern confederacy." Ten years later the Yankee secessionists were still at it, angered by what they saw as a Virginia-based hegemony in politics. It took a victory in war, the Battle of New Orleans in 1815, to impress the world (and Americans) with the durability of federal power, and in so doing end the talk of northeastern rebellion.

The South's fateful contribution to the idea of secession and states' rights was to bind the idea tightly—treacherously—to the question of race and slavery. The Founders in Philadelphia knew they would lose the argument for a federal constitution if the document decreed the abolition of slavery. They also knew that the Southern states, dependent on the plantation economy, would use every ounce of their power to protect their economies as they knew them. The Founders did what President Bill Clinton called "kicking the can down the road." They proposed that no slaves could be imported, but postponed the effective date of the ban for twenty more years (or until 1808). Other than that, everything was up to the states.

Slavery turned Madison's optimistic vision of continental stability into a nightmare. Rather than securing peace and prosperity, as Madison had hoped, the growth of a coast-to-coast country stoked the fire of war. In the first half of the nineteenth century, as each new territory sought to enter the Union, the same questions would arise: slave or free, who should decide? The Founders had kicked the can down the road thirty-seven years to 1820, when Henry Clay fashioned the Missouri Compromise, which lasted another thirty, until the Compromise of 1850, which lasted only ten. Abraham Lincoln's Republican victory in 1860 sparked the secession of South Carolina and ten other slaveholding states. Northerners call the result the Civil War; the Southern name, "the War Between the States," better reflected the way most Americans saw the conflict at the time.

It remains the deadliest conflict in our history. Our habit of arguing slipped the bonds of reason, and the farm fields ran red with blood. You can't use the term "American Argument" without pausing in reverence over this one. As the war fades further into history, it becomes harder to appreciate the nightmarish scale of it. Nearly a million Americans were killed or wounded—almost as many as in World War II. In relative terms, it was far worse. The equivalent casualty figure, measured against today's population, would be *10 million*. The percentage of soldiers killed in combat was more than twice as high as in any other American war; the Confederate rate was nearly *four times* higher. In the landscape of our politics, this was an upheaval unlike any we had ever known or, we had to hope, would know.

The war, and the regional identity it confirmed even (if not especially) in defeat, continues to shape our public life. Anyone who tells you the South is not a separate place has not spent much time there, or has not looked at an electoral college map in recent decades. The South remains demonstrably (and demonstratively) more patriotic and religious; more at home with the culture of combat, whether in war or sports; more open about social hierarchies, both within the races and between them; more willing to use corporal punishment; and more given, over the course of time, to offer sweeping allegiance to one party or another.

Southerners are more likely to give their hearts to their state as well. In Pennsylvania or New York or Illinois, the local citizens tend not to think of themselves as Pennsylvanians or New Yorkers or Illinoisans. In the South, the state is still the reference point. Politically ambitious boys (and now girls) tend to grow up wanting to be governor, not a United States senator. Coming across the state line into Kentucky from Tennessee in the southern Appalachians, you can still see billboards that proclaim, "We're Proud to Be Kentuckians!" The state did not pay for the ones I saw; the local cola bottler did.

Race polluted the virtue and usefulness of "states' rights" in the federal scheme of government, and continues to do so in some sad cases. After Reconstruction, the Southern states—and some Northern ones, too—devised schemes for denying black suffrage and political participation, and not only countenanced but also encouraged Jim Crow laws and Klan-led acts of racial terrorism. It took the "Second Reconstruction" of the civil rights movement—and the court cases, federal laws, and presidential actions it prompted—to weld the country into "one nation, indivisible" on issues of voting rights and educational opportunity.

Communications and commerce, and not just laws and war, welded us together. The South was bound to the rest of us by railroads and Reconstruction; railroads and land grants spread cultural uniformity through the Midwest and tied one coast to the other. As states and regions competed with each other for investment, they sparked a "race to the bottom" in terms of accommodation to business. With few exceptions (New York and Massachusetts being the main ones), states kept supervision of working conditions minimal—eventually sparking a Progressive Movement at the turn of the twentieth century, which in turn forced Congress to pass the first national standards. Depression and wars in the century weakened regional distinctions and brought new national laws to regulate the flow of currency and commerce. In 1957, we marked two related milestones on the road to uniform nationhood. In Arkansas, the Little Rock public schools were desegregated; in Missouri and Kansas, the first stretches of the interstate highway system opened to traffic.

At last America was safe for McDonald's.

It was the shoes, Lee Atwater told me. This seemed like a laughably trivial notion, but not to Atwater. He insisted that the shoes (and the rest of the outfit: khakis and a black Lacoste tennis shirt) were a dead giveaway. The pair of preppy-looking Topsiders convinced him that the man wearing them in the wire-service photograph, Governor Michael Dukakis of Massachusetts, did not have a chance in hell of defeating Atwater's candidate, Vice President George H. W. Bush, in the 1988 election. Desperate to "pick the Republican lock on the South," as one of their strategists put it, the Democrats had staged their convention in Atlanta and had featured speeches by a parade of Southern governors. (One of those speeches turned out to be a famously interminable one by Bill Clinton of Arkansas). Dukakis had chosen a patrician with a Southern drawl, Senator Lloyd Bentsen of Texas, to be his running mate and aimed to run as a moderate and unassuming family man.

Dukakis had reason to think, or at least hope, that he and his Republican rival were not that different culturally. The governor was the son of Greek immigrants, but, in other ways, he and his to-the-manor-born WASP opponent shared roots. Both were reared in well-off circumstances in a New England suburb: Dukakis in Brookline, a country-club town outside of Boston, Bush in Greenwich, Connecticut, in the orbit of New York City. Both were Ivy Leaguers: Dukakis from Harvard, Bush from Yale. Both had spent years in politics. Both liked to relax along the New England seaside: Dukakis in Nantucket, Bush in Kennebunkport.

Bush had taken his Eastern establishment background with him when he moved to Texas to go into the oil business and, later, into politics. His father had been a senator and a golfing friend of Ike's, and Bush had initially shared his father's middling political views. Bush's early political handlers in Houston had advised him to dress a little more "Texan" by getting rid of the button-down Brooks Brothers shirts and box-cut suits. He had refused. He remained true to his heritage, from the quirky, self-deprecating bravado on the tennis court ("Time to unleash the Chang!") to his requests for a "splash more coffee."

All of which posed tactical headaches—problems of region, problems of culture—for Atwater, who was Bush's presidential campaign manager. A gifted tyro, only thirty-six at the time, Atwater had a mission that was the mirror opposite of Dukakis's: to preserve the "lock" on the South, which Reagan had forged, by selling Bush there. That was all the more crucial because the Democratic convention had worked nationally: Bush was seventeen points behind Dukakis in the polls. The modern GOP was being built upon the rock of the South. Bush had to defend it.

Atwater worked hard to Dixify his candidate. There *was* material to work with. Bush liked country music; Atwater made sure that country-music stars were in the entourage. Lee Greenwood became Bush's unoffi-cial vocalist, showing up to sing "God Bless the USA" at event after event. Bush liked to fish; Atwater made sure that the vice president paid more than one visit to the bass fishing outlet in Springfield, Missouri, a town that had the added benefit of being the national center for the Assemblies of God Church, one of the Southern evangelical denominations. Pork rinds became the official on-the-plane snack food.

Recasting Bush was not enough. The Republicans had to take Dukakis apart, especially in the South and the border states.

But that is what Atwater did. He commissioned his research staff—the "thirty-five excellent nerds," he later called them—to assemble a short list of attack lines. The resulting infamous 3-by-5 card contained the fol-lowing: Dukakis had vetoed, on constitutional grounds, a state bill re-quiring students to recite the Pledge of Allegiance. He was governor of a "high-tax, high-spend" state and had opposed most major defense pro-grams. He had at some point or other expressed doubt about the Monroe Doctrine. He was a "card-carrying member" of the American Civil Lib-erties Union. He opposed the death penalty. He had run a prison-furlough program that had let a convicted murderer—the infamous Willie Horton—out of jail for the weekend. At a GOP conference that spring in Atlanta, Atwater had previewed the list and scoffed at the no-tion that Dukakis would win a single state in the Old or New South.

The governor, Atwater told me, was a "northeastern Ivy lib," which meant that he was too concerned with "rights" (though not enough with guns), too eager to promote the role of the national government in do-mestic affairs, too wary of open displays of patriotism, and too leery of the use of force in law-enforcement or world affairs. Only an operative with the chutzpah—or cynicism—of an Atwater could have presumed to make Bush (a Mayflower descendant) the regular guy in comparison with Dukakis (the son of a Greek immigrant).

The cultural semiotics were crucial, in Atwater's view. He was a crea-ture of popular media. He would brag that he found his most powerful political clues not in polls on focus groups but in the images of super-market tabloids, wrestling magazines, grade-D horror movies, and the ravings of late-night television pitchmen. His mind was a "middle-of-the-middle" (his term) mélange of gossip, sweat, campy theater, and Veg-O-Matic infomercials. In this milieu, Dukakis would never sell, Atwater informed me one day. How did he know?

The Dukakis vacation picture. Why? First, it was taken in Nantucket: an effete, northeastern elite no-no. Bush, in just-as-snooty Kennebunkport, was always careful to be photographed hot-rodding around in a high-horsepower cigarette boat. Here Dukakis was not doing anything macho at all. He was just sitting around on the porch, which was sensible enough, but passive, as Atwater saw it. Worse—better from Atwater's point of view—was what the governor of Massachusetts was wearing. The ensemble made him look like a New England elitist, which is precisely the caricature the GOP was aiming for. "As soon as I saw those Topsiders I knew we were going to win this campaign," he told me later. "There was just no way they were going to buy the guy in the South."

In the fall, Dukakis seemed eager to prove Atwater right. What would he do if his wife were raped? he was asked at a debate. An opponent of the death penalty, he unspooled a long, technocratic answer; whatever chance he had had to connect with voters in the South ended at that moment. On election night, Dukakis won—narrowly—one state below the Mason-Dixon Line, West Virginia, on the way to being routed by Bush from coast to coast.

George W. Bush ran for president in 2000 as a conservative from the proudest of all states-as-state-of-mind, Texas. He was far more Texan than his dad, who always was regarded by the locals as a Yankee transplant. Bush II was born in Connecticut and sent "Up East" to Andover and Yale, but his approach to life was formed on the playgrounds of Sam Houston Elementary and San Jacinto Junior High in this family's adopted hometown of Midland, Texas.

Covering him as he campaigned for governor in 1994, I saw a candidate who reveled in the idea that he could be accepted by Texas. He had not been successful in the oil business, but he knew enough about it to be able to talk knowledgeably with men who had. He took special pride in knowing a thing or two about the local geology wherever he went. He did not run as an oilman, however, which is just as well, since he was a bust at it. At the time of the campaign, he had a job that was just as good, and just as symbolically Texan: managing partner of the Texas Rangers in Dallas. As governor, Bush proudly wore a belt with a giant silver buckle, given to him by the Texas Rangers—the police force, not the baseball team. It fit the swagger of his gait.

All the syrupy Texan-ness notwithstanding, the Bush who came to the presidency was not a "states'-rights" man. From the start, he was a federal-power man. His signature domestic initiative, the "No Child Left Behind Act," called for the most aggressive expansion of the federal role in nearly forty years—since the heyday of the last president from Texas, Lyndon Johnson. The proposal, which the Republican-controlled Congress enacted in 2001, called not only for setting national test standards, but for a regulatory regime to oversee what had been a state responsibility: elementary and secondary education.

The Bush administration moved aggressively to expand federal influence in other spheres. Vice President Dick Cheney's energy task force is a good example. For years, energy companies had argued that local and state officials were blocking the stringing of new high-capacity electrical, oil, and gas lines. For just as many years the companies argued for more federal power to "preempt" state law. The Cheney task force gave the companies the opportunity to make their case—in secret. Not surprisingly, the group adopted the companies' view. It was not surprising in part because both Cheney and Bush agreed with them. Four years later, Congress wrote the measure into law.

Bush held firm views on education and energy long before he came to Washington. Events in 2000 and beyond gave him new reasons to expand the authority of the federal city. Lingering controversy over the 2000 election led him to sign the "Help America Vote Act." Despite its benignly anodyne name, HAVA was, in fact, a sweeping takeover of state control of federal elections.

In 2001, Osama bin Laden did more to centralize government power in America than anyone since FDR. The attacks on 9/11 led the president and Congress to erect a vast new edifice of federal bureaucracy in the name of security. The relationship between the FBI and state and municipal police agencies, long a delicate and contentious one, changed fundamentally after 9/11. Successive versions of the Patriot Act gave federal authorities, from the FBI to the NSA, dominion over investigative and arrest powers that once had belonged to the locals. Bush initially opposed creation of a federal Department of Homeland Security, but quickly relented in the face of congressional demands. The resulting bureaucracy instantly became the second largest in government, ranking behind only the Pentagon, with broad new powers over another province of traditional state power: public response to disasters.

The 9/11 attacks, combined with concern over a flood of illegal immigrants, added urgency to the effort to create an official "national identity card." It was an ideal foreign to American history. In a hypermobile, continental nation, a driver's license was the standard form of identification for nearly a century. No one was required to carry one—or any other form of identification, even a Social Security card. That would change if the law were passed. The document would be federally issued. You could be fined for not carrying it. As of early 2008, Congress had not voted for such a card, but the assumption was widespread that any new immigration bill that reached the president's desk would require one.

It always was hard to get the governors of the fifty states to agree on anything, but they found common ground in the summer of 2006: an administration proposal to give the president extensive new powers to use the National Guard as he saw fit. Under the proposed statute, any president could order any state Guard unit sent on a military mission or dispatched to the border, or deployed for any other purpose—all without the consent of the state's governor. As one, the governors protested the idea in Congress, pointing out that in thirteen cases the Guard units (they used to be called "militias") predated the Republic itself. Under pressure from the White House, however, Congress in 2007 tweaked a two-hundred-year-old law to give the president the new power. It was buried in a 439-page, $538 billion defense bill. The change made no headlines in Washington, but the governors noticed. They called it a "dramatic expansion of federal authority." They were right.

As a candidate, Bush claimed to have been inspired by Barry Goldwater's famous book, *The Conscience of a Conservative.* The Sage of Arizona was a staunch believer in states' rights, and in the idea that the government that governs best is the government that governs least. If Bush was a "conservative" as president, then the word had acquired an entirely different meaning in a generation.

If the meaning of "conservative" had changed, the image of states' rights had changed, too. With Republicans in charge throughout Washington, Democrats suddenly took an interest in political platforms elsewhere—and in a theory that they had spent a generation attacking. In Boston, state legislators legalized marriage between same-sex couples, basing their action on the broad language of the Massachusetts constitution. With federal funding for stem-cell research blocked, states eager to attract top-level talent and investment rushed to establish stem-cell programs of their own. The largest was in Democratic California, where it was championed by Republican governor Arnold Schwarzenegger. Some states—again, Massachusetts was one—sought to take the lead on health-care policy, extending medical coverage far beyond the federal norm, in part as an object lesson to Washington on how it could be done nationwide.

The new emphasis on the states cut both ways politically. Blocked at the federal level, religious conservatives focused on state capitals and state referenda in their efforts to ban same-sex marriage. By the fall of 2006, they had succeeded in doing so in twenty-six states. Given added leeway to administer costly federal programs such as Medicaid, some states sharply curtailed spending on them. In some areas, the president was only happy to once again be a champion of states' rights. One was in disaster recovery. After Hurricane Katrina, he said, Washington had allocated billions to Louisiana for homes and neighborhoods. "But what actually is done with that money is up to the state," he said, "and that's the way it should be."

Indeed, the states were hardly withering away. By 2005, the combined budgets of state and local governments was $1.7 trillion. They employed a staggering 19.2 million workers, more than any other sector of the economy. The state and local sector actually grew more than twice as fast as the federal one between 1947 and 2005. In 2005 the Feds accounted for 26 percent of all economic activity, but the state and local governments accounted for fully 18 percent.

The Founders probably would be chagrined to know that what we now call the "public sector" comprised 44 percent of the entire economy—many multiples of what it was in colonial times. But they would see that the states remained going concerns, and for that they would presumably be grateful.

"States' rights" isn't just a Southern idea; it is an American one. And race does not always have anything to do with it. In fact, there is no place in the country more proud and protective of its local prerogatives—or with a longer history of protecting them—than northern New England, especially along the Connecticut River, which separates Vermont and New Hampshire. Every four years, Americans catch a glimpse of that fierce localism in the New Hampshire primary, where "retail" politics still mattered, and the state's legions of independent voters (they registered "undeclared" so they could take either ballot) tended to decide the outcome. As for Vermont, it most recently had given the nation Governor Howard Dean, M.D.—who nearly won the Democratic nomination in 2004 on the first wave of protest to be generated by America's newest "local" frontier, the new West of the Internet.

The superficial image of Vermont was of a landscape of Birkenstock-shod tree huggers, but the reality was far more idiosyncratic. Yes, Ben and Jerry settled there. On the other hand, Vermont is the only state in the Union with no year-round gun-control law—only one for deer-hunting season. You can shoot a deer on the lawn of the state capitol in Montpelier, so the saying goes, as long as you use the proper-gauge shotgun. On a per capita basis, Vermont has sent more soldiers and National Guardsmen to Iraq and Afghanistan than any other state. On a per capita basis, it has suffered more casualties. Over dinner in Middlebury in the summer of 2005, I talked to Governor Jim Douglas, the mild-mannered Republican who succeeded Dean. At the time, eleven Vermonters had been killed. "For us, that is a devastating number," he said. "Everyone knows everyone, and we feel it." (The total reached eighteen by the summer of 2007.)

The war was an example of the kind of grand plan that skeptical Vermonters had always resisted (unless, frankly, it involved federal schemes for protecting dairy farmers and milk prices). As every Vermonter knows, their state was an independent republic for fourteen years after the Declaration of Independence, and even went so far as to exchange ambassadors with . . . Pennsylvania, among other foreign powers. At the time, the French were still making mischief via Quebec, but the Vermonters' desire to remain unattached had less to do with the Great Power geopolitics of the day than with the desire of the natives to remain as free and unencumbered as the riches of the land and their fortunate position on Lake Champlain would allow. They envisioned themselves as "the Switzerland of North America," or at least some did. They were only willing to seriously consider joining the Union *after* the passage of the Bill of Rights—and after it became clear that Kentucky, a slave state, would join the Union, too.

New Hampshire has the reputation for ornery independence, summarized by its license plate motto, "Live Free or Die," but it was the Vermonters who actually did both. Their belief in human freedom was precociously advanced, even by American standards. Vermont was the first state to ban slavery in its constitution—and was the first to send a member of the Republican Party to Congress. That was the first time, and essentially the last, that Vermonters were for what we now call "big government." "We think that there is a huge risk in thinking that the federal government can do everything," said Pat Leahy, the first and only Vermont Democrat ever elected to the U.S. Senate. "You have to protect the states because that is where the innovation is."

Americans tend to think of "secession" as a Southern invention, but it's no surprise that the Vermonters have taken up the idea again. Only half tongue-in-cheek, some provocateurs in Montpelier in 2007 published a "Green Mountain Manifesto," subtitled "Why and How Tiny Vermont Might Help Save America from Itself by Seceding from the Union." They hoped that town meetings, held twice a year, would consider the idea. Rob Williams, editor of a newspaper and website that favors secession, declared that the United States was collapsing of its own weight. "The argument for secession," he told the AP's Montpelier correspondent, "is that the U.S. has become an empire that is essentially ungovernable—it's too big, it's too corrupt, and it no longer serves the needs of its citizens." None of the state's leading politicians supported the idea, but Leahy explained where the interest in it came from. "People in Vermont are individualists," he said. "They like their privacy. They like to be left alone. But they also expect to have a voice in things, and they feel like they have been shut out in the Bush years."

Only one major political figure supported Vermont secession. That would be Bill O'Reilly, the conservative talk-show host. He even offered to raise money.

Senator Patrick Leahy was no secessionist, but rather than leave the Union, he wanted the Union to leave Vermont—that is, he wanted his state to win back from Washington some of the freedom and independence he thought the Feds had taken. It was a small matter to some, but an urgent one to Leahy: the question of who controlled the National Guard. The Vermont Guard traced its heritage to the Green Mountain Boys of the Revolution. After the law had passed, Leahy took to the Senate floor to denounce it as a power grab, and to argue that the "constructive friction" between Montpelier and Washington was not only mandated by the Constitution, but a moral necessity in an Age of Terror. The president alone could not decide whether the young (and not so young) men and women of Vermont could be dispatched—with no assent from the governor—to war abroad or police duty at home.

Besides, he said, the notion that fighting terrorism was solely a federal responsibility was contradicted by record. Local cops in places such as New York City had done a far better job—given their savvy and their feel for the local terrain—than the FBI. "Basically, after the attacks on the Trade Center in 1993, the FBI blew it," said Leahy. "What you need is good, traditional law-enforcement. Al Qaeda is decentralized, shouldn't we be, too? Big, centralized responses don't work."

It turns out that you need to know the lay of the land, and for that you need the locals.

Nine

PRESIDENTIAL POWER

The first thing you noticed about Jimmy Carter was that there was no aura and very little entourage. In the aftermath of Richard Nixon's "imperial presidency," the country in 1976 had turned to an unassuming peanut farmer turned Georgia governor— a man of the soil and of the Bible Belt—to lead it back to humble, law-abiding ways. The Democrats ran Congress and seemed to run all of Washington, too. President Carter was a member of their own party, of course, but they showed little deference to him, passing legislation with his input but not his leadership. As for Carter, he seemed deferential to the entire world: the first president officially known by a diminutive. "Jimmy" was on his stationery.

The aura and clout of the presidency had waxed and waned over the centuries. This particular mini-era of presidential humility had begun with Republican Gerald Ford, the former House leader and accidental president who had moved into the Oval Office after Nixon's departure. He instantly became famous, if not beloved, as the Chief Executive Who Made His Own Toast. Carter followed in the same unassuming vein, carrying his own suit bag as a candidate, overnighting in the homes of Iowa voters when he was seeking votes there.

During the Ford-Carter years, the Congress passed a War Powers Resolution in an effort to reclaim, or assert, its role in decisions about the use of our armed might in the world; all but dismantled the CIA for its misdeeds; passed laws aimed at enhancing Congress's own power to con-

trol administrative spending; and demanded new openness in the proceedings of federal agencies. If Carter saw in any of this a catastrophic loss
of the power of the office he held, he didn't say so. For much of the time,
he was too busy worrying about more technical matters.

In the summer of 1977 Carter came to Louisville, Kentucky, to tour a
coal-fired power plant that had been retrofitted with new environmental-
control systems. In the years after the Arab Oil Embargo of 1973–1974,
energy "independence" was an urgent matter, and no issue involving it
(or anything else) was too technical for Carter, a navy engineer by training, to study. As an environmental writer for *The Courier-Journal,* I drew
the assignment to cover him. It wasn't a difficult administrative matter.
You showed up, flashed a press pass to a Secret Service agent, and were
whisked into the small entourage. At its center was a smallish man of serious mien who asked lots of questions and who, from time to time,
would flash a blindingly friendly grin. I walked along beside him in a
small group of officials, asking questions as we walked. To my surprise,
he asked me questions, too, about the plant, about the beat. The Secret
Service agents—and there were no more than a handful—stayed in the
background. He was the president as average guy, or at least average engineer.

The visit was endearing if not inspiring. Carter had his foibles, and he
could be self-righteous in a determinedly small-minded way, but reporters liked his unassuming approachability—and at first, so did the
country. After all, he had won the job by promising to restore decency and
trustworthiness to the office. "I will never lie to you," he had declared,
and people seemed to believe him, which was an accomplishment in itself
after what many Americans viewed as Nixon's shredding of the very idea
of presidential leadership.

But before long, voters came to doubt not Carter's honesty but his ef-
fectiveness, his ability to inspire: his strength. He gave speeches in which
he seemed to beseech and complain, not command. In one infamous televised set speech, on energy, he wore a cardigan sweater that made him
look more like Mr. Rogers than the leader of the free world. Carter eventually sought to blame the voters themselves for his declining political
standing, telling them that they had been infected with a "malaise." The
word was foreign-sounding, abstruse, and created in the public the very
emotion it was intended to exorcise.

None of this might have mattered to Carter's fate—to his chances of winning reelection in 1980—had events in Iran not turned him from commander in chief to the man who could not command. Radical Iranian students, inspired by a revival of fundamentalist Islam, overthrew the American-backed Shah in November 1979 and took fifty-two American diplomats hostage in the embassy in Tehran. Five months into the siege, Carter dispatched a daring secret rescue mission, which ended in failure—and humiliating worldwide publicity—when the aircraft carrying American commandos crashed in the Iranian desert.

Even before the crisis in Iran, Carter had been forced to endure a rare political crisis at home. He had become one of the few sitting presidents ever to face a serious fight to be nominated to seek a second term. (In that decade of presidential low tide, Gerald Ford had faced a similar situation.) Senator Ted Kennedy's challenge had fallen short, but it diminished Carter further.

The Democratic convention in New York in 1980 turned into a presidential antipageant, robbing Carter of dignity even as he was being officially launched on his reelection campaign. Kennedy dominated the show, and won the hearts of the delegates, with a speech that invoked the tragic grandeur of his family of fallen heroes. Sitting in the press stands as he spoke, I saw a Madison Square Garden crowd overcome with nostalgia, and longing.

When Carter spoke, the hall was drained of energy, enthusiasm, and hope. His speech was dutiful, sober, and weary, with the travail of the American hostages on everyone's mind. "My own heart is burdened for the troubled Americans," Carter said. "My thoughts and my prayers for our hostages in Iran are as though they were my own sons and daughters."

He enumerated the burdens of the office, even though he hadn't convincingly showed that he was up to dealing with them. "The life of every human being on Earth can depend on the experience and judgment and vigilance of the person in the Oval Office," Carter said. "The president's power for building and his power for destruction are awesome. And the power's greatest exactly where the stakes are highest—in matters of war and peace."

The political strategy behind this passage was clear: The aim was to frighten voters who might be considering casting their ballots for a retired movie actor named Ronald Reagan. But at least Reagan had played a commander in the movies, and he seemed to have that bearing—and, in the end, that was enough. Trust was one thing, but presidential leadership was more than that.

I f we all are created equal, how is any one of us entitled to lead the rest of us? The American answer is a presidential election, the only collective choice in which we all can participate as citizens. But that begs questions and fosters arguments. If we believe in the Individual—and we surely do—shouldn't we trust the individuals we elect to lead without restraint? And if we don't fully trust them—and we don't—what is the best way to hold them accountable for their actions? To what extent is the president, especially in wartime, free to make decisions alone, in secret, with no oversight from Congress or courts? When, if ever, is he free to interpret the Constitution as he sees fit? How can we tell which skills and traits are best suited for the job? And what, essentially, *is* the job—military commander, educator, or magistrate?

In no country is wise leadership more necessary; in none is it harder to find and sustain. Representative democracy is not an easy business to conduct. We distrust authority but cannot live without it. We need leaders but resent them. We distrust elites but cherish the freedom of talent and ambition to rise to the top of the American meritocracies of mind or money. We celebrate, even fawn over, great men (and women), but can't resist the thrill of humiliating them, or at least reducing them to mere celebrity. So here is the American Argument about leaders: Do our public (and private) leaders have too much power—and leeway—or more than they deserve? Can leadership temper the excesses of democracy, and protect us from our enemies (and ourselves) without becoming the tyranny we overthrew to become who we are?

Americans have never been fond of kings. Authoritarian, divinely sanctioned royal power was anathema from the day we started calling ourselves Americans. We tolerated, even lionized, commanders, however. We knew that war would require them, and that we had no alternative but to trust them, at least as long as we had some hand in choosing them. We had a companion hope, which was that war would not become a perpetual state. For if it did, history told us, a leader could morph into a despot. Early Americans feared a standing army because they thought it would be all too potent a tool—not for our security, but for dictatorial power.

For a host of reasons, presidential leadership or the lack of it has come to dominate the discourse of American public life. One explanation is that war, and rumors of war, and a national crisis that can be *defined* as war, stir yearning for a leader to master the situation, a commander in chief.

That is how George Washington became our ideal. We see him as the perfect unassuming democrat and commander who could lead us firmly in battle and yet not rob us of our freedom, which is why a fresco of him enthroned in heaven (in the role of Christ) frames the oculus of the Capitol dome. It is why, periodically in our history, we have sought out military leaders as presidents—from Jackson and Taylor to Grant and Eisenhower.

The Washington touch has become harder to find and maintain. The American Argument over leadership is urgent now because of something the Founders saw and feared, but could not quite imagine happening. They thought they had carefully limited the president's role as commander in chief by giving Congress the sole authority to declare war, to raise money for it, and to end it by starving it of funds or by approving a treaty. The president was not a bystander in all of this, but, rather, an official pledged to see that the "laws are faithfully executed." His oath, prescribed by the Constitution, was not to protect the country per se, but rather the Constitution itself—a document that carefully limited his own powers. He was as much administrator as anything else. White horses were for Washington alone.

War, the Founders assumed, was a sometime thing, at least it would be in America. But what if war became perpetual? What if war, not "peace," became our life? What if wars and the weapons that might be used in them required not only intelligence, secrecy, and surprise—tools of war always—but *instantaneous* decisions in an atmosphere of secrecy both fateful and permanent? And what if the war "over there" arrived on our soil? And what if there was no "enemy" in the form of a nation with an army in uniform, but an enemy that was and could be here, in the United States, anywhere at any time and in any place?

If all of that were true, then the commander in chief role's could (would have to) overtake all others in the office of the presidency, and the presidency could (would try to) overtake all other branches and functions of government as it sought out the enemy in the midst of ever-present war. The Second World War, and the Cold War that followed it, led to, or gave an excuse for, the most radical expansion of the powers of the presidency since the Civil War; by 2007, the "war on terror" led to another exponential leap in the power of the office.

Political leadership was indispensable in the chaos and challenge of colonial times. The *Mayflower* passengers were engaged in a proudly communal mission, but they would have foundered without the redoubtable John Winthrop; in the South, their contemporaries, the Virginians, would have been lost on the banks of the James had it not been for Captain John Smith. Colonies were commanded by larger-than-life figures: William Penn, John Carroll, the Virginia royal governors. Colonial leaders saw impressive role models in the forests around them, especially in the shrewd chiefs of the Iroquois Nations.

Respect for leadership never extended to monarchy. By the middle of the eighteenth century, Americans were beginning to agree with Tom Paine about not only the "evil of monarchy" but also the evil of "hereditary succession"—by which, of course, he meant the English crown. The Declaration of Independence was an eloquent summons to the cause of freedom and human rights—the trumpet blast that heralded the arrival of the modern world—yet it also was a parade of horribles about the many abuses of power by a leader who, among other things, had become a commander without conscience. Thomas Jefferson and his compatriots complained that King George III had "kept among us, in times of peace, Standing Armies without the Consent of our legislatures"; that he had "affected to render the military independent of and superior to the Civil Power"; that he had been guilty of "quartering large bodies of armed troops among us"; that he had brought mercenaries to our shores, and forced American citizens to serve against their will in his navy.

With those and other, civil and legal, transgressions in mind, our first government fashioned after the Revolution was a weak confederation—and essentially one without a "president" at all other than the person who would preside over legislative meetings. And as if to emphasize their main worry—that despots arose where armies and navies were—the Articles of Confederation said that "no vessel of war shall be kept in time of peace by any state, except such number as shall be deemed necessary by the United States in Congress assembled, for the defense of such state or its trade." In other words: a navy of nothing.

Washington had no interest in leading the confederation, even though he had nothing against it. He had left his farm to fight the war, done his duty in it, and returned home. There were those who wanted to deify him; he would have none of it.

Then Shays' Rebellion broke out, and Washington changed his mind about the need for a strong federal government—and a strong executive to lead it. Events in the post–Revolutionary War frontier of western Massachusetts convinced him. In 1786, Daniel Shays led a revolt there by a band of debt-ridden farmers against the banks and other moneyed interests in Boston. The governor could not raise a public militia, so he raised a private one of mercenaries. The confederation government was powerless to assist in the effort. The "national" government had no army and no commander to lead it. Washington, in a series of letters, fretted about the weakness of the Congress. That brought him back into the field, not of war but of politics. He agreed to leave Mount Vernon—again—for Philadelphia, there to preside over the convention that wrote a new constitution with substantial presidential powers.

The delegates in Philadelphia wanted to create a powerful "executive," but not *too* powerful. Frankly, they were more concerned with other, more pressing matters, the most important of which was how to make sure a new central government could actually function without hopelessly antagonizing the states. The presidency was almost, but not quite, an afterthought. Alexander Hamilton had held forth for hours on the need for a strong "executive"—named for life, with absolute veto power—but the delegates ignored him. They also ignored the New Jersey delegates, who went in the opposite direction, proposing that a new "executive branch" be composed of a rotating committee of appointed nonentities with limited managerial functions and no veto.

The convention settled on one person, with veto power that could be overridden, and very few defined powers. By far the longest section of the Constitution was the first, setting out the enormous powers of Congress, which was the guts of the bargain between the states, and between the People and their new government. The president would have the "executive power," but that wasn't defined, and very few specific ones were enumerated. He was given two important tasks: to be commander in chief of the military, and to oversee the management of foreign affairs by negotiating treaties (which still had to be approved by the Senate) and nominating ambassadors (who still had to be confirmed by the Senate). And that was about it for the presidency.

Not that big a job. But for all their foresight in other matters, the Founders did not foresee, perhaps could not foresee, how the commander-in-chief function would consume all others and, in the early twenty-first century, all but consume the government.

The ironic pattern since 1789 has been for presidents to come to office claiming to worry that the job possessed too much latent power, only to be moved by fate or their own evolving views to expand presidential power even further. Usually, war, or the acquisition of new territory or commercial interests abroad, was the proximate cause of the turnaround.

Washington was famously reluctant to acknowledge the blandishments of office. Yet, in 1794, he personally led a federal militia force of 13,000 over the Allegheny Mountains into western Pennsylvania to put down a revolt by frontiersmen who objected to a new federal tax on whiskey. He did it under the powers granted by Section 2, Article II of the Constitution, which says that the president "shall be Commander in Chief of the Army and Navy of the United States, and of the Militia of the several states, when called into the actual service of the United States." Two years earlier, in one of its first important war-powers acts, the Congress had spelled out procedures for "calling up" the militias to federal military service. The force Washington amassed in a matter of months was larger than the entire Continental army he led during the Revolutionary War.

Thomas Jefferson came to the presidency worried about the corrosive effect it might have on his vision of a democracy of rural yeomen. The sight of Federalists such as Washington, Hamilton, and Adams laying federal taxes and calling out the troops had vividly reminded Jefferson why he distrusted centralized power—especially in the hands of a president and commander in chief. In office, however, Jefferson did not hesitate to exercise the powers of the office in sweeping fashion: dispatching the navy, without a declaration of war, to fight the Barbary pirates; and engineering the Louisiana Purchase without prior authorization from, or consultation with, Congress.

It took only a few years for the idea to be accepted that a president was virtually omnipotent in foreign affairs—and that such omnipotence might pose a danger to democratic freedom. In "external relations," Chief Justice John Marshall declared, "the president is the sole organ of the nation . . . and directs the force of the nation." Prophetic as always, Tocqueville warned that "if the existence of the American union were perpetually threatened, the executive would assume an increased importance." Senator John Calhoun was, as always, more apocalyptic. Were America to become an imperial nation, he warned, "all the added power and patronage which conquest will create will pass to the Executive. In the end, you put in the hands of the executive the power of conquering you."

We tend to forget that presidents—especially the ones that historians view as great or near-great—often did what they wanted, Congress or the courts notwithstanding. Indeed, depending on their politics, historians tend to reward the presidents who acted most boldly, and independently—as long as that bold and independent action brought results. The classic example: the Louisiana Purchase, which Jefferson engineered without consulting Congress in advance. Andrew Jackson, a hero to progressive historians, shut down the national bank, and defied congressional censure in doing so. He and the Congress agreed to "remove" the Native Americans to the West, and he scoffed at the Supreme Court decision that attempted to block the measure.

The latitude has always been widest in times of war. Jackson's fellow Tennessean James K. Polk ordered the invasion of Mexico without ever getting a declaration of war from Congress. In theory, lamented John Quincy Adams, "the power of declaring war is given exclusively to Congress." After the Mexican War, he complained, "it is now established as irreversible precedent that the president of the United States has but to declare that War exists, with any nation upon Earth, by the act of that Nation's Government, and the War is essentially declared."

This is precisely the argument, in fact, that George W. Bush used after the 9/11 attacks, when Americans suddenly heard more than they had in decades about Abraham Lincoln's wartime attitude toward the scope of presidential power. The issue then—and 150 years later—concerned a revered idea of medieval English common law. It held that any subject who claimed to have been wrongly arrested by local magistrates could ask royal authorities to check the case for at least minimal procedural validity. A privilege, but a near-sacred one, the freedom to file such a "writ of habeas corpus" was enshrined in Article I of the U.S. Constitution. The privilege cannot be suspended, the Founders wrote, "unless when in Cases of Rebellion or Invasion public Safety may require it." It was up to the Congress—not the president—to suspend the writ. At least that is what Chief Justice Marshall ruled in 1807.

At the onset of the Civil War, Lincoln secretly suspended the writ in Maryland, freeing military officers to make arrests of American citizens—not enemy soldiers—without worrying that the captives would be able to challenge their imprisonment. The Supreme Court, following the earlier Marshall opinion, declared in late 1861 that only Congress could suspend the writ. Lincoln ignored the decision, and, some historians think, may even have contemplated issuing an arrest warrant for the man who wrote it, Justice Roger B. Taney. Citing President Jackson's earlier expressions of contempt for the Court, Lincoln declared that he would rather ignore the ruling than see "the government itself go to pieces." Only two years later—after Lincoln had suspended the writ in many other places and ignored many other court orders—did the Congress finally validate his actions by passing a statute to suspend the writ throughout the Union.

Lincoln continued to defend his action, which was perhaps the single most sweeping extension of presidential power in our history. "I felt that measures otherwise unconstitutional," he wrote, "might become lawful by becoming indispensable to the preservation of the Constitution through the preservation of the nation. Right or wrong, I assumed this ground, and now avow it." Yet we continue to revere him. And even though we think of him as a reticent, humble, even self-doubting man, the memorial we built to him in Washington is meant to evoke a sense of almost religious awe. It's patterned after the Temple of Zeus.

A t the turn of the twentieth century, the presidency assumed center stage again after a period of relative obscurity, this time propelled not by war at home but conquest abroad: the chance to seize assets—in the Philippines, Puerto Rico, and, by proxy, in Cuba—of the crumbling Spanish empire. To the usual commander's bravado Teddy Roosevelt added a new domestic theme: a "progressive" agenda to tame the abuses of unbridled industrial capitalism. T.R.'s "new nationalism" was a brashly presidential project. His vivid showmanship fed and captivated the new engines of publicity—big-city tabloid newspapers—in a way a mere congressman could never manage. Not shy about his own abilities, Roosevelt explained later that he promised not to "content himself with the negative merit of keeping his talents undamaged in a napkin. I declined to adopt the view that what was imperatively necessary for the Nation could not be done by a President unless he could find some specific authorization for it."

Still, T.R. was the exception. Presidents from Taft through Hoover often found themselves buffeted by what amounted to congressional government, even and sometimes especially in foreign affairs. In reaction to World War I, Congress not only rejected President Woodrow Wilson's League of Nations, but also shaped America's neutrality-and-disarmament-oriented foreign policy. In 1923, when Henry Luce launched *Time* magazine—and a new era in coverage of politics—the person he chose to grace the first cover was not the president. Rather than the eminently forgettable and virtually powerless Warren G. Harding, Luce and his editors decided to lionize the man who really ran Washington at the time: Speaker of the House Joseph "Uncle Joe" Cannon.

It took another war—a metaphorical one—to justify constructing the foundation of the modern administrative presidency. Preparing to assume office in 1933 in the midst of the Depression, Franklin Roosevelt was urged to use extraordinary measures to revive an economy in ruins. "A mild case of dictatorship," wrote Water Lippmann, the widely respected columnist (and someone who did not admire Roosevelt), "will help us over the rough spots in the road ahead." In a private meeting, Lippmann told FDR the same thing.

In his inaugural address, FDR did not go that far, but he adopted the language of war to portray himself as a new kind of domestic commander in chief. He vowed to seek "the one remaining instrument to meet the crisis: broad executive power to wage war against the emergency, as great as the power that would be given to me if we were in fact invaded by a foreign foe."

It was the biggest applause line of the speech.

Privately, FDR may have at least considered the possibility of following Lippmann's advice. With the nation's banks bracing for new assaults by frantic depositors, FDR used his first radio speech as president to speak to the American Legion. It was the nation's leading veterans group, with no official role in government, but its members had signed pledges to help "maintain law and order." In a draft of the address unearthed recently by my *Newsweek* colleague Jonathan Alter, FDR was prepared to say to the Legionnaires: "As new commander in chief under the oath to which you are still bound, I reserve the right to command you in any phase of the situation which now confronts us." In other words, he could turn them into his own personal army.

If Roosevelt stood at such a brink, he quickly stepped back from it. The line never made it into the American Legion speech. Soon thereafter FDR passed word to Lippmann to cut out the dictator talk. But the basic notion survived, which was that the country needed a new kind of domestic economic commander in chief, and Congress and the courts had to accept that fact. Congress did; the Supreme Court, of course, did not, striking down key features of the New Deal's regulatory machinery. That, in turn, led FDR to propose adding new, younger members to the high court—which finally prompted Congress to shout "enough!" to the domestic commander. However, most of the economic bureaucracy that exists today dates to FDR's time.

Another war, this one in Vietnam, led Congress to try to reassert its role in foreign affairs and national security. Widely seen as the first conflict that America had lost, Vietnam reversed the usual pattern of presidential history. Rather than augmenting presidential power, as other wars had done, Vietnam resulted in new limits on the White House. As the war ground on to its dismal conclusion, Congress passed the War Powers Resolution in 1973, insisting that it is "the intent of the framers of the Constitution of the United States to insure that the collective judgment of both the Congress and the President will apply to the introduction of United States Armed forces into hostilities." As a "resolution," the measure did not require a presidential signature, which was the point. President Richard Nixon would not have been willing to sign it. No president since has even hinted at a willingness to let the resolution govern his actions as commander in chief in any way.

Fueled by an unpopular war and Nixon's remorseless approach to politics, the American Argument between Congress and president reached a furious climax in 1974. For the first time in more than a hundred years, a congressional committee voted articles of impeachment; Nixon openly defied federal courts and his own Justice Department, refusing to turn over evidence and raising the specter, in some feverish minds, of a coup. "I expected to hear gunshots in the streets," recalled Representative Jane Harman, a young Hill staffer at the time. In the end, he chose to save himself, and, arguably, the office itself, by agreeing to resign.

Nixon remained unapologetic, however, in his view of the prerogatives of the presidency. Three years after his departure, Nixon was asked by interviewer David Frost whether some of the domestic spying activities he had approved were legal. "Well," Nixon answered, "when the president does it that means it is not illegal." Nixon went on to elaborate, in ways that echo down through the years to today, "If the president, for example, approves something because of the national security, or . . . because of a threat to internal peace and order of significant magnitude, then the president's decision in that instance is one that enables those who carry it out, to carry it out without violating a law." In other words, to paraphrase King Louis XIV: *La loi c'est moi.*

When he published his memoir the following year, Nixon argued that he had been forced by the tumultuous times to be an almost monarchial president, who would do whatever it took—constitutional niceties aside—to keep the country from sliding into chaos. "My reading of history," he wrote, "taught me that when all the leadership institutions of a nation become paralyzed by self-doubt and second thoughts, that nation cannot long survive unless those institutions are reformed, replaced or circumvented. In my second term I was prepared to adopt whichever of these methods—or whichever combination of them—was necessary."

It was a low point in the presidency, but also, paradoxically, a high point. Nixon, operating at the height of the broadcast television age, dramatized the presidency as a national obsession. We distrust leaders, and he gave us ample reason to do so. We also love riveting stories, and he gave us those, too. We are drawn to narratives about heroes, but also about heroes who fall from grace and land with a thud back on Earth. No one is above us. We raise people up, and tear them down—for we believe in equality in both the noble and the cynical sense.

The presidency, in fact, is the ideal theater for this never-ending cycle of glory and shame, hagiography and soap opera. Here is another reason why the office has come to dominate our political culture. In a nation of individuals, if not individualists, the Oval Office is made for narratives, and our historians and popular writers have obliged from the start. Parson Weems constructed the mythology about George Washington that endures to this day; more books have been published in America about Abraham Lincoln than any other historical figure besides Jesus. Bill and Hillary Clinton had been out of office for only five years when the two-hundredth book was published that focused on either one or both of them.

The presidency is a laboratory for state-of-the-art communications, its prominence the accumulated work of its most media-savvy occupants. George Washington carefully fashioned himself into a parade-ground and drawing-room icon as a superb equestrian, a fastidiously attired figure, and an ardent letter writer. His image was made for the medium of public display and the word of mouth that stemmed from it. His life was a Federalist's royal progress. Jefferson was the premier pamphleteer at a time when that printed medium was the opinion-shaping Internet coffeehouse of its day. Lincoln was steeped in the biblical cadences of speechmaking, and in the wry, sharp techniques of courthouse debate. The "copy" he produced kept the telegraphers busy, and the country's newspaper pages full. Teddy Roosevelt's exploits were camera-ready for the new mass-produced big-city tabloids (web presses were the cutting-edge media technology); later, the soothing and optimistic timbre of his cousin's voice was made for the medium of radio, which came into its own in FDR's day. Kennedy commanded the then-new medium of live television; Reagan the set-piece Technicolor theatrics of the made-for-TV movie; Clinton the fast-paced "war room" call-and-response of confessional cable television. In 2008, Senator Barack Obama made his bid to dominate the *YouTube* era with Web-based fund-raising prowess and vivid, easily sound-bite-able speeches.

Congress cannot often compete in the arena of political theatrics, except as a backdrop for the manufacture of scandal scripts for committee hearings. Its comparative obscurity posed a challenge for even its mediasavviest inhabitants. When I first started covering the Hill in the early 1980s, the best of them was Chris Matthews—yes, *that* Chris Matthews. He was one of the top aides to Rep. Thomas P. "Tip" O'Neill, the Democratic Speaker of the House. Matthews was steeped in the ways of the Congress—he had begun his career as a Capitol police officer—and he also had been a speechwriter for President Jimmy Carter. He knew both ends of Pennsylvania Avenue.

O'Neill was competing for attention with fellow Irishman Ronald Reagan, who not only had a gift for the blarney but also had been a movie actor and TV-show host. O'Neill could be warm and jovial behind closed doors. He was charming in public in a gruff sort of way. A product of clubhouse Boston politics, he did not see wooing the national media as part of his job. O'Neill thought his main goal in talking to reporters was to tell them what would be happening legislatively on the floor. "Tip's idea of a press conference was to give them a rundown of the schedule and that was it," Matthews says. "We had to change that."

Matthews understood the quickening pace of the news cycle and the shorter attention spans of readers, viewers, and editors. The term "sound bite" was coming into vogue to describe the new up-tempo cadence in political speech. He studied the feeding habits of TV and print reporters, and made sure they had a fresh quote from Tip that would fit into their filing schedules. More important, he soon realized that the only way Tip could work his way into a story was to take on the president. "Reagan was always the story," Matthews says. As Matthews pointed out, Congress was designed to be the "first branch," its powers denominated in Article I of the Constitution—the center of gravity of government. "It's supposed to be the starting place and the center, but the president dominates the media, which means that he dominates the whole process. The presidency is so powerful, so central to the media narrative of everything, that the only way your guy can get any ink is in *relation to* the president. That's how I operated."

Matthews picked his spots. Quick with a tart remark, he mimicked the Boston Irish humor of his beloved boss. One day the White House spokesperson accused the Democrats of attacking too harshly. "It's McCarthyism," declared Larry Speakes. Matthews was ready with an instantly manufactured reply from Tip. Speakes, "said" Tip, was just parroting whatever he was told to say by Republican strategists, in the manner of a famous ventriloquist's equally famous dummy. "That's McCarthyism, all right," O'Neill was claimed to have said. "*Charlie* McCarthyism."

Congress itself is at fault, too. It has become the "broken branch," in the words of political scientists Thomas E. Mann and Norman J. Ornstein. The committee system—which Woodrow Wilson (a political scientist) saw as the indispensable engine that made the institution work—has been destroyed by iron-fisted party rule, Mann and Ornstein write in their book *The Broken Branch*.

Rather than looking inward to the institution and its duties, working out deals with each other, members of Congress look outward, toward the White House, the party machinery, and its donors. The result, say Mann and Ornstein, is "arrogance, greed, venality, condescension toward the minority," and a Congress able to do only one of two things: rubber-stamp a president's program, or block one. Congress has the form of a parliament now, but without any of the powers parliaments possess. Tellingly, the use of impeachment as a normal tool of business is growing—a trend that in itself stresses the relative dominance of the presidency.

First the Democrats, then the Republicans, gave away power that was not theirs to give, especially after the GOP won control of the White House and both chambers of Congress in 2000. At that point, say Mann and Ornstein, the "majority abandoned their institutional identity and independence with barely a second's thought." Congress essentially rubber-stamped George W. Bush's decisions as commander of the war on terror, and much else. American government, they write, "works best when both executive and legislative branches are strong and protective of their institutional prerogatives and comparative advantages. But Congress has largely abdicated that responsibility as party and ideology trumped institution."

Bush fostered that abdication by ignoring the Democratic minority altogether and by strong-arming the Republican leaders on the Hill. They became at best mere appendages to White House policy. The president himself, used to dealing through intermediaries with the Texas legislature, never developed a close relationship with members of Congress—and never thought it was important to do so. "There might have been more debate among Republicans over, say, the war in Iraq, had the White House not intimidated everybody into silence," said Republican conservative Craig Shirley. "Members were afraid to ask questions."

It was the Thanksgiving after 9/11 and the country was at war. Not at war as we once thought of it, but certainly no longer what we used to think of as peace. A mysterious new enemy or enemies had arisen in the world. An anxious era had begun, leading us we knew not where. Still, there was comfort in ritual. So on the day before the holiday, George W. Bush would fly to Fort Campbell, a sprawling army post along the Kentucky–Tennessee border, to share a turkey-and-trimmings dinner with the 101st Airborne, which was deploying to the war in Afghanistan.

The pageant at the post had been carefully choreographed for two presidential money shots: one of Bush speaking to the troops, the other of him serving the turkey. A vast open field had been cleared so that thousands of soldiers could gather in front of a stage to greet him on the bright, clear afternoon. The only other people who were to be on the stage with the president were the post commander and leaders of the 101st Airborne.

The Republican members of Congress—even such dignified figures as Senators Fred Thompson and Bill Frist (nominally two of Bush's closest allies)—were relegated to a rickety wooden viewing stand to the rear of the crowd. (Bush had never bothered to consult senators of either party about foreign policy. Just after his inauguration, he invited Senator Joseph Biden—the Democrats' senior man on the topic—to the Oval Office for a chat. But all the new president wanted to talk about was raw politics. "What do I need to do to keep your guys quiet on the foreign relations committee?" he asked a stunned Biden.)

On cue, to shouts of *"hoo-ah,"* Bush strode onto the stage. He was wearing an open-necked shirt and a brown leather bomber jacket of the 101st. The young GIs crowded into the field smiled and pumped their fists. The soldiers—men and women—seemed to be genuinely inspired, not just by the goal but also by Bush's presence at their home base. Their upturned faces were innocent, unblemished: a harvest of youth filling a former farm field.

As for the president, he was in his role and in his element, and seemed to draw strength from both. The role was the one fate had handed him, that had given his presidency a sense of urgent purpose, and that he was determined to make the most of: president as commander in chief. Bush loved the "hoo-ah" part, and the soldiers loved that he loved it.

Bush's speech was one of the most remarkable of his presidency: equal parts war cry, pep rally, and bellicose foreign-policy directive—Prince Harry at Agincourt, reading a text provided by the most neo of the new American neocons. The Taliban was on the run in Afghanistan, he said, but that was just the beginning. "I believe good triumphs over evil," he said, all but shouting. "And I believe in the fearless hearts of the United States military! *[Hoo-ah!]* We will fight terrorists and we will fight all of those who give them aid. America has a message for the nations of the world: If you harbor terrorists, you are terrorists! *[Hoo-ah!].*" To enforce that policy, Bush laid out his new theory of "preemptive" war. "Wars are won by taking the fight to the enemy," he declared. "America is not waiting for terrorists to try to strike us again. Wherever they hide, wherever they plot, we will strike the terrorists!" Warning given, he finished with a paean to the young men and women in front of him. "Every one of you is dedicated to something greater than yourself. You put your country ahead of your comfort. You live by a code and you fight for a cause. And I am honored to be your commander in chief!"

But by the summer of 2007, even some Republicans—and many traditional conservatives—had become concerned about the nature of
the presidency as it had been defined since 9/11 by George Bush. No one
in the inner circle of political, diplomatic, military, or legal advisers acted
as a brake on Bush's (and Dick Cheney's) commander/caudillo instincts.
Citing the exigencies of wartime—and the global, borderless battle
against a strange, new, hard-to-find-and-define terrorist enemy—Bush
and his lawyers attempted to assert presidential power in startling ways
through an expansive reading of both congressional resolutions and the
commander-in-chief powers of the U.S. Constitution.

The president, they said (harking back to Lincoln), had the power
under the Constitution to imprison without charges American citizens
captured taking part in terrorist actions on foreign soil. The Supreme
Court said no, with the most vehement no coming—lo and behold—
from the staunchest and generally most pro-administration conservative
on the Court, Justice Antonin Scalia. Bush claimed the right to secretly
wiretap and monitor overseas calls, even though Congress had passed a
law in 1978 specifically barring the practice. Once again, the Supreme
Court said no. The president claimed the authority, delegated by him to
the armed forces, to put "enemy combatants" on trial in secret proceedings that would have very few, if any, procedural protections called for by
the Geneva convention. Again the high court said no.

Bush's aggressive attempts to expand presidential power drew sharp
criticism from Democrats on the Hill, and from editorial writers around
the country. Some likely Democratic presidential contenders in the early
states of the 2008 race complained about Bush's aggrandizements, but not
too loudly. They vowed to have a different attitude about habeas corpus,
but were otherwise silent. After all, there was a chance that one of them
would wind up as commander in chief.

None of which slowed Bush down. His administration continued to
push the conceptual limits of presidential power. His lawyers came
up with a novel constitutional theory. They called it the "unitary executive." As they explained it, mostly through the compliant vision of a law
professor (and onetime administration lawyer) named John Yoo, the president had total control of the administrative functions of the government
created by Congress. Once Congress created a department—say, the De-

fense Department—Congress had very little say over how it was being run, except that they could cut off funds for it altogether if they dared. If accepted (and it was not), the theory would reduce the Congress to afterthought status.

His oath of office was to "faithfully execute the office of President of the United States, and . . . to the best of (his) ability, preserve, protect and defend the Constitution of the United States"—not the homeland per se, but the Constitution. In the view of Bush's critics, Bush had forgotten about the latter in the name of defending the former. If a commander-in-chief president was presiding over a "unitary executive" government in the middle of an unending "long war," what were the limits, if any, of the power of the presidency in the twenty-first century? We had come a long way from Jimmy Carter—so far we could hardly see him anymore.

Ten

THE TERMS OF TRADE

Smiling hostesses in long skirts swept into the Great Hall of the People in Beijing carrying trays of champagne flutes. They were celebrating two U.S.-China trade deals, but Al Gore, caught by surprise, looked more than vaguely ill.

He had reason to be. This was in the spring of 1997, and he was launching a long march from the vice presidency to the Democratic presidential nomination. I was one of a handful of reporters who followed him and Tipper on a state visit to China. He had to be careful about the political semiotics of his dealings there. His visit was sensitive in diplomatic terms: He was the first top-ranking U.S. official to visit the People's Republic since the infamous and brutal events at Tiananmen Square, eight years earlier. The tanks had rolled on the vast plaza just beyond the walls of the Great Hall in which we stood. The U.S. government, like most others, had denounced the action but had done little in the meantime to change the Chinese.

For Gore, the visit also was sensitive politically, but for a different reason. As a Democratic candidate-in-waiting, he had to be careful about seeming to be too chummy with the Chinese—not because of their human-rights record, which was awful, but because of what his cold-smiling hosts meant to American industrial workers, most of whom were Democrats. For those workers, there was some good news in the proceedings in the Great Hall: the announcement of new deals with Boeing (to purchase planes made in the United States) and General Motors (to build new auto manufacturing facilities in China). But the machinists and auto workers unions back home in America knew the deeper, more profound story: that the PRC was an industrial power on a rocketlike trajectory. Sooner or later, lower-wage workers in China, following in the footsteps of the Japanese and South Koreans, would drain away most of the high-wage manufacturing jobs in the American industrial heartland.

Gore had long since committed himself to a position that was at odds with the industrial unions of the Midwest. At Harvard, Jack Kennedy was his hero, and Kennedy had been a free-trader at heart. As a young House member and senator from the right-to-work state of Tennessee— and as a self-described post–New Deal Democrat—Gore was skeptical of most protectionist deals, and voted accordingly. He was a founder of the Democratic Leadership Council, a "centrist" group designed and financed by Wall Street Democrats with two aims in mind: to diminish the clout of the party's antiwar crowd, and to wrest control from the old-line industrial unions. In his first presidential campaign, in 1988, Gore left the serious courtship of labor unions to other candidates, whom he regarded as prisoners of 1930s-era Old Think. They rewarded him accordingly: He was out of the race, fast.

As Bill Clinton's vice president, Gore had led the charge to expand trade (what the Street wanted and what most sensible corporate CEOs wanted) with new low-tariff deals: the North American Free Trade Agreement with Mexico and Canada in 1993; two years later, the entrance of the United States into a new global alliance, the Brussels-based World Trade Organization. In both cases, Gore had been forced to square off against the industrial unions (not to mention Ross Perot). Now he needed their support, or at least their neutrality, if he wanted to be president.

The last thing he wanted was a wire photo of himself clinking glasses with the Chinese. But that is what, to his chagrin, he got. For reporters it was a chance to view an all-too-rare unscripted moment. We watched it unfold from the back of the Great Hall, a cavernous building with a central ballroom large enough for military maneuvers. Fifty-foot-high maroon velvet drapes framed the doorways; the chandeliers illuminated a central area where Gore stood with the leaders of the Communist Party of the PRC.

Gore had no idea what was coming. It was morning in Beijing—about 11 a.m. The last thing that he or his entourage expected was a champagne ceremony. The speeches were about to begin when the hostesses arrived, carrying their silver trays. Gore had no choice but to raise his glass. The cameras flashed.

The picture made the wires.

The image was not forgotten. Nor were Gore's other actions as an administration team player. In 1999, he led the push to permanently "normalize" trade relations with China. The ancient technical term for what Gore was proposing was "most favored nation" status, but no matter how bland the bureaucrats tried to make it sound, the idea was an incendiary one to the industrial unions. That was especially true of the United Auto Workers. The UAW's rolls were shrinking fast, but in 2000 they still had 1.5 million active and retired members, most in key Midwest states.

The UAW was in no hurry to endorse Gore. They considered supporting his main rival, former senator Bill Bradley, and wound up refusing to go along with the rest of Labor in endorsing Gore after he wrapped up the Democratic nomination in May 2000. The reason, UAW president Steve Yokich told anyone who would listen, was that Gore was supporting China "normalization." "How are we supposed to believe that Gore really cares?" he said that spring. "Why do him any favors?" Publicly, Yokich was even harsher. "Vice President Gore," he said, "is holding hands with the profiteers of the world."

Next: the equivalent of a punch in the nose. To underscore their dissatisfaction, Yokich and the UAW suggested that the UAW might endorse a third-party candidate, specifically, Ralph Nader. (To anyone with a knowledge of industrial history, this was an ironic turn of events, to say the least, since Nader began his career by attacking General Motors.) For several months, the UAW remained aloof from Gore. After much cajoling from other union leaders and Democratic strategists, the UAW board, in August of 2000, endorsed the vice president.

The presidential election that November was so infamously close that any one of a hundred factors could have cost Gore the victory over Governor George W. Bush. Many observers, however, focus on one key reason in several industrial states: the 2.6 million votes won, nationwide, by the Green Party candidate, Ralph Nader.

Champagne, anyone?

W e were born in trade and born to trade, built from the fertile ground up for global commerce—which explains why we argue about it so much. We started as seventeenth-century heirs to a statist, zero-sum theory. Our role was to grow and harvest, not invest and manufacture. Value would be added, and profits retained, in the "mother" country. We chafed at this mercantilism, trading with Native Americans and colonial freelancers on our western flank. Then Adam Smith proposed a new paradigm: Let every nation be scot-free to import and export as it wished and all that it wished; rid the world of medieval barriers—tariffs, duties, quotas, subsidies, exclusive shipping, and port rules—and world trade would grow exponentially as each country maximized its "comparative advantage." *The Wealth of Nations* was published on March 9, 1776; not coincidentally, we declared our (economic) independence four months later. The Founders believed that free trade would lead not only to profits, but to peace.

There was a hole in Smith's theory, however, as the Founders knew. Trade was good for nations, but its benefits were not distributed equally *within* nations—especially one as large, diverse, and raw as ours. The resulting American Argument has raged ever since, between "free trade" and "protection." In truth, we've never come close to Smith's ideal, and we only formally (and theoretically) accepted his teachings in 1934 in the Reciprocal Tariff Act. The conflicts are deep—between North and South before the Civil War; between the Coasts and the Rust Belt a century later. The issue now is China, the largest mercantile power ever. Wal-Mart shoppers are entitled to buy Asia's cheap products—but at what social cost? The Argument, as always, is about: What's in it for us?

The Founding Fathers thought we were lucky to have settled in a place that lacked gold (or so they thought). As a result, they wrote in the eighteenth century, we were peopled not by conquistadores ravenous for quick profits in precious metals, but by patient, peaceable men who wanted to establish steady trade. "Our plan is commerce," wrote Tom Paine in *Common Sense,* "and that, well attended to, will secure us the peace and friendship of all of Europe." American free trade, he said, "will always be her protection, her barrenness of gold and silver secure her from invaders."

It was a comforting thought. Yet for whatever calm trade might produce in the world, it can produce an equal measure of conflict at home. The reason is that trade alone cannot satisfy every social need. No nation on the planet is as buffeted by capital flows as we are; yet none expects more social stability in the economy—a stability that trade forever undermines by its very nature. We expect jobs, Social Security, and a sense that we are being treated fairly, but when a tractor factory closes in a mill town in the Midwest (or anywhere), it is not just the jobs that are lost. "A closure like that takes a blowtorch to the spider web of social relations in the community," says Rick Sloan, the communications director for the International Association of Machinists. "There's nothing left."

By 2007, that "blowtorch" had destroyed half of the country's industrial base—a base that had been nurtured from the late eighteenth century onward not by "free trade" but by a firm wall of barriers to imports. Those barriers were slowly but steadily dismantled after World War II, and are now at their lowest level in history. As a result, we are enjoying (and being overrun by) a flood of cheap imports from nations—especially China—that have advanced as global traders by pursuing the same protectionist policies we alternately deplored and deployed for centuries.

The result: Wal-Marts bulging with bargains; a withering away of high-paying, stable, middle-class jobs; a world awash in the dollars pumped into the global trading system on the strength of loans largely from the same foreign countries (China and Japan) that are selling goods to us in the first place. To keep their own costs down, the Chinese have developed a brutal auction system for their domestic suppliers, forcing them to bid against each other ferociously. Given their growing clout, there is no reason to think that the Chinese will not extend the practice to the world at large—and drive down wages further.

In the early seventeenth century, most people in most places on the planet rarely looked beyond their hedgerow, river bottom, or High Street. America was born with the world in view. Our trade was "global" before it was "local." Founded after the Age of Discovery had mapped the seas, we rose in an age of unsurpassed seamanship as a colony whose main purpose was to take part in global commerce. Our founding American minds may have looked like rustics, but they were cosmopolitans of capital, business, and labor.

We were, essentially, a commercial trading enterprise from the start, administered not so much by government directly, but by men of enterprise and profit with franchises. In royal palaces and parliaments sovereign governments carved out territory for exploitation and development; they took the monopolistic profits. The governments were operating, however, in an era when new theories of capital and commerce were undermining the old, the static, and the monarchial. Even though chartered by royal authority, a private stock company was a new, independent creation: a force of its own, with more loyalty to its shareholders than to the crown and court. The place where they were investing—North America—also threatened the old-think of king and corporation. How could they impose a straitjacket—mercantilism—on a continent so large, so various, so easily entered by land or sea?

The Europeans tried; the lure of profits was too great not to, and, with that desire, the first acts of nation building began. It is inspiring to think that we were set in motion entirely by a more noble purpose: the search for religious freedom or the empire of God. But in 1609, when Henry Hudson sailed the *Half Moon* up the broad river that would later bear his name, he had a less lofty goal in mind: doing some business. Surveying the dreamlike vistas of natural plenty—the cathedral-like forests, the striped bass leaping unbidden onto the deck, the teeming animal life—the sharp-eyed Dutch captain was eager to find in the unimagined splendor a bottom-line commerce to cheer his corporate sponsors back in Amsterdam. These men, puffing on their pipes in the coffeehouses of the Prinzengracht, were traders on a global scale, and Hudson understood that they wanted him to find the seventeenth-century version of the New New Thing.

He did so in the form of . . . beaver. Clad in dense fur coats, beavers lived comfortably in water; not so human beings. A few decades earlier, hatters in Europe had begun using beaver pelts, mostly from Russia and Scandinavia, to make state-of-the-art waterproof headgear. In the rain and gloom of a European storm, the well-to-do wanted a hat fashioned of beaver pelts that could be beaten into a felt more impervious than wool. In the rushing rivers and streams of the New World were beavers enough to keep the whole Old World dry.

The result was a new international commerce—and conflict. The Dutch famously "bought" Manhattan from the Native American locals, who soon felt cheated of their grounds. The British muscled in, pushing the Dutch aside by treaty and by sheer bullying presence. The chief New World prize then, and for a century thereafter, was the trade in beaver pelts—those the Native Americans wore (the better, more useful kind for the hatters) and those the trappers harvested from rivers and lakes. The trade was the cause of war upon war, between Indians and British, French and British, British and American, backwoodsmen and federals.

From the seventeenth century onward, America's role in the world of commerce was defined by the tug-of-war between restrictive rules and raucous freedom—the former more the result of political than profit-making calculations. The dependence on global trade made its restriction—by taxes or outright barriers—a powerful tool, one that officials were all too often tempted to use.

The British came to understand its explosive power. After fighting the French in the 1760s, they faced mounting government debt, and wanted to extract more revenue from their expensive-to-run colonies in America. Lord Grenville, the First Lord of the Treasury and Chancellor of the Exchequer, came up with a plan: Collect more tax revenue on the cheap molasses that the colonists were importing from French plantations in the Caribbean.

It took only another dozen years, and several more import duties and taxes, for the Revolution to begin. After it, we bought even more molasses from the French. At the same time, however, the Continental Congress began imposing duties on imports—from Britain. Our national government has seesawed between "free" trade and "protection" ever since.

As in much else, Alexander Hamilton and Thomas Jefferson squared off on the details. In his *Report in Manufacturers* of 1791, Treasury Secretary Hamilton suggested that high tariffs on manufactured imports would spur the growth of industry here. The Jeffersonians, farmers who liked the idea of more than one source for the manufactured goods they needed, vehemently opposed the idea. Hamilton's full tariff scheme did not pass, but some specific quotas did—and much of Congress's work ever since has involved fiddling with limits on everything from fabric to steel to motherboards.

Congress was a trading floor from the outset. One of the first acts of the new Continental Congress after the Declaration of Independence was a treaty extending "most favored nation" status to our new best friends at the time, the French. And the first substantive—as opposed to administrative—law ever enacted by the U.S. government was Hamilton's tariff bill. His dual aim was, as the legislative language said, "the discharge of the debt of the United States, and the encouragement and protection of its manufactures."

The resulting schedule of duties is the simple, two-page ancestor of the telephone-book-size list that any trader can find on the government's website today. One of the heaviest duties—fifty cents per pair—was on imported shoes. The tanners and shoemakers of New England, some of which still exist, needed help. Then, as in our day, nothing was more important in America than transportation.

As always in American Arguments, party labels over the centuries are not consistent, or reliable, guides to who believed (or claimed to believe) what on a certain topic. The Republican Party from Lincoln through McKinley was the champion of protection—all the better to secure the strength and markets of Union industry. The Democrats in the South, as heirs to the Jeffersonian view, were the free traders. The parties had entirely switched places by the time Ronald Reagan was president.

Ottumwa, Iowa, in the dead of winter was not a pleasant place. In January of 1988, the temperature was 0 degrees and felt colder. The town's streets and sidewalks seemed frozen. The stiff wind penetrated anything with ease, including the train shed in which Dick Gephardt, who was running for president, stood with a group of labor-union friends.

Gephardt knew the weather. He was from Missouri, and he had been campaigning in Iowa for years. He came prepared, clad in a parka and work boots. He not only knew the territory and the temperature, he knew what he wanted to say, which was that the American worker was losing his place in the world and the marketplace, drowning in a sea of imports from Asia. He was for "fair trade."

"Trade" was one of those campaign-trail topics that made reporters' eyes glaze over. It evoked an image of bureaucrats in Brussels haggling over the impenetrable fine print of tariff agreements with unpronounceable acronyms. It seemed to be merely about things—sales figures, "balance of trade," whatever *that* was—and not about the lives or real people in real places such as Iowa.

In Ottumwa, Gephardt was determined to show that "trade" was about real life and real jobs. He aimed to convince voters of the urgency of the threat, and, most important, he wanted to show the union rank-and-file—whose get-out-the-vote muscle he was counting on—that he was One of Them.

At first glance, Gephardt seemed rather miscast as Tribune of the Working Man. He had been reared in a St. Louis neighborhood of severe German orderliness and respectability. He graduated from Northwestern and the University of Michigan Law School. In the House of Representatives, where he had served for twelve years, he wore his blond hair short and his button-down dress shirts blindingly white.

Nevertheless, St. Louis was an industrial town, and Gephardt was a Democrat. He was comfortable with the union guys—especially the shop-floor types—and they liked his determination and unassuming style. They had gone primarily for Ted Kennedy in 1980 and Walter Mondale in 1984, and now they were with him.

To make his point, Gephardt and his staff had to come up with a way to make the loss of industrial jobs seem not only vivid, but also outrageously unfair and obviously the result of un-American forces. A little xenophobia never hurt. Gephardt's brain trust had come up with the slogan for the campaign: IT'S YOUR FIGHT TOO! The idea was that not just union jobs were at stake—so was America's standard of living. How could he show that in a TV ad? One of his handlers came across a newspaper article about South Korea's trade policies. The Koreans, the article said, imposed such massive duties on imported American cars that a $10,000 Chrysler cost the equivalent of $48,000 in Seoul. Of course, there was not much demand for Chryslers in South Korea, and an independent estimate put the correct figure at $30,000, but that was not the point. Here was an example of what America was up against in the world of brutal trade.

The ad hit the airwaves with a couple of weeks left until the caucuses. It said that Gephardt was "tired of hearing American workers blamed" for U.S. export woes and concluded that if the Koreans refused to drop their trade barriers, he would retaliate in kind. "They'll know that we'll still honor our treaties and defend them," Gephardt said, "because that's the kind of people we are. But they'll also be left asking themselves: How many Americans are going to pay $48,000 for one of their Hyundais?" The ad generated tremendous coverage, and controversy, which is precisely what its sponsors had wanted.

Gephardt's strategic problem in Iowa was that it was really two states: an industrial one and an agricultural one. The industrial one was heir to all the invasive forces about which he was warning. There were auto-parts plants, washing machine and refrigerator plants, farm-machinery plants, and so on. But Iowa was also an "ag" state, and farm exports were a healthy and growing part of its economic life. Iowa exported vast quantities of corn and soybeans, among other products. And Iowa was also rapidly becoming an insurance state—there would soon be almost as many insurance companies in Des Moines as in Hartford—and the white-collar workers there tended to like free trade in the abstract and in the reality of, say, a Japanese car.

Meanwhile, a surprising competitor was emerging to challenge Gephardt: Governor Michael Dukakis of Massachusetts. A lifelong government technocrat, Dukakis was running on the wave of the so-called Massachusetts Miracle. Spurred by computer and software design and by medical technology, business activity and employment were booming in Boston and its suburbs. Dukakis had positioned himself as the avatar of this "new economy" and was trying to advertise his gift for out-of-the-box thinking to Iowans. Farmers were among his targets, on the reasonable theory that they were the real innovators despite the seemingly conservative nature of their business.

At one campaign stop, Dukakis suggested that Iowa farmers should make a cash crop of Belgian endive. The comment elicited gales of derision from the press corps, local and national. Dukakis nevertheless had a point, even if he did not know how to make it in Iowa. It was, simply, that the future was the future. (And, by 2008, many Iowa farmers had become devotees of organic techniques and some were growing boutique crops— including endive.)

By the time I caught up with Gephardt in Iowa, he was talking like a member of the Industrial Workers of the World, the old IWW "Wobblies" of the early twentieth century. His advance men had scouted the state for camera-ready industrial locations. They found one in south central Iowa in the Ottumwa train shed. With a huge American flag in the background, Gephardt stood with a row of labor leaders in front of a colossal locomotive engine. He ticked off a list of Iowa factories in which workers had lost jobs: the Farm-All tractor plant, the J. I. Case plant, and the Caterpillar machinery plant. The fight to save these jobs, he shouted, did not belong just to the workers themselves, but to all of America.

"IT'S YOUR FIGHT TOO!" he declared.

Gephardt won the caucuses, barely, but Dukakis finished a surprisingly strong third—and went on to win the nomination. I always wondered about the wisdom of Gephardt using that railroad-repair shed as a backdrop for his message. It won him Iowa, to be sure, but wasn't a locomotive a symbol of the economy of the past? Wasn't it true that voters liked to think about the future? The answers, I realized later, were no and yes. Trains were as important as ever—to get Iowa's farm products to market, and import the cheap goods that most Iowans were very happy to buy.

It would be left to Bill Clinton to sell a new future of free trade as a Democrat in the White House.

For a political person, Frank Greer was a modest-seeming sort, with sandy blond hair and the forgettable regular features of the insurance agent down the street. His looks were deceiving. He was a steely customer. The son of schoolteachers, he had been reared in Tuscaloosa, Alabama, a Kennedy Democrat in a sea of segregationists. The sight of George Wallace blocking the doors of the University of Alabama in 1963 turned the sixteen-year-old into a political crusader. He came to Washington in 1977 to be communications director in Jimmy Carter's Department of Labor.

Greer took what he learned about labor and made it a calling card of his new business, political consulting for Southern Democratic candidates running for governor and U.S. Senate. In those days, that meant teaching them how to swim upstream in the tide of Reaganism.

Among the candidates Greer tutored in political survivalism was a man born to become, in the end, the Master Survivor of them all, Bill Clinton. A thoughtful tactician with national media contacts and a good feel for how to structure a speech or cut a TV spot, Greer was the kind of guy that Clinton needed as he prepared to make the long jump from "boy governor" of Arkansas to presidential candidate. In the late eighties, Greer and pollster Stanley Greenberg carefully studied the polls and Reagan's appeal. They concluded that they could forge a candidacy—a Clinton candidacy—on a new appeal to the "forgotten middle class." As Clinton would later put it, these were people who "worked hard and played by the rules." The sales pitch would ditch the shopworn us-versus-them frame that Democratic strategic thinking had comprised since the days of FDR. Clinton really was not a traditional liberal in any case. He would prove it on cultural matters by supporting the death penalty and the idea that able-bodied people needed to work to get welfare (an idea that had been considered, but rejected, during Roosevelt's New Deal).

In the fall of 1991, what would Clinton say about economics that was smart, innovative—and Un-Liberal?

He would talk about trade. He would run for the Democratic nomination as a "free-trade" foe of high tariffs on imports, including imports that came from low-wage countries such as Mexico. This idea was, in essence, a Republican one. President George H. W. Bush had broached it, asking Congress for new authority to negotiate a barrier-free trade zone that would encompass all of North America. The goal was nothing less than a grand new vision of global commerce.

As a concept, "free trade" appealed to Clinton. It was internationalist in tone, and he thought of himself as an internationalist, in the mold of one of his Arkansas idols, the late senator William Fulbright. Clinton was a Rhodes Scholar, in itself a bridge to global perspective. As an Oxford student, he had traveled in Europe. He would dispel Big Labor's grim gloom. We would trade ourselves to a new prosperity. In saying so—even at the risk of losing labor-union votes—he would demonstrate how bravely Un-Liberal he was.

As Bill Clinton's union-savvy political handler, Greer knew just the place and time for his Arkansas Daniel to enter the labor lion's den: Detroit, November 12, 1991, at the convention of the 13-million-member American Federation of Labor-Congress of Industrial Organizations. The AFL-CIO had been a pillar of the party since the FDR days, even if, in recent years, it had acquired a reputation for backing losers and failing to deliver the labor vote. But the federation still mattered, and it was sponsoring a debate in front of its own top-ranked members among the six candidates for the 1992 Democratic nomination. The audience would cheer for their favorites, Greer knew, men such as Senator Tom Harkin of Iowa. But Clinton wouldn't really be speaking to the crowd; he would be using it as a prop to define himself to the country.

Before the debate in the pressroom that day, Greer worked the rows of reporters like a sheepdog herding a flock. "Watch what Clinton is going to do here," he told me, leaning over my shoulder in conspiratorial fashion. "He's not going to say what they want to hear." That was precisely what happened, although Clinton, typically, chose his words with great finesse. "Whether you like it or not," he told the crowd, many rank-and-file workers were voting Republican because they had decided that Democrats were tied to outdated economic policies. He promised to create "an America that can and will compete again." Precisely how was not clear, but the real message—his willingness to take on a powerful party constituency—was. "You should accept as Democrats the challenge to change," he said, "so that all of us can be part of an economic revival." There was no applause in the convention hall.

On that day in Detroit, most members of the press entourage, including me, were more interested in whether Clinton's "bimbo eruptions" would occur. No one saw it at the time as a turning point in the presidential campaign. Looking back, it was even more important than that. Having committed so publicly and confrontationally to a policy of free trade, he could not turn back—as Greer later suggested he do. By the end of April 1992, Clinton had wrapped up the Democratic nomination. Now he was faced with a crucial decision: whether he should formally support President Bush's call for the North American Free Trade Agreement. Clinton was about to give a speech on economic policy in Washington. Up or down? Clinton and his advisers met in the presidential suite of the Washington Hilton to map out their strategy. "I told him, 'No, you can't be for NAFTA,'" Greer recalled in 2006. "I thought it was too big a risk. I knew how industrial unions would react. My reasoning was: You have wrapped up the nomination, Labor wants to be with you, why give them a reason to go the other way? But Bill Clinton was adamant. He believed in it. There was no telling him otherwise."

The result was a fateful decision of the Clinton years. As soon as he moved into the White House, the new president set about taking over the NAFTA sales job from his Republican predecessor. Greer would not be part of the effort. Out-maneuvered in the late stages of the 1992 campaign by other (more free-trade-oriented) consultants, he was cut loose. Instead, Clinton appointed another Democrat, William Daley of Chicago, to drive the trade deal. The devoted son and brother of mayors of Chicago, Daley—with his balding pate, deep-set blue eyes, and square jaw—was the embodiment of the old-school Democratic Party politico. Yet he preferred business to government, perhaps because he had seen what the latter had done to his dad during the late sixties. It had turned the old man, an FDR Democrat, into a reviled caricature of political reaction.

Clinton teamed Daley with Vice President Al Gore to keep corporate America on board while at the same time selling NAFTA to the skeptical Democrats who ran Congress. It was not an easy job, and there were many who thought that the combination of Big Labor and traditional Democrats would kill the bill. But then the administration got lucky in its enemies. The most visible NAFTA foe turned out to be a bantam-rooster billionaire named H. Ross Perot.

The year before, Perot had run for the presidency as a third-party candidate, tapping into a river of middle-class resentments. To Perot, free-trade deals, especially with Mexico, would destroy the manufacturing underpinnings of the American economy. NAFTA would generate a "giant sucking sound"—the sound of American jobs draining south.

Perot was running neck-and-neck with Clinton and President Bush—leading in some polls in 1992 when it occurred to him that he hated the spotlight into which he had thrust himself and his family. He was a fixture on CNN's *Larry King Live*—at the time, the only cable TV game in town. That was a gig he liked, and could control. He was a big hit on *Saturday Night Live,* too, with Dana Carvey playing him to perfection. Snooping reporters and Republican "oppo" guys—those he could not control. So he turned squirrelly and quit the race in early summer after charging that secret agents were spying on his daughter's wedding.

But no sooner had he left the stage than he missed it. He was more than happy for a return engagement in 1993, this time as the leading critic of the NAFTA plan. And no sooner could you say "giant sucking sound," than Larry King had cleared time for a prime-time debate between Perot and Gore on his cable show. This was perfect, as far as the Clintonites were concerned. They had two goals. One: to tell, in human terms, how the NAFTA deal would help create jobs in America. Two: to make the volatile Perot look like a flake and a hypocrite. "Perot turned out to be just the kind of foil we needed," Gene Sperling, an economics adviser in the Clinton White House, recalled. "You couldn't have invented him."

For the "up" side of their NAFTA argument, Daley and Sperling looked for the sweeping and the personal. Gore would portray NAFTA as a confident bet on a prosperous global future, a big, expansive commitment on the order of the Louisiana Purchase, NATO, and the acquisition of Alaska. Then Gore would cite a stack of academic studies, each concluding that ending trade tariffs with Mexico would produce a net *increase* in industrial jobs in America—at least 400,000. To personalize the numbers, the vice president would explain the detail through the eyes of one Gordon Thompson, a personal friend who worked at a Bridgestone tire factory near Gore's home district in central Tennessee. Abolishing the

Mexican tariffs on American-made tires would secure ole Gordon's job, because "they'll make more tires, sell more tires."

That was the nice stuff. For the nasty stuff, the Daley-Gore-Sperling team loaded up on leftover "oppo" from the 1992 campaign, plus new items that they scoured the landscape to find. They would adopt a classic tactic: Make Perot, not NAFTA, the issue. In high-minded fashion, Gore would demand that Perot disclose the finances of his anti-NAFTA campaign. Gore would accuse him of trafficking in the politics of "negativism and fear." They would accuse Perot and his son of having a personal interest in the defeat of NAFTA, a duty-free airport zone near Dallas that would lose its allure in a free-trade world. As for the theatrics, Gore would choose the seat on *Larry King Live* farther away from the camera so he could play a mocking role while Perot was speaking. Gore would interrupt Perot at will—and often. There would be room for ridicule. When Perot talked about job losses to cheap-wage Mexico, Gore would show the cable audience pictures of two antique, congressional representatives—the Smoot and Hawley of the infamous 1930 tariff bill that helped deepen the Depression. "I framed this so you could put it on your wall," Gore would say.

The debate plan worked to perfection. Gore was droll and dismissive, and sounded like the Future. Perot, jammed uncomfortably downstage, nervously eyeing Gore over his shoulder, sounded like a relic of an earlier age—even though the computer-based business in which he had made billions was as innovative as they come. Perot sputtered as he tried to parry Gore's thrusts on the airport. "Do you guys ever do anything but propaganda?" Perot demanded. "Would you even know the truth if you saw it?" he asked. With Perot backed into a corner, Gore moved in for the kill, demanding to see the books on "the financing of the anti-NAFTA campaign." Perot exploded. "See, again, he throws up propaganda! He throws up guerrilla dust that makes no sense!" Perot yelled. "It has nothing to do with what's going to happen to our country!"

End of debate. Within two weeks, Congress had approved the measure. In both chambers, majorities of Clinton's fellow Democrats voted against it. He had won the day because of overwhelming, though not total, Republican support with just enough Democratic votes to give the deal a veneer of bipartisanship. A number of Frank Greer's clients and friends had voted no, and Greer had deep doubts. "I wasn't sure it was good for the country," he said years later.

H ere is where we were, in sum, in the summer of 2007. Trade with Mexico had more than tripled. In 2004, the year NAFTA became law and tariffs and other trade barriers came down, the United States sold more to Mexico ($50 billion in goods and services) than we imported from it ($49 billion). But after that, the numbers literally went south. In 2006, according to U.S. Census estimates, America was expected to sell $126 billion worth of goods and services to Mexico, while the growing low-wage, low-cost Mexican economy was pumping $180 billion worth of goods and services north. In Tennessee, Gore's friend Gordon Thompson was still working at the Bridgestone tire plant. According to the most reasonable and unbiased studies available, NAFTA spurred enough export business to create at least 1 million new jobs between 1994 and 2006.

But the lure of relocating plants and service jobs in low-wage, low-cost Mexico has sent American investment, and many jobs, south of the border and made the bottom-line numbers more problematic. According to the studies, imports from Mexico "displaced" at least 2 million jobs, about two-thirds of them in manufacturing, and most of those in the industrial heartland. "There has been a hollowing out in the Midwest, no doubt about it," Sperling said in 2006. "It's sad but true." Greer remains ambivalent about the original Clinton decision to tie his candidacy to free trade in general and NAFTA in particular. Greer and his wife had long since settled in Seattle. "I guess I feel more positive about it because Washington State is one of the few that is a net gainer of jobs from NAFTA." Was it because they exported computers? No. "We sell them apples," he said.

Eleven

WAR AND DIPLOMACY

The roots of the war lay in the garden of the Texas governor's mansion in Austin. There was nothing cowboy about the place. It was a stately home of white stucco and tall pillars, more Southern plantation than dude ranch. Nor was it an isolated spot on the prairie. It sat perched on a small hilltop, a few blocks from the state capitol, in the midst of the bustle of a university-and-government town. Buses wheezed along outside the garden walls. The noise and exhaust fumes wafted over the patio on a day in November of 1999 when Governor George W. Bush sat in a metal lawn chair and talked about his view of the world and history.

On foreign policy he was, for the most part, a blank slate. He made no claim to expertise, only to the names of heroes and role models. In recent months, he had been attending tutorials arranged for him by former secretary of state George Shultz, and an academic protégé of his from Stanford named Condoleezza Rice. All of this seemed at the time rather pro forma, almost unnecessary. The Soviet Union was long gone; the American economy was booming; the country's problems seemed primarily domestic, moral, and even spiritual.

Bush did not claim to be an expert, or even to know much about the world as a tourist. He knew that it would have been a waste of time to try to claim otherwise. Over the years he had occasionally mused aloud about his meager world travels. As a teenager he had worked as a farmhand on the estate of a family friend in Scotland. After his years at Harvard Business School, he had hung out with his parents in Beijing, where his father was in charge of the first American mission. As a young sports-equipment sales representative he had made one trip to South America, and one other when he was in the oil business. "Oh, and I've been to Japan," he told me. That, he conceded with a smile, actually was a stopover at an airport in Tokyo.

His reading was not much broader or deeper. The only course at Yale he liked to talk about was the one in political science he had taken from John Morton Blum about "great leaders." At Harvard, his focus was on the teamwork required to handle casebook marketing exercises. If there were theories of history he knew—of diplomacy or of war—he did not mention them. Bush never was a man for theories in any case. He was proud of that.

Baseball and Texas were his windows on the world, or at least the Spanish-speaking part of it. As managing partner of the Texas Rangers, he came to appreciate the Latinization of "America's Pastime," and perfected sound-bite Spanish in his role as goodwill ambassador for the team, kibitzed on roster moves that involved ballplayers from countries such as the Dominican Republic and Venezuela and relished his locker-room relationship with the Latino players, bumping fists and joking in pidgin Spanish with his favorite, slugger Juan Gonzalez of Puerto Rico.

One foreign trip loomed large in Bush's global education. In the summer of 1998 he had traveled to Israel with other American politicians on one of the yearly field trips arranged by the American Israel Public Affairs Committee. A tradition in American politics, the AIPAC trips for decades were a way for up-and-coming candidates to see and hear Israel's side of the Middle East story—and to signal openness, if not friendship, to that country's American supporters.

For Bush, the key moment was a helicopter trip across Israel with Ariel Sharon, the hard-line defense minister in the otherwise dovish administration of Yitzhak Rabin. From the air, Sharon showed him Israel at its narrowest point—a mere nine miles across—and the paths of troop movements in wars from 1948 through 1973 to protect it. Sharon's unspoken but obvious message: This is why we can never rest militarily and never give an inch. At the time, Israel was preparing to do just that, as it was deeply involved in peace negotiations with the Palestinians under the auspices of the Clinton administration. Sharon never questioned those talks as he played tour guide to Bush and the entourage. Sharon dutifully supported the negotiations even as he managed to signal his doubts. This, more than the terrain, is what impressed Bush. "I saw a guy demonstrating loyalty," he told me. "He didn't try to go behind Rabin's back."

Still, Bush admittedly was a neophyte on issues of national security, diplomacy, military affairs—all of the topics that would turn out to be the primary focus of his presidency. After he was reelected as governor in 1998, he knew enough to know that he needed an education—fast. In the Bush family way, that education came through friends, and the friends of friends. The innermost circle (basically, Karl Rove) knew that the choice of tutors was of the utmost importance. The carefully considered choice was George P. Shultz. He had the right blend of pedigrees. He had been Ronald Reagan's secretary of state, but was not thought of as a wild-eyed ideologue. He was quite close to neoconservatives such as Paul Wolfowitz, who wanted to remake the Middle East in the image of America, but Shultz was also close to Bush the Elder, whom the neocons saw as an all-too-sober "realist" too willing to play ball with the sheikhs for the sake of expanding American corporate interests in the Persian Gulf. The governor pointedly avoided contact with his father's closest and most trusted foreign policy adviser, Brent Scowcroft. The former national security adviser was way too much of a "realist" to be trusted in Austin. It was a fateful choice of tutors.

By the time Bush sat down in the garden to talk foreign policy, he had been through the Shultz-Rice tutorials. Even so, he impatiently fidgeted and drummed his fingers on the tabletop like a delayed passenger at a ticket counter. He disliked interviews. Even worse, he had a cold, and nothing mattered more to Bush than a sense of physical well-being. "He's a little off his game," warned his press secretary, Karen Hughes.

Who were his role models in the management and strategy of foreign affairs? He did not hesitate to name two. "Winston Churchill and Harry Truman," he said. "Churchill, because he wasn't afraid to say unpopular things, and he rallied his country," he said. Bush had recently read David McCullough's biography of Truman. "People underestimated him," Bush said, leveling his gaze as if to say *Everyone is doing the same with me.* "He turned out to be one of the most important presidents. He was not afraid to confront the communists, and he set up a framework for world peace and American prosperity that lasted for the next fifty years."

He grew vague when the topic shifted to specific challenges. One was the violent Islamic theocrats in Afghanistan. The Taliban rulers there were generating alarming headlines: smuggled-out news of brutal executions; repressive rules to constrict the rights of women in their society; and threats to destroy two colossal, deeply revered statues of Buddha carved into a rural hillside centuries earlier.

What should the United States do about the Taliban?

Bush looked a bit stunned. He grimaced, folded his hands, and stared at the ground, seemingly lost in somber reflection. Several seconds of silence ensued. Then he shook his head, as if in weary acceptance. "We have to be patient," he said. Applying military muscle was not something he had in mind—or, if he did, he did not say so. We had to "be humble" in foreign policy, he said, and in the projection of American military might. He did not reject President Bill Clinton's decision to send U.S. troops to Bosnia to protect Muslim minorities there, but we had to pick our spots with utmost care, and resist the temptation to "do nation building" and remake the world in our image.

As he rose to walk back to the governor's mansion, one more question remained to be asked. Could he name the foreign-policy experts with whom he was consulting? Bush declined to give a full roster, other than Rice and Richard Armitage (who eventually became Colin Powell's deputy secretary of state). Bush was waving good-bye as he was about to disappear into a doorway when he wheeled and gathered himself for what he evidently deemed to be an important disclosure. "One of the people I talk to," he said, pausing for dramatic effect, "is Paul Wolfowitz." Bush raised his eyebrows, as if to say *This is significant.*

It was. "They never really wanted to listen to what I had to say," Scowcroft later told me, especially about the decision to go to war in Iraq.

A mericans have never really thought that we could live in "isolation" from the world. How could we? We were created by global forces: colonialism, immigration, seaborne trade, and the planet-wide rivalry of seventeenth- and eighteenth-century superpowers. True, we were "guarded" by oceans, but these were routes of connection, not separation. We knew that we needed to understand the world. Farmers watched commodity prices; immigrants tracked politics in the old country; Yankee traders mapped not only the ocean currents but diplomatic ones.

Today, American youths may not know where Germany is, but they possess a planetary consciousness, the legacy of everything from *YouTube* to the Iraq War. The American Argument over foreign policy isn't about *whether* we should engage the world. It is about *why and how* we should use government power (military, diplomatic, informational) to protect our way of life and even our conscience.

The root question: Do we need to change the world to survive in it? The conflicting answers we give stem from the same forces that vie for our allegiance elsewhere in American life. The Market cares only about ready access to materials and customers; justice is beside the point. Faith—secular and religious—urges us to insist on freedom for every soul in the service of democracy and salvation. Tribes—Poles, Germans, Jews, Hispanics, and now Arabs and Muslims, to name a few—long have jockeyed for policy influence. Science tells us that planetary survival depends on new forms of diplomacy. As for the State, its goals are survival and the accumulation of bureaucratic power in the twilight of endless war. The logic of "security," once accepted, knows no limits. Ike warned us: A "military industrial complex" would result. He was right. In 2007, congressional analysts scoured the federal budget (not just the Pentagon's) for everything the government was spending on "defense." The total: 1 *trillion* dollars.

The Argument began in earnest with a speech, one of the most famous in American history. President George Washington was expressing a hope as much as describing a reality in his Farewell Address of 1796. It is remembered for its sobriety, good sense, and optimism, but equally for its suggestion that our newborn nation should be, to use his word, "detached" from the brutal politics of the planet.

The text, truth be told, was not a testament to Washington's Cherry Tree honesty. True, he was recommending policy: studied neutrality in the world, distance from the ancient feuds of Europe. But the speech was also a campaign pitch. Washington warned against the "fury of party spirit" and the "mischief of foreign intrigue," knowing that he was stirring, however subtly, that very "fury" and that the country had been buffeted by "foreign intrigue" ever since the adventurers of the Virginia Company waded ashore at Jamestown in 1607.

It is true that we were the only great nation ever to think it had the option of remaining aloof from the world. We *were* different. Oceans separated us from the war-scarred continents of Europe and Asia. To the north and south were empty quarters, vast, lightly populated territories that posed no strategic threat. The continent itself was largely unexplored and unsettled, an expanse capable of absorbing our energies for generations. Our resources were so plentiful, we could thrive on our own.

Ideas were as crucial as geography. At the end of the eighteenth century we thought of ourselves as having started history anew. The very idea that a country *could* be "new" was itself new. In addition, this new country had been designed to operate differently from all that had gone before: free, based on the will of the people, every action of state subjected to the rule of reason.

Uniquely constructed, blessed with an unfathomable store of resources, isolated from ancient armies and conflicts, we could stand alone—or so Washington said he hoped.

"Our detached and distant situation," he told the Congress, would soon produce an Elysium of independence. "If we remain one people under an efficient government," he said, "the period is not far off when we may choose peace or war, as our interest, guided by justice, shall counsel. Why forgo the advantages of so peculiar a situation?" he asked. "Why quit our own to stand upon foreign ground? Why, by interweaving our destiny with that of any part of Europe, entangle our peace and prosperity in the toils of European ambition, rivalship, interest, humor or caprice? It is our true policy," he declared, "to steer clear of permanent alliances with any portion of the foreign world."

Why would we ever "stand upon foreign ground" or make any irrevocable commitments in "the foreign world"? We are the only global power ever to ask such questions at the time of our founding. That view was summarized in 1821 by the son of Washington's Federalist ally, John Adams. America, said President John Quincy Adams, "goes not abroad in search of monsters to destroy. She is the well-wisher to freedom and independence of all. She is the champion and vindicator only of her own."

That tradition, however, does not mean we have ever really stood aloof from the world. The ironic result of our sense of isolation most often has been just the opposite: to foster headlong plunges onto "foreign ground" or into the kind of entangling alliances Washington claimed to worry about. As for "isolationists," they usually do not oppose involvement in the world per se—but merely favor employing a different theory of involvement from the one their opponents favor. We do not go searching for monsters, but we find them anyway.

That certainly was how Washington's speech was viewed by many of those in Philadelphia and in the country. They did not think he was an "isolationist" of any sort. (Indeed, the word "isolationism" wasn't invented until the Civil War, and wasn't used extensively until the period between the world wars.) Just the opposite was true. They saw him as having taken sides: for the monstrous British.

As the 1796 election loomed, opinion was divided into two camps, each accusing the other of treasonous devotion to a foreign power that was manipulating our government.

The countries were Britain and France, and the political fight was proxy for a conflict that had occupied the New World for centuries, and that even continued down to our time, when French president Charles de Gaulle, in 1967, declared from the steps of the city hall in Montreal: *"Vive le Québec libre!"*

Washington had issued a "declaration of neutrality" in 1793, aimed at keeping the five-year-old Republic out of the latest version of an Anglo-French war. He wanted to "exhort and warn the citizens of the United States carefully to avoid all acts and proceedings whatsoever, which may in any manner tend to contravene" the message of detachment. The president knew precisely whom he was warning the country about: Thomas Jefferson and his fellow admirers of France and its new Revolution. Inspired by that event, Secretary of State Jefferson had opposed the neutrality declaration. How could he not? The French, he said, were embarked upon "the most sacred cause that ever man was engaged in," and America had a duty to support it. (There was also the possibility, perhaps, of better cuttings from the vineyards of Bordeaux.)

The political conflict turned nasty in 1795 after the Washington administration negotiated, and the Senate ratified, a treaty with its former enemy. The Jay Treaty compensated American ship owners for war losses in exchange for reimbursing Loyalists for property seized during the American Revolution and giving Britain navigation rights on the Mississippi River. To the practical Washington, this was nothing more or less than good business; to the Jeffersonians, it was a sellout. It was an "infamous act," declared Jefferson, "which is really nothing more than a treaty of alliance between England and the Anglomen of this country against the legislature and people of the United States."

Despite the furious opposition of the pro-French Jeffersonians, another "Angloman"—Vice President John Adams—won the 1796 presidential election. It was the first, but certainly not the last, American election to be dominated by foreign policy. "For Jefferson, as for subsequent American statesmen, the desire to change the world was at war with the desire not to be corrupted by the world," commented historian Robert W. Tucker. Jefferson had chosen change.

The American Argument in foreign policy always has been about, and often between, reasons, rationales—and excuses. As with other ongoing disputes, we generally are fortunate when justifications and motives vie with each other, and no single one predominates. When they join forces in lockstep to propel us toward "foreign ground," the result is war: "good" ones, such as World War II, and questionable ones, such as the American-led invasion and occupation of Iraq.

For historians of foreign policy, the challenge (and sometimes the obsession) has been to name and explain "the roots of involvement." Two of the more influential analysts at the turn of the twenty-first century were Walter McDougall and Walter Russell Mead. In *Promised Land, Crusader State,* McDougall divides the history of our relationship to the world into two biblical eras, "Old Testament and New Testament." In the first, which lasted until late in the nineteenth century, our aim was primarily defensive, to protect the liberty and prosperity—and example—of our own "promised land." In the twentieth century, and now in the twenty-first, we have moved out to the world on crusading missions, to change it or manage it—or inspire it with missionary zeal.

Mead, in his book *Special Providence,* divides America's foreign policy traditions into four categories. Wilsonians (our role is to make the world safe for liberty); Hamiltonians (we must make the world safe for commerce); Jeffersonians (we fear that either type of involvement might undermine liberty at home); and Jacksonians (we believe in destroying America's enemies and defending our sovereignty at all costs, world opinion be damned).

There is another pattern, and perhaps a more fundamental one, than any of these sets of labels suggest. The same elemental forces that constantly battle throughout history for the allegiance of humanity—the Church, the State, the Market, the Tribe, and Science—vie for control of our foreign policy, too. Each has shaped American policy over the centuries, and each had a role in sending us abroad.

Start with the "Church," broadly defined. Americans have always engaged the world in the name of saving souls through Christ or freedom or both. The missionary zeal—secular or religious (often in tandem)—has been a driving and defining force for engagement. Baptist missionaries, for example, were venturing from their rural homes in Upstate New York to as far away as Burma by the early days of the nineteenth century. Protestant denominations, especially of the more evangelical stripe, made early inroads in China. Mormon missions increasingly took members of the Church around the globe. These Americans brought along not just the Gospels but also their faith in the ideals of the new country that had trained them. The message was choice: Humanity must be free to choose, and especially free to choose Christianity.

Religious missionaries never drove American foreign policy in an official sense. It was never State Department policy (even in the second Bush administration) to put the weight of the U.S. government behind the propagation of the faith. The Church pulled us into the world nevertheless. Protecting American citizens in China, many of them missionaries, was a concern of our Pacific forces for decades. More generally, the zeal of the missionaries and their message of redemption through Christ amplified, and justified, our secular ardor to bring the benefits of what we thought of as "civilization" to the world.

The missionary spirit was mostly secular—but no less fervent. Thomas Jefferson was anything but an "isolationist." He yearned to see "this ball of liberty . . . roll round the globe." Having served for years as the Continental Congress's minister to France, he was deeply immersed in French politics, engaging in "nation building" there centuries before that term became familiar. As secretary of state in George Washington's first term, Jefferson was a close adviser to leaders of the French Revolution, advising the Marquis de Lafayette, for example, on the drafting of a French Declaration of Rights. Jefferson wanted good relations with the new government, of course, but he wanted something more: to install the machinery of liberty in Europe. Late in life he supported the overthrow of Ottoman rule in Greece. "Possessing ourselves the combined blessings of liberty and order," he wrote to one of the Greek insurgents, "we wish the same to other countries, and to none more than yours, which, the first of civilized nations, presented examples of what man should be."

The two types of missionary spirit—Christian and Jeffersonian—coalesced in the person of another Virginia-born president, Woodrow Wilson. Born and reared in the Bible Belt (he lived as a boy in Georgia and South Carolina), Wilson was the devout, studious son of a Presbyterian theologian. A lifelong churchgoer and a Bible reader, he fervently believed people needed to be free so that they could find their own way to God's grace. The Bible, he said in a speech in 1911, "is a book which reveals men unto themselves, not as creatures in bondage, not as men under human authority, not as those bidden to take counsel and command of any human source. Whenever a man sees this vision he stands up a free man, whatever may be the government under which he lives, if he sees beyond the circumstances of his own life."

Wilson came to the presidency in 1913 promising to reverse the aggressive, empire-building policies of his Republican predecessors (although he didn't hesitate to invade Haiti in 1915). He won reelection in 1916 on a slogan of "He Kept Us Out of War." Nevertheless, in a campaign speech, Wilson foreshadowed what would become his own aggressive foreign policy—one based not on imperial ambition but on morality. "We believe these fundamental things," he said. "First, that every people has the right to choose the sovereignty under which they live. . . . Second, that the small states of the world have a right to enjoy the same integrity that great and powerful nations expect and insist upon." And third: "The world has a right to be free from every disturbance of its peace that has its origin in aggression and disregard of the rights of peoples and nations." Within a year, he asked Congress to declare a "war to end all wars."

Moral idealism led Wilson to argue not only for war, but also for a system of world government that he hoped would make war impossible. He pleaded with the Senate to ratify the Treaty of Versailles, which contained the Covenant of the League of Nations. "Dare we reject it and break the heart of the world?" he asked. It failed by seven votes. The crusade failed; the idea of Wilsonian idealism remains.

Religious faith was an even more central and direct influence on the rise of anticommunism in America. By the time of the Russian Revolution in 1917, millions of immigrants from Eastern Europe and Russia had flooded into the United States. Most of them were either Catholics or Russian Orthodox—two denominations brutally suppressed by the ferociously secular Union of Soviet Socialist Republics. Soon thereafter, Catholic churches in America and elsewhere began to recite weekly prayers for the "liberation of the Church in Mother Russia," prayers that were amplified by the Soviet occupation of the Eastern bloc after World War II. A generation of Catholics grew up with a creedal belief that the defeat of communism was a goal and dream—and it was. Senator Joseph

McCarthy was the preacher-in-chief of that sentiment. He was a weak and spiteful character but nevertheless an influential man, and a hero to millions of Catholics who saw him as fighting the good fight for the Church against Evil.

The concerns of the State are geographic, demographic, and bureaucratic: the defense (and, sometimes, the expansion) of territorial integrity and national identity—even if that means going to "foreign ground" to do so. Jefferson had no abstract ideals in mind when, as president, he sent James Monroe to Paris to engineer the Louisiana Purchase at fire-sale prices from a bankrupt France. Jefferson's goals were national security—and a place in which to relocate Indians. He didn't have "human rights" in mind; arguably, the opposite.

The definition of borders was, and remains, a motivation of State. After the War of 1812 ended, a newly feisty America began expanding its borders and influence. Monroe bought Florida from the Spanish for $5 million after sending Andrew Jackson there on the pretext of suppressing Seminole raids. Three years later, Monroe declared his famous Doctrine, telling Europe to butt out of the Western Hemisphere—forever. Monroe and his contemporaries said that he had made the declaration in the name of freedom and national self-determination.

At the dawn of the twentieth century, the triumph of Republican "Manifest Destiny" thinking was at its height. The concept of the American State stretched throughout the hemisphere, or so Teddy Roosevelt asserted. It was the right and duty of the United States, he said, to extend its police powers throughout the region. "Chronic wrongdoing," T.R. said, "or an impotence which results in a general loosening of the ties of civilized society may in America, as elsewhere, ultimately require intervention by some civilized nation." That "civilized nation," of course, was us. "In the Western Hemisphere the adherence of the United States to the Monroe Doctrine may force the United States, however reluctantly, in flagrant cases, to the exercise of an international police power." We are always reluctant, but cases are flagrant—and we have to play cop.

The Market has been such a durable, pervasive force in American foreign policy that it is almost invisible in its sweep. It is everywhere, and always has been. Profit from trade—or the lack of it—had spurred the Revolution, and the earliest actions of Congress focused on treaties and rules for global trade. And it *was* global. The geography that made America "detached," in Washington's word, also bound it instantly to the entire planet, because our livelihood depended on world trade on safe seas. We needed a navy to project power, at least enough power to protect the flow of seaborne commerce.

The new federal government's first war was sparked by controversy over the principle of free navigation for American merchant vessels on the high seas. Pirates along the North African coast had preyed on shipping for decades, capturing cargoes and ransoming crews. President Washington signed a treaty of "harmony" with the Muslim pirates. The treaty was not worth the quill pen used to write it. John Adams was forced to pay tribute to the Barbary pirates—by 1800 it amounted to the then-huge sum of $2 million. "We ought not to fight them at all unless we determine to fight them forever," Adams wrote. Thomas Jefferson thought just the opposite. When the pirates declared war and captured an American naval ship, Jefferson sent the navy and the Marines to the "shores of Tripoli." The war ended in 1805, as did the North African habit of preying on American shipping.

As European empires collapsed at the end of the nineteenth century, American leaders began to talk more of markets than morality, more of profits than prophets. "We do not mean to be content with our own market," declared President Benjamin Harrison in 1889. We had no desire to "dominate these neighboring governments," he said—of course not. All we wanted were "those friendly political, mental and commercial relations which shall promote their interests equal with ours. We should no longer forgo," he said, "those commercial relations and advantages which our geographical relations suggest and make so desirable." The idea, said President William Howard Taft, was to substitute "dollars for bullets." It worked. One piece of evidence: The total foreign securities held by Americans quadrupled between 1900 and 1909. "True stability," said Taft's secretary of state, Philander Knox, in 1910, "is best established not by military but by economic and social forces." Knox had reason for faith in commerce. As Andrew Carnegie's lawyer, he had helped organize United States Steel—which had begun to sell its products worldwide.

The emotional attachment of Tribe—in the national as well as ethnic sense—is a powerful engine in American foreign policy. We have a national Us and an ethnic Us. Usually they go together, but not always. They can impel us to adventure overseas, or argue that we should go nowhere, lest we end up confronting the distant cousins we left behind when we came here. They can also lead us to the right war, as they did when Winston Churchill and Franklin Roosevelt linked arms as brothers in World War II, summoning their respective national Tribes in the name of what Churchill called a "great purpose and design."

The list of Tribal attachments—and fears—is long. The first "lobbyist" for American ties to Poland was General Thaddeus Kosciuszko. A Polish military officer who served in the American Revolution, he later helped lead a revolution in his country that drew widespread support here. That history resonated later, in important ways, after millions of Polish immigrants arrived here early in the twentieth century. With more Poles than any city besides Warsaw, Chicago (with Cleveland and Pittsburgh not far behind) became a pivotal bastion of support for President Ronald Reagan's aggressive anti-Soviet policy. Americans of Eastern European descent hated the very idea of the Warsaw Pact, which purported to bind the region to Soviet will. Lech Walesa was a hero to many Americans, but practically a patron saint of the industrial Midwest.

After the Second World War—and the Holocaust—Jewish Americans urged Washington to support the creation of a modern State of Israel. President Harry Truman, both out of personal ties and get-out-the-vote calculations (especially in New York, Pennsylvania, and Illinois) committed to doing so. The United States was the first to recognize the new Jewish state in 1948. Jews, already a mainstay of the Democratic Party because of the influence of Franklin Roosevelt, remain largely loyal to the party to this day.

By early in this century, the largest immigrant wave from a single country had arrived in America. Mexicans did not have to cross an ocean to get here. The growing commercial ties between the two countries made their journey all the more logical—and, for many Mexican families, urgent. No one knows precisely what role some 20 million Mexican Americans will play in shaping foreign policy. But the methods of influencing policy already have changed. The political border between the countries seems almost to have vanished. In 2006, candidates for president of Mexico campaigned *in the United States* among immigrants who still held Mexican citizenship. At the time, the sitting president, Vicente Fox, campaigned *in the United States* against a proposal in the U.S. Congress to place strict new limits on immigration from the south. The U.S. government, meanwhile, quickly recognized the legitimacy of the disputed presidential election *in Mexico*—even as the losing candidate in the race refused to accept the final vote count as valid.

For most of our history, Science and its real-world consequences were not an independent force guiding American foreign policy, although technology always influenced its course. Confronting the vastness of the oceans around us—and the needs of trade—we focused on the speed of our sailing ships and, later, of our steamers. The very size of our continent sped the development of aviation and air forces; success at it has shaped American military thinking ever since. Our determination to beat the Soviets to the moon, and our victory in that race, gave us capabilities in space and satellites that no other country can match.

In recent decades, however, Science has gone from enabler and enhancer to a factor in deciding not only what we *can* do, but what we *should* do. The development of atomic weapons during World War II changed the discourse on the meaning of war itself. It gave new impetus to the idea of pacifism—the new conviction that "all-out" war could simply never be an instrument of policy. Paradoxically, Science also gave rise to a new theory of threat: Henry Kissinger's famous theory of "mutual assured destruction." The "weaponization" of nuclear energy had made annihilation of countries not only possible, but inevitable. Fear, Kissinger saw, could preserve peace—as long as the potential "enemy" was rational enough to want to avoid doom. Luckily for the planet, the Russians, as a people, are merely untamable—not suicidal.

Nuclear power made Science an organizing principle unto itself. Now it is bidding to set the American agenda, and the planet's, as we seek to understand, and react to, changes in the global environment. In 2007, Americans had to ask themselves: Did they really want the People's Republic of China to continue opening a new coal-fired power plant *every week* of the year? How long before we, and the rest of humankind, suffocated in the heat of our own prosperity? Did we dare tell China to stop? There was a new "monster" in the world—not the Chinese, who mostly wanted to make lots of money (a motivation we applauded), but the air pollution they produced in the process.

The American Argument over foreign policy is usually best served when one or more of the Five Forces is in conflict. The drama—and the danger—arrives when all forces are pointing in the same direction. That is precisely what happened in the run-up to the war in Iraq. In the aftermath of 9/11, President George W. Bush, already steeped in a Wilsonian attitude toward the Middle East, saw a chance—and an urgent reason—to remake the region in America's image. He drew upon theories that had been offered to him in his earliest briefings, by Paul Wolfowitz, Dick Cheney, and others. World peace, they advised him, required that Arab and Muslim nations be modernized and democratized. They had to be remade, or at least reformed, to understand if not fully accept the Western idea of pluralism and secular democracy. That was the only way to avoid what Bernard Lewis of Princeton had first called, in 1990, a new "Clash of Civilizations" between Islam and the West. Lewis's model of reform was Turkey, once the center of a Muslim empire, and now a secular country with deep ties to Europe and the United States.

The forces of history were lining up in a fateful way. The Faith crusaders were on the march, too. Jeffersonians and Christian evangelicals alike feel kinship to the ancient Jewish state—the former because of its commitment to democracy, the latter because of the central role of a reconstituted Israel in New Testament prophecy. Supporters of Israel saw a chance to eliminate a foe of the Jewish state, Saddam Hussein, who had been paying $25,000 to the kin of each suicide bomber there.

Corporate America saw a chance to secure access to oil, the sales of which would be counted in dollars. (In Iraq, Saddam Hussein and his United Nations allies had begun to write contracts in euros.) Finally—and crucially—there was the State: electoral politics. Bush's political mastermind, Karl Rove, saw in a war in Iraq a chance to keep his client front and center in the governmental role of commander in chief defending the homeland from threats in wartime.

In John Adams's terms, Bush took us abroad, where we thought we found "monsters to destroy." There is a problem, however. In Donald Rumsfeld's terms, we had "no metric" for knowing whether we were creating more terrorists than we were destroying. By the end of 2007, the answer was clear to almost everyone beyond the walls of the Oval Office. A "surge" of American troops may have calmed the streets of Iraq, but another, more numerous, generation of terrorists was on the rise.

A s the ranking Democrat on the Senate Foreign Relations Committee, and a U.S. senator since 1972 (he was elected at the age of twenty-nine), the voluble Joe Biden was one of Washington's leading voices on foreign policy. He had traveled to more countries more times than anyone else on the Hill, and as part of a quite possibly quixotic bid for his party's 2008 presidential nomination, he had prepared a long critique of Bush's tenure—and of America's position in the world five years after the 9/11 attacks.

The idea that America stands for freedom, he said, is all that is protecting us in the world. That remains as important as military force, so-called hard power. Our ideas were our power, too. "Strategically, when you think about the notion of 'soft power,' it starts with big ideas," he told me. "The idea that means the most is freedom—and the idea that we really do care about it. There is a piece of the world that is relying upon our naiveté and optimism about freedom. That, to them, is an important element. It allows them to be cynical about us without despairing."

Bush may well have been properly and justifiably within the freedom-as-a-crusade tradition when he launched the war in Iraq—Biden joined most of his fellow Democrats in authorizing it—but Biden argued that the execution of it had undercut the world's sense that we really cared about the goal at all. "That is the most damaging thing that Bush had done, or that the administration has done," Biden said. "The world has no faith in our judgment! We're like the surgeon who killed the last fifteen patients." He told a story about his short-lived baseball career, and finished with the famous line about the results of ineptitude. An error-prone player, the manager says, "screwed up center field so badly no one can play it."

Bush, in Biden's view, did not really fit into any categories of foreign policy known to scholars, journalists, or diplomats. "He's sort of a combination of the Monroe Doctrine and Manifest Destiny and Woodrow Wilson, but he has screwed them all up. He's got pieces of them all but they don't fit together.

"Ultimately, to him the only thing that matters in international relations is power and force. Unlike any other school of thought, I think he thinks that force can produce—and this is the irony of the guy—force can produce ethical conduct. All you got to do is force someone's head around to look into the Light of God and he will be seized with the rightness of this approach. That's how he thinks about democratization."

Wolfowitz, Cheney, Lewis, and others had a worthy idea, Biden said, but failed to acknowledge—or convince the president—that implementing it would take time. "What you have are the Wolfowitzes of the world who think democratization can happen, but that it is a process. And it *is* a costly, time-consuming but I agree worthwhile process."

Bush, said Biden, is not into process. "At first I thought that he was trying to appeal to guys like me who are out there, and average Americans, that he was taking Jack Kennedy at his best but just saying it badly. I have come to believe that he actually does think in terms of black and white. He has this bizarre notion that idealism can be spurred by sufficient punishment. This guy thinks you take the sinner and make him look into the eyes of God and it is done."

All that said, Biden reminded me that he agreed with Bush on one essential point. "I start from the premise that we are the indispensable nation," he said, folding his hands ceremoniously on his desk. "There is no hubris in that. It's just a fact."

The George Bush of the garden in Austin was not the same George Bush who rode on Air Force One two months after the terrorist attacks of September 11, 2001. He no longer suggested that we had to be "patient" with the Taliban; in fact, he had ordered its destruction in the aftermath of 9/11. And he no longer was reluctant to engage militarily the world; no longer would we have to be "humble" in foreign policy. Instead, we were in the midst of the biggest expansion of spending and military force structure since Vietnam, the latter to be accomplished in part through the deployment of Reserves and the National Guard.

Bush had said that he admired Truman and Churchill. Now he had downloaded their combined histories and tried to fashion himself as a defiant defender of the faith—not the faith of antifascism or anticommunism but of something he called "Islamo-fascism." Most profound and consequential was his declaration that there was evil in the world and that nothing less than its eradication was the aim of American foreign policy.

In the solemn calls to arms, he delivered this message in the days and months after the 9/11 nightmare. He gave perhaps his most moving—and memorable—statement of this new orthodoxy in an address at the National Cathedral in Washington. He summoned the power of prayer and the name of God. "Just three days removed from these events," he said, "Americans do not yet have the distance of history, but our responsibility to history is already clear: to answer these attacks and rid the world of evil." In lofty, lilting language that echoed Christian prayers for grace, Bush asked that God "bless the souls of the departed" and "guide our country" in the war against evil that the commander in chief had just declared.

Two months later, I was flying on Air Force One with Bush. As he sat in the conference room of the Boeing 747—a conference room like any other, except that the tall chairs were on tracks and each had a seat belt—he spoke of the existence of evil, and the foreign-policy consequences of it. He had been using the word repeatedly in his speeches, describing the terrorists who had attacked and the Taliban leaders we were in the process of destroying.

So was Saddam Hussein "evil"? The president's advisers gazed intently at him, then nervously at their notepads.

He didn't answer.

Again, the question: "Is Saddam Hussein evil?" Again, he gave no reply, and the conversation moved on to other topics. A few minutes later, unprompted, Bush—evidently unable to contain himself—answered the question.

"Saddam is evil," he declared. The rest, as they say, is history.

Twelve

THE ENVIRONMENT

I t was August in Washington. In Vice President Dick Cheney's West Wing office, the air-conditioning was on full blast, which was appropriate, because the topic he wanted to discuss was energy, specifically his view that America needed to drill and mine its way to a larger supply of it. The cool air in his office was an example of how the system should work. Coal was strip-mined in West Virginia, shipped by rail to a power plant in northern Virginia, which burned it to generate electricity, which was then sent to the White House on Pennsylvania Avenue. In the argument about the management of American resources—how to balance what we needed to use against what we needed to save—Cheney knew where he stood: for air-conditioning.

Earlier in that year of 2001, in one of the new Bush administration's first official acts, Cheney had convened a task force to study the country's energy needs, and how to meet them. Its membership and meetings were shrouded in secrecy, but there was no hiding Cheney's personal agenda, which he had brought with him from his job at the energy company Halliburton and from his upbringing in the oil town of Casper, Wyoming. He conceded that conservation was important; he noted in speeches that there had been much progress on that front since the Arab Oil Embargo of 1973, especially in the efficiency of electrical appliances and some of Detroit's fleets. Still, he said, we could not meet our needs, secure our country, unless we could dig and drill our way out of whatever "crisis" we might face.

Coal was an important part of the equation, and it was something that he knew about. The Powder River Basin in his home state of Wyoming had become a leading source for low-sulfur coal. It was mined by colossal "dragline" cranes that slowly crawled along the moonlike landscape. The mining of Western coal was a relatively new phenomenon, but one Cheney applauded.

Seated in front of a large (nonworking) fireplace, Cheney was a calm, avuncular presence. His manner was friendly in an impersonal sort of way, and gravely knowledgeable. He seemed to know so much, almost too much—like the college dean informing you that you have been placed on probation. He was still trying to dig himself out of the rubble of a wire story out of Toronto. He had been speaking to the Associated Press about energy. He had given the usual nods in the direction of conservation and research, but wasn't able to resist taking a swipe at the administration that he and George Bush had recently replaced—the one in which Vice President Al Gore had been the leader on the topic of energy and the environment. "Conservation may be a sign of personal virtue," the vice president had told the AP, "but it is not a sufficient basis for a sound, comprehensive energy policy."

Of course he was just stating his version of the obvious, but something about the tenor of the remarks—his seeming disparagement of the *societal* virtue of conservation—had driven the environmentalists nuts. He had been forced to send his wife, Lynne, out to repair the damage the next day, when laryngitis (they said) kept him home. "Conservation is a must," she had said. "We must become more efficient in energy use, for efficiency helps us to make the most of our resources. It softens the impact of high process, and reduces pollution."

In his office, Cheney was unbowed. The quote had been taken out of context. Of course conservation was important, but we had to drill in Alaska, lay new natural gas pipelines, and preempt the states from being able to object to the stringing of new power lines for electricity transmission. "We cannot wait for the next crisis to take action on these things," he said. "We have to move."

Still, it wasn't as if Cheney didn't care about the environment. He had been born and reared in Wyoming. His father was an official of the Soil Conservation Service, and had spent his career studying the lay of the land of the state. After flunking out of Yale, Cheney had worked as a lineman for the power company. He appreciated handsome natural vistas, wherever they were. In fact, after he and George W. Bush won a second term, Cheney purchased a $2.67 million home on the eastern shore of Maryland in the town of St. Michaels. The town was built on slips of land jutting out into the Chesapeake Bay. St. Michaels and the surrounding areas were known for their sumptuous, unspoiled vistas and the shoreline and the bay. Much of the land along the water was protected from development by scenic easements or state parks. From the Cheneys' house, there were no power lines visible. He had beautiful, unobstructed views.

In America, land meant freedom. It had no past (as we understood "past"); it was roamed by people who made no claim to own it (as we understood "own"). From the beginning, land—emblematic of what we now call "environment"—drew immigrants yearning for the freedom and opportunity it could afford them. The lure of land remains, even if the virgin earth does not. We still look to nature as a source of possibilities.

We revere the *idea* of available land, but less often particular pieces of it. Why? For one, because there still seems to be so much of it; second, because our forebears were taught to believe that God wanted us to possess it the way He wanted ancient Israel to possess Canaan. It was ours to use or use up—a disposable commodity, not a sacred place. The result is an Argument that is uniquely American: a vigorous contest between practicality and awe.

We hold three basic, and basically antagonistic, views. Virginia planters embodied the dominant view: You grew tobacco, you depleted the soil, you moved west. Yet, from the start, there were other, competing visions. Perhaps because William Penn was trying to sell Pennsylvania titles to German farmers, who prided themselves on meticulous husbandry of hard-won, limited plots, he laid out Philadelphia as a "city in a garden." Jefferson, at Monticello, occupied this same "middle landscape," as cultural critic Leo Marx famously called it. A third concept, which honored untouched nature, surfaced with Emerson and Thoreau. They feared what rampant "industrialization" would do; the "conservation" movement was the eventual result. And now? Have we finally "used up" nature—consumed our eons-deep heritage of hydrocarbons? Are we now to be punished in a biblical flood? Having cut the timber, extracted the oil, and strip-mined the coal, will we choke on our own CO_2? Or is this the hysteria of those who underestimate our possibilities?

The reigning idea of early America was that this was our Eden to consume and, as the Bible says, "subdue." For roughly three hundred of our first four hundred years as a people, the goal was to "settle, cut, slaughter, and sell," in the words of environmental historian David S. Wilcove of Princeton. "We saw an endless frontier out there, or what seemed to be one. You could always move to someplace new."

The resulting attitude toward what we now call "the environment" was rapacious. Throughout most of our history, the resource in short supply was not land, but labor. The search was constant for ways to use the former to compensate for the lack of the latter. In Virginia, local squires soon discovered that their wildly lucrative cash crop—tobacco—rapidly sucked nutrients from the soil. Rather than replenish those fields, a labor-intensive task in an already labor-intensive business (that is what the slaves were for), they just moved west: from Jamestown to the Piedmont, over the Blue Ridge into the Shenandoah, through the Cumberland Gap to Kentucky (still Virginia then).

Visitors sometimes marveled—or were aghast—at the wanton waste. In European eyes, wood was valuable. Indeed, it was one of the first things that caught the eye of the earliest visitors here, who knew only an Old World in which tending fires was an arduous and expensive proposition. Here it was no problem. Europeans especially noted the practice of "driving a piece," writes historian William Cronon. Lumberjacks cut weakening notches in good trees beneath the giant ones they wanted to fell. The smaller trees were trashed.

It was the felling of trees that finally ignited the argument over resources. In the late 1880s, the last of the majestic virgin forests of the East, in the Great Lakes region, were cut down. Vast wildfires swept through the deforested land. Meanwhile, an economic boom created a dramatic timber shortage—and the first legislation to establish federal forest preserves.

Meanwhile, Americans' sense of their continent was changing. It was not really limitless. The U.S. Census of 1890 declared that there was "no longer a frontier line." Three years later, Frederick Jackson Turner delivered his famous thesis about individualism and the West. He was not concerned with resources per se, but readers got the message: Perhaps something valuable—and uniquely American—resided in our never-ending confrontation with the wilderness.

That was now gone.

By 1901, President Theodore Roosevelt declared, "the preservation of our forests is an imperative business necessity," and the National Committee of the Audubon Societies (now the National Audubon Society) was formed. In 1905, Gifford Pinchot became the first head of the new U.S. Forest Service. By the time he left office, T.R. had overseen the creation of 42 million acres of national forests, including 16 million that he ordered set aside moments before Congress passed legislation designed to stop him. He also created fifty-three wildlife refuges and eighteen areas of "special interest," including the Grand Canyon. T.R. was not only a hands-off fellow. For example, he supported legislation that led to the damming of virtually every river in the arid West. Still, he is widely regarded as not only America's first "environmental president," but the best. "He's still the standard," said Gene Karpinski of the League of Conservation Voters.

Teddy Roosevelt and his cousin Franklin had pursued conservation largely in the name of economic prosperity. No one thought that we were really destroying nature or our place in it. The idea was to ensure a steady supply of timber and, in later years, a place where Americans could vacation. The Roosevelts' agenda had less to do with reverence than with commerce.

You can find the roots of what we now call "environmentalism" deep in American soil. In a New England town, a commons was more than a convenience. It embodied a social ideal of Puritan community, a patch of land owned by all. The related notion was that the acreage should not be abused or overgrazed; detailed rules were written in an attempt to ensure that it was not. As early as the seventeenth century, authorities in some New England jurisdictions expressed concerns about declining herds of deer and other game in the forests; officials wrote ordinances to limit hunts—as their medieval English forebears had done. In the seventeenth and eighteenth centuries, a few town planners at least paid homage to nature as it more or less was, or as the mind of landscape gardeners wanted it to be.

Some among us adopted the attitude of the Native Americans, which was at once more casual and more worshipful. A rare nineteenth-century American who belonged in their camp was Henry David Thoreau, who found spiritual solace in the natural surroundings of Walden Pond. "The pine," he wrote, "is no more lumber than man is, and to be made into boards and houses is no more its true and highest use than the truest use of a man is to be cut down and made into manure. There is a higher law affecting our relation to pines as well as to men."

Even the Transcendentalists didn't take the next, scientific step: to consider the actual, ecological relationship between man and nature. Americans were slow to consider the notion that the human race was part of something called an "ecosystem," let alone a global, interactive one. The word "ecology" entered popular discourse only when the writer John Steinbeck waxed eloquent about the Gulf of California in 1940. "The tide pool stretches both ways," he wrote in *The Log from the Sea of Cortez,* "digs back to electrons and leaps space into the universe and fights out of the moment into non-conceptual time. Then ecology has a synonym, which is ALL." In 1960, zoologist Marston Bates published *Forest and the Sea,* now considered a classic denunciation of the old American attitude. "Man's destiny is tied to nature's destiny," he wrote, "and the arrogance of the engineering mind does not change this. Man may be the most peculiar animal," said Bates, "but he is still part of the system of nature." Two years later Rachel Carson published *Silent Spring,* which made a convincing case that the pesticide DDT was killing birds by thinning their eggshells.

The idea that the earth itself was in danger—that we could not only mismanage but destroy our Eden—remained foreign to our politics until the end of the 1960s. In 1968, a prestigious group of European scientists and bureaucrats produced a manifesto called "The Limits of Growth." The central, Malthusian notion: that Earth would soon reach its population-carrying capacity. It was a bestseller worldwide and in the United States, but not in itself a political watershed.

In 1969, environmentalism suddenly reached a critical mass as a new brand of politics. It did so at the convergence of five vivid events: the Santa Barbara, California, oil spill; the seizure by Wisconsin and Minnesota of eleven tons of cans of DDT-laden tuna fish; the application by oil companies for permission to build a pipeline across Alaska; an industrial fire that briefly but famously flared on the Cuyahoga River; and a medical order in Los Angeles declaring that children there could not "run, skip, or jump inside or outside on smog alert days." The media attention suddenly added up to more than the sum of its parts.

"Earth Day" was inaugurated the next year. So was the Environmental Protection Agency, promoted by Democrats but signed into law by a

Republican president, Richard Nixon. The Clean Air Act was greatly strengthened, too.

At first, "environmentalism" did not provoke much partisan argument. Drawing on the Teddy Roosevelt history, the conservation tradition in the Republican Party, and a desire to pacify the "Eastern Establishment" that had turned against him on the Vietnam War, Nixon ran for reelection as an environmentalist in 1972. He supported passage of the first serious national water-pollution control law that year. One radio spot produced by his ad team, for example, proudly noted that he had used his historic trip to Moscow (the first by an American president) to sign an environmental agreement. Democrats such as Senator Gaylord Nelson of Wisconsin pushed Nixon and the GOP to accept landmark environmental legislation—Nelson is also considered the founding father of Earth Day—but historians give Nixon credit, too, not to mention longtime conservation advocates such as the Rockefellers. "The laws enacted in that time were landmarks we need to appreciate today," said Carol Browner, who headed the EPA in the Clinton years. "They were huge steps forward."

It took time for the issue to generate partisan heat. The energy came out of the West, where resource issues always had been at the forefront of politics. After all, nearly half the West's acreage was federally controlled. As far back as T.R.'s time, Washington had played the leading role in designing and paying for massive water projects there. For the first time, the locals were thinking of what *not* to develop. In Colorado, a young lawyer named Gary Hart spearheaded a successful drive to block the 1976 Winter Olympics from being staged in the state. In the Old West, such an attitude would have been unthinkable, but it made sense to a new generation of Coloradans who wanted to save its still-pristine environment. Hart, who hailed from Kansas and graduated from Yale Law, wore jeans and looked like a cowboy. The message: This ain't no hippie crusade.

The first flat-out national "environmental" candidate was a Westerner, too. Representative Morris Udall of Arizona ran for the Democratic presidential nomination in 1976 as a tribune of the Old Old West. His brother, Stewart, had been secretary of the interior in the Kennedy administration. The brothers saw themselves as guardians of their native soil and its carefully conservationist values. Udall didn't win, but the man who did—former governor Jimmy Carter of Georgia—touted his work in protecting his state's "wild" rivers. Carter touched a deeper chord about the land, too, although being "green" was not the objective. He and his family had been peanut farmers. Running as someone who would purify Washington of the stench of Watergate, Carter was photographed in overalls, examining a handful of reddish soil. The message: *I am of the earth, and therefore a man you can trust.*

It was Carter, with great fanfare in the Rose Garden, who signed the first federal strip-mine bill into law in 1977. With that, and other regulatory measures, he and his Democratic allies provoked a political counterreaction in the West. It was called the "Sagebrush Rebellion," led by Ronald Reagan, James Watt, and Cheney. These were leaders who always claimed to distrust "big government" and who saw the environmental movement as a stealthy bureaucratic attack on the soul of man and the profits of business. They cited the writings of their philosophical heroine, novelist and critic Ayn Rand. "Observe that in all the propaganda of the ecologists," she wrote, "amidst all their appeals to nature and pleas for harmony with nature there is no discussion of man's needs and of the requirements of his survival. Man is treated as if he were an unnatural phenomenon."

One of Watt's first acts in 1981 as Reagan's new secretary of the interior was to demand the resignation of all of his department's top officials, including those charged with overseeing the new strip-mining law. Under Watt, the government propounded the "wise use" policy, which really was the "more use" policy: far more leasing of public lands for timber, mining, and oil, and the opening of wilderness areas for more recreation.

On these and other issues, the Argument rages on, but this much is settled: Branding someone a "polluter" can be an effective tactic. Oilman George H. W. Bush deployed that weapon in his 1988 presidential race against Michael Dukakis, who was running on his record as a pragmatic, can-do governor of Massachusetts. Dukakis's Boston enemies saw an opening: the slow-moving, mismanaged federally mandated cleanup of Boston Harbor.

The Bush campaign planned its attack for the days immediately after the Democratic convention that nominated Dukakis. Bush, who was vice president at the time, flew to Boston, toured the harbor by boat, stressing not only the massive pollution problems—which Dukakis had inherited—but also the billions it was costing to clean up. For eight years, environmentalists had blasted the Reagan-Bush administration for laxity in the face of court-ordered action. Without a trace of shame the Bush campaign turned that cannon around, claiming that the state government had been so slow to act that a federal judge had been forced to assume control of the project.

The campaign launched a companion ad, one of the most effective—that is, disingenuous—of the campaign, blaming Dukakis for failing to clean up the harbor. It had been polluted since colonial times, but a voice-of-doom narrator in the ad called it "one of the filthiest harbors in America" while the screen showed a lurid vista of oil-like water and floating debris. The ad showed a sign that read "Danger/Radiation Hazard/No Swimming." Long afterward, word surfaced that the sign was located at a nuclear-submarine repair facility. Dukakis's ad team wanted to respond with an ad attacking Bush's environmental record, according to media analyst Kathleen Hall Jamieson of the University of Pennsylvania, but Dukakis declined to do so. The spot was too negative, he said.

Dukakis may have been reluctant to fight on that ground (or water), but four years later Al Gore was not. By 1992 he had published *Earth in the Balance,* his jeremiad on global warming. He thought of himself as *the* leader on a topic about which his Democratic running mate, Bill Clinton, cared little. One of Gore's first stops as a vice-presidential candidate was in the Ohio River town of Weirton, West Virginia. A huge hazardous-waste incinerator was located in a floodplain across the river in East Liverpool, Ohio. It was one of the largest of its kind, scheduled to burn 70,000 tons of waste a year in a location not far from homes and a school. The candidate hammered the Bush administration for its plans to give the facility an air-pollution permit. "The very idea is just unbelievable to me," he declared. He vowed to create "an environmental presidency"—a new phrase in national campaigns. "We'll be on your side for a change."

For the first time, "environmentalism" became an issue of its own in a presidential campaign. Beleaguered on other fronts, President Bush depicted Gore as "ozone man," an extremist bent on dismantling the fossil-fuel economy, from Detroit cars that ran on gasoline to electric power plants that burned coal.

After 9/11, the argument returned in more urgent form. The second Bush administration was insisting after the terrorist attacks that the country should burn more, not less. After renewal of war in the Middle East, they said, our deep dependence on foreign oil—more than half of total consumption—looked far riskier than ever. They had a point. The argument was over the best way to reduce that dependence. Environmentalists, and a new generation of technologists and investors, believed that radical, inventive new conservation measures offered the most hope.

The Bush administration had a rather different view. One way out of the crisis, the administration said, was to rely on new technologies that "liquefy" the coal in ways to limit the pollution it produced. The deposits of coal beneath the continent were almost too enormous to calculate. We had all we needed, and could make tons of cash by selling much of it to China. The only foes of such a sensible idea, they said, were "the elite environmentalists."

The catch was depressingly simple: Even when you "liquefy" coal, you still have to burn it. And even if you eliminate most of the toxic chemicals and gases (which liquefaction can do, although at a steep price), you're doing nothing about the carbon dioxide that is the main by-product. It is the carbon dioxide that everyone is worrying about. It's the CO_2 that creates the "greenhouse effect" that traps the air that is heated by sun, leading to global warming. The only remaining skeptics of this theory, Gore said, were "corporate polluters."

French is not a language native to eastern Kentucky, which may explain why the The La Citadel restaurant had an extra definite article in its name. It was perched on a mountain above the town of Hazard, the county seat of Perry County, through which coal trucks rumbled on their way to loading docks outside of town. By law, their cargoes were supposed to be covered and tied down, but sometimes, on bumpy roads, coal lumps would fly free, bouncing along the asphalt, landing on windshields, or worse. Hazard lived up to its name.

It was a long way up a winding road from the main streets of town to the restaurant, where, in the spring of 1977, Bill Gorman was explaining his views on the environment. The Arab Oil Embargo of 1973—and the subsequent doubling of crude oil prices worldwide—had made coal, the most problematic of fuels, a very hot commodity. Short-term "spot" prices for a ton of clean-burning, low-sulfur coal doubled. Suddenly everybody in the mountains was rushing into the coal "bidness," reopening old mines, carving new "wildcat" surface mines with rented bulldozers. Almost anyone could make a good living just driving a coal truck.

Good times, but there was another side to the story. Nowhere else in America was the clash so dramatic—or, sometimes, so violent—between the forces of the Market and the sanctity of the living environment. In eastern Kentucky, the trade-offs were deadly. It was entirely possible that the local industry—especially in frantic, blast-every-coal-seam boom times—would shake loose a five-ton boulder that would roll down the hill and flatten your new "double-wide" trailer, maybe even with you inside.

Such immediate dangers were among the many reasons (acid-water pollution was another) why, after many years of crusading, and the election of Jimmy Carter in 1976, environmentalists around the country had pushed through Congress a sweeping federal law. The new measure would, for the first time, set national rules for strip mining, far tougher than any Kentucky would ever write. A political war was about to break out in the mountains, a war that continues to this day over the regulation of an ever-more-crucial industry.

Gorman sat at a table near a wall of windows at The La Citadel. It was a sunny, clear day. The phrase "takes your breath away" is a cliché, but it is true: You are suddenly hit with the recognition of a greater force. I saw undulating carpets of lush green mountains marching into the distance to an almost musical cadence. Since there were so few strip mines close to town, the view was unspoiled. Of course, there was no guarantee it would stay that way. Even if mines were out of sight, their effects were not. Strip-mined land, denuded of its trees and topsoil, cannot absorb rainwater the way a forest does. In the spring, the floods came, and came harder and faster each year.

A thoughtful fellow whose family business interests ranged from TV broadcasting to banking, Gorman was no firebrand. He did not denounce the environmentalists as "abolitionists"—a loaded word meant to warn of an impending federal shutdown of the entire industry. The year after I met him, Gorman was elected mayor of Hazard. He conceded that the environmentalists had valid points, and that they were going to win a legal round. The greedy coal operators brought troubles on themselves with sloppy—sometimes openly defiant—practices. He knew that the coal industry as a whole might benefit from careful, wise regulation, however dubious he was about the ability of bureaucrats in Washington to provide it.

Still, he shook his head as he watched me take in the breathtaking scene. "It's beautiful, but that's not enough," he said. Poverty, everyone knew, had long been endemic to the region. The area was a national symbol of that. In 1968, just weeks before he was assassinated, Robert F.

Kennedy had come to Hazard to draw attention to the region's plight. Gorman had been with him that day. Folks had to do what they had to do. "First priority for the people here is to make a living," he said. "I know it's beautiful. I love the mountains. This is my home, too. But you can't eat beauty."

It was a memorable declaration, obviously, but a misleading one. Yes, aesthetics play a part and actually an increasing part (because of tourism) in the American Argument over our relationship with the natural world. But even though our earliest settlers often thought of themselves as immigrants to a New Eden, they didn't come because it was pretty. They came because the land offered almost unimaginable abundance. And the abundance was not just the land itself, but what lay beneath it. At the same time, they did not want to make the very land upon which they lived uninhabitable. And all too often that was exactly what happened in eastern Kentucky.

In many ways, the American Argument over the environment is really an argument about the uses and abuses of carbon and the carbon-based fuels that are our geological inheritance. Much of our country's prosperity and growth has been colorfully carbon-based—from the shipbuilding and mast-cutting industry to timbering for construction to oil and natural gas. Our freedom was nurtured in forested wilderness that we saw when we arrived and that we can still see in many states, but also in the forests of eons ago, the remains of which form the lodes of carbon-based fuels we mine, drill, and tap. It is an inheritance that we must use, that we have no choice but to use, but that we must find a way to use without endangering ourselves by filling the air with the pollution that fossil fuels create.

That's the coal boulder rolling down the hill on a global scale—or at least that is how a young congressman from Tennessee explained it not long after he arrived in Washington in 1977. Albert Gore Jr. had spent his boyhood summers on a farm in the foothills of those same coal-filled southern Appalachians. At Harvard in the late 1960s, he had been inspired by Roger Revelle, the pioneer researcher in the new study of global climate change. Using careful measurements, Revelle was the first to show that the levels of carbon dioxide in the planetary air were escalating steadily, and one of the first to suggest that the resulting "greenhouse effect" could trap too much heat for our own good. In 1981, newly elected to the U.S. Senate, Gore cosponsored the first congressional hearings on the possible dangers of climate change.

The American public (and press corps) paid little attention. Gore was ahead of his time—even his own time. In 1988, he mounted a confused, futile bid for the Democratic presidential nomination—confused because Gore was reluctant to make the environment his main calling card as a candidate. By his next presidential campaign, in 2000, he had decided who he was, at least as a public man. He had published *Earth in the Balance,* which sounded an alarm about global warming—and became the first bestseller by a sitting senator since John F. Kennedy's *Profiles in Courage.* Activists criticized the record of the Clinton-Gore administration and, indeed, Gore had looked the other way when some antigreen deals went down. No one doubted his commitment to, even obsession with, convincing the country that burning fossil fuels threatened the planet's survival. And yet he did not make the environment the centerpiece of his 2000 campaign, either. One reason: He wanted to win coal-rich West Virginia. He lost it, and the election, anyway.

By 2006, Gore had become a public environmental institution of sorts, a kind of public media icon. He was the subject of a shrewdly presented documentary movie called *An Inconvenient Truth,* an understatedly slick, Hollywood version of the PowerPoint presentation Gore had been giving for years. In a convergence of profit and politics, the producers staged an East Coast "premiere" at the National Geographic headquarters in Washington. Gore was the star of the event; the buzz was about whether a movie could make a president.

Patrolling the fringes of the event were scouts for "The Competitive Enterprise Institute," the other side of the argument. Funded largely by Exxon—the most prodigious hydrocarbon business on the planet—they derided the movie as a hodgepodge of bad science, rank speculation, and alarmism in the guise of altruism.

Science was merely a part of the counterattack. In the abstract, Gore's foes knew, the environmentalists' goals—high-mileage cars, strict air- and water-pollution controls—were popular. No, derailing Gore would require more. You could hear it on the talk shows: People such as the former vice president, critics said, did not care about good jobs or national security because . . . they were not us. They were "elitist environmentalists" (a phrase that was taking over from the more hysterical but less surgical "extreme environmentalists").

It was shrewd and cold-blooded. Big business now would try to isolate and demonize its opponents with the same resentment-laden, us-versus-them tactics that Karl Rove had perfected in the service of George Bush. The business message: If Gore really wanted to turn global warming into a campaign issue, they would respond in kind. Be careful what you wish for—you might get it.

But the issue *was* in the mainstream. Later that year, NBC's Tom Brokaw—nobody's idea of a nutty crusader—presented a television special on global warming that offered many of the same conclusions that Gore had long since reached. There were even conservative Republicans and evangelical Christians who had come to decide that we were despoiling the garden God had given to us. If we were a New Eden, we needed to renew it, not burn it up.

As for Gore, he found himself ascending into the pantheon of global humanitarians, at least as judged by the Norwegian Nobel Committee. In October 2007, they awarded the Nobel Peace Prize to the UN's Intergovernmental Panel on Climate Change and to "Albert Arnold (Al) Gore, Jr., for their efforts to build up and disseminate greater knowledge about man-made climate change, and to lay the foundation for the measures that are needed to counteract such changes." The Nobel committee congratulated the UN panel for its research, and Gore for his skills as a publicist and environmental politician. "He is probably the single individual who has done the most to create greater worldwide understanding of the measures that need to be adopted," the panel said. After the announcement was made, the White House issued a backhandedly congratulatory statement. Dick Cheney had nothing to say.

It was time to talk to Bill Gorman again. He had been serving as mayor of Hazard for nearly thirty years. From an old local family—his grandfather had owned more than a score of mines—Gorman, at eighty-two, had seen boom times come and go . . . and come again. With crude-oil prices in the stratosphere (touching $100 a barrel in January 2008) and electricity demand setting new records every month, "the coal industry is booming," he told me. "We got coal trucks coming out our ears."

Over the years, as Hazard had grown, the mountains and valleys had changed—literally changed. Gorman had supported passage of the federal strip-mining law, but the key, he soon discovered, lay not in the broad language of the statute but in the regulations that had been written—and rewritten, and argued over endlessly—to implement it. In the earliest days, officials had all but ruled out a practice that came to be called "mountaintop removal," which involved slicing off the peaks of ridges to get at the coal seams beneath. Officials also wrote strict rules on what to do with the debris that mining creates, the so-called overburden. Whether stripping hillsides or hilltops, it did not make sense—or so Gorman and others argued—to put everything back as it was. In fact, it was pretty close to impossible, even if it was cost-effective, which it was not.

The hills and hollers of Hazard have been rearranged over the years since I first visited Hazard, with the new flatland put to use. On a series of "hollow-fills"—the name means exactly what it says—and strip-mine benches and mountaintops, the community has built schools, shopping centers, hospitals, and tracts of new homes ("Some of them are pretty fancy," Gorman said with pride). New roads have been carved through hills that blocked the way. The place was abuzz with news that Wal-Mart was coming in—on a hollow-fill. One of the hollers that had been filled in was Gorman Hollow, named for Gorman's granddaddy. The mayor estimated that $1 billion worth of construction has been placed on such sites. Water pollution was a problem (coal waste can leach acid into watersheds), and rock slides were possible, even if the work was done properly. The La Citadel was bought by a civil-engineering firm, whose employees enjoy the panoramic view as they plan new roads, water lines, and the like. "Hazard had no potential room for growth," Gorman said. "We needed the earth for something other than trees. We had to go in and move mountains."

A FAIR, "MORE PERFECT" UNION

In a sense, Senator John S. McCain III had no standing to complain about his rival in the 2000 presidential campaign, being the son of a powerful, famous father. As McCain himself readily would concede if you asked him, he probably would not have been admitted to the U.S. Naval Academy had his father and grandfather—both named John S. McCain—not been Annapolis grads and top-rank officers. The elder McCain was in the Pacific during World War II, the younger in the South China Sea during Vietnam. The youngest was a feisty wrestler and talented partier but not much of a scholar at Episcopal High School in the Virginia suburbs of Washington. Still, he had made it to—and through—the Academy.

On the other hand, McCain's celebrated lineage nearly got him killed. In 1967, on his twenty-third mission as a navy fighter-bomber pilot, he was shot out of the skies over Hanoi. He spent five years as a POW, much of it in solitary confinement. His North Vietnamese captors were all too aware of his background. They beat him repeatedly, viciously, determined to turn any "confession" into a propaganda coup. Near death, McCain signed a vague statement of guilt, an understandable act that nevertheless tormented him ever after. In prison, he would not and could not think of asking for a shred of special treatment. To do so would have destroyed his self-respect, but also his standing in the eyes of his fellow prisoners.

Returning home in 1971, his left arm rigid and his knees still weak from his injuries, McCain began a long political climb. Most military vets applauded his sacrifice and his ambition, but a few did not, harboring resentment at the special consideration he never, in fact, received. Their unjustified antagonism pained him deeply. McCain was a proud and resilient man, but a permanently angry one.

All of his history had turned him into a rare but characteristically American figure: the reform-minded son of privilege, suspicious of the powers of his own kind. He was born to the elite, but forever ambivalent about being one of them. Through his prison experience, he had come to identify with the powerless because he had been one of them for so long, in such extreme circumstances. He could never lord anything over anyone, and he had a hair-trigger resentment of anyone who did.

So when it came time to run for president, Senator John S. McCain, Republican of Arizona, found it infuriating and almost physically intolerable that the man he would have to defeat was a "Son Of." And George W. Bush was not just *any* Son Of. He was the son of a former president. And he was not just *any* Son Of a former president, he was the eldest son—an arrogant kid who had spent his Vietnam years patrolling the air space over Houston.

It was the Bush money, however, that really got to McCain. Because Bush's father had been president only eight years earlier; because the Bushes were relentlessly friendly networkers, Christmas card mailers, and record keepers; because of the way they so carefully assembled the new Bush campaign from the inside out, collecting and hoarding all the fat-cat, big-donor money—because of all that, Bush the Younger was in the midst of raising the then-unheard-of sum of $100 million for his Republican presidential campaign.

McCain could not collect anywhere near as much. His wife, Cindy, had family wealth (her father had the Budweiser distributorship in Phoenix), but McCain did not possess a vast web of wealthy acquaintances when he ran for the House and, later, the Senate in Arizona. He never liked the process of cozying up to contributors, and he had gotten in trouble for doing so when he went in search of sugar daddies one at a time. One of them was a savings and loan executive from Cincinnati named Charles Keating, a man as generous as he was insistent on the need for favors from the recipients of his cash. McCain was one of those recipients. As one of a group that came to be known as the "Keating Five," McCain lent his name to an effort to pressure regulators to back off from an investigation of the banker. Keating was eventually convicted of fraud;

McCain was never reprimanded, let alone accused of any illegal activity, but he seethed over the damage he thought that the incident had done to his reputation for integrity.

Now, as the 2000 campaign began, McCain felt he faced the hard labor of having to unearth a hundred clean Keatings—each a potential risk if not properly vetted—while his main rival had the luxury of easily tapping his father's ready-made, longtime donor list. The emerging shape of the campaign wasn't fair. Beyond that, the whole process was corrupt. He wanted to change it.

McCain vented his anger at Bush and at the campaign-finance system one night at dinner early in the campaign. Sitting at a big, round table in the back of a restaurant in Manchester, New Hampshire, he didn't so much hold forth as mutter. "All Bush has to do is ask 'daddy' to go down the list of all the people he ever appointed to an ambassadorship," said McCain. "All of those people feel obligated to the father—a former president, for Christ's sake. Of course they are going to give the maximum to his son!"

The absurdity and unfairness of the money chase merged in McCain's mind with his sweeping critique of the political system as a whole. There was, he said, something profoundly out of whack about American public life at the dawn of the twenty-first century. The political parties were locked in an endless, downward cycle of accusation and recrimination; spending priorities were badly askew; the money chase itself was corroding the arteries of the body politic. And, after eight years of the smooth-talking and mendacious Bill Clinton, it was time for a president who was honest, even if honest to a fault.

McCain ran as the embodiment of the insider turned outsider, a plain-speaking man of reform who had been in Washington long enough to see the light. He rented a tour bus in New Hampshire, christening it the "Straight Talk Express," and made himself almost promiscuously available to the press corps. He would sit in the back in a red leather swivel chair; they would be arranged around him on benches and on the floor, like eager schoolkids at library hour.

At some stops, he would be engulfed by an audience filled with what seemed to be almost magical hope for a new level of candor in politics, and for the kind of change that would engender a renewed spirit of public service of the intensity, if not the kind, that he had shown when he went to Vietnam to fly bomber jets. College and high school students would show up at events and arrange the folding chairs for the war veterans who would come to sit in the first row. There was a promise, hard to identify but palpable, a new respect for the decency and common sense of average folks.

When McCain won the Republican primary in New Hampshire in 2000, he pulled off one of the bigger upsets in recent political history. Bush managed to survive later on, in part by co-opting McCain's message of political reform and making it his own. As governor of Texas, Bush argued, he had been a reformer, too—a "Reformer with Results." The slogan worked.

Back in the Senate, McCain channeled his experience into an ongoing drive for campaign-finance reform. He joined with Senator Russ Feingold of Wisconsin to sponsor new limits on the kind of money that big-buck contributors could pour into the coffers of political parties—a phenomenon McCain saw as one of the most egregious abuses of the previous decade. He brushed aside the notion that this would somehow limit free-speech rights, or that it would weaken political parties. "We have to give the political system back to the people," he said.

As of 2007, the people were still waiting, but the idea of reform—that there was a better, fairer way to do things—was alive. At least McCain thought so, for he was running for president again.

Born in revolt against unaccountable power and undeserved rank, born in a desire to remake the world along new lines, dedicated to creating "a more perfect" union, Americans perpetually wage, or think they should be waging, a war for reform. In a theoretically egalitarian country, the idea of reform is almost always the same: to dismantle the power of the elites who have rigged the system against the little guy. We want reform to prevent *them*—a ubiquitous and sinister *them*—from tilting the playing field of life, liberty, and the pursuit of happiness. Americans will grudgingly accept most deals if they feel they have had a chance to be heard. In our democracy, the elites' power is not money per se, or the might of the police. It is the power to control the discussion—and stifle voices other than their own.

Here is the paradox that produces an argument: We need elites, even admire them. We even designed a meritocracy to produce them in what we regard as a democratic way. But we never fully trust them. We know that at least some of *them* are necessary, even laudable. After all, our own

Revolution was led by gentlemen of education and means. Lacking a hereditary aristocracy, we create elites of money, learning, military prowess, or mere sociability. They promise to rise above the ruinous thinking of the Mob. But while elites can be deserving of their clout, they can also be (or become) merely corrupt. They can win Nobels and invent iPods, but they also can smother competition in steel or spark a war in Mesopotamia. We look to our favorite advocates to champion our causes, yet decry everyone else's insiders as "special interests."

We always ask the same urgent question: Who is getting screwed? In the name of fairness, we have launched crusades against "insiders"— from colonial merchants to the railroad magnates of the nineteenth century to twenty-first-century bureaucrats and lobbyists. The anti-elitist critics bubble up from everywhere: farms, big-city labor movements, college campuses, church-based prayer groups, and the Internet. Many of their concerns are valid; some are mere paranoia.

This ambivalence about elites generates an ongoing Argument: between Main Street and Wall Street, grass roots and powers that be, republican theory and pure democracy, insiders and outsiders, the best and brightest and the forgotten man. The Argument lures us down byways of hatred, fear, and division, but mostly it has led to a fairer, more open America. We keep staging revolutions, real or imagined, against a status quo with which we claim to be unsatisfied. Are we there yet? That is, have we arrived at the "more perfect union" of which the Founders spoke? The answer, of course is usually no. The question is always whether we can or should try to do better. The answer is usually yes. At least we can include more people in the conversation. In this country, it is the journey that matters.

I n ancient Athens, only 14,000 of the 70,000 inhabitants could vote; far fewer had a hand in distributing riches and power. In Rome, the "P" in the Roman standard, SPQR, stood for the People, but in reality it was the "S," senators—and later, the emperors—who held the real reins of power, the occasional riot notwithstanding. More than a millennium later, England gave birth to our modern ideas of freedom, but that kingdom, too, was stratified by feudal custom and waves of conquering invasions.

Here in America we started with a different idea, at least when it came to free white men. It did not take us long in the seventeenth century to realize that no single person, and no group, had a God-given right to literally "lord it over" other men. The concept of divine right was crumbling in Europe; it was beside the point to pioneering settlers from England, Holland, France, or even Spain, who confronted a vast continent of opportunity and danger. What mattered was not who the commander was, or what the king said, but what the individual, or group of individuals, could do to wrest a living from and build a community. You could become a person of power and position—an elite, if you will—through your own hard work and fearlessness.

Such apparent freedom of opportunity was inspiring, but also a permanent irritant, stimulating constant struggles to encourage but limit the power of determined, ambitious groups within our society. If the challenge was to "make something of yourself," you needed a venue in which the rules were fair, and in which others were not rigging the game. Fairness—not equal outcomes, but a fair chance for individual and group achievement—early on became an American watchword. In Eastern societies, such as the Japanese, "harmony" is all. In the theory of levelers and communists, a strict equality of rewards is the ideal. We just want a fair game. Ensuring one is an American preoccupation—and it produces an American Argument over the role of elites and their relationship to the rest of us mere strivers after the Dream.

The ever-perceptive James Madison fretted about the tension between the freedom to succeed and the power of the successful. Safeguarding individual ambition was "the first object of government," he said in his famous *Federalist No. 10.* But "diversity in the faculties of men"—their differing abilities—inevitably produced "division of the society into different interests and parties." An "unequal distribution of property" was inevitable; the problem was one or another faction of wealth throwing its weight around in an attempt to commandeer or manipulate the majority. Preventing them from overreaching—balancing competing "factions" against each other—"is the principle task of modern legislation." The best venue for doing so, he said, was in a decentralized, continental republic, with "greater security afforded by a greater variety of parties."

Madison's notion—the saving cacophony of faction—was a noble one, reflecting his faith in the ability of countervailing forces to produce useful, elegant machines, from clocks to governments. But it was naive, or at least a little too optimistic. The clockwork can be broken—or can seem to be broken, which in politics can amount to the same thing. For every American who believes in the overall "fairness" of the system, there is another who thinks that he or she is being trampled by powers beyond control, seen or unseen, or simply ignored.

There is a fine line in America, sometimes nonexistent, between legitimate grievances that foster earnest reform, and what historian Richard Hofstadter called our "paranoid style" of movement politics. We see elites that are real, and dangerous; we also see, and fear, groups that merely are exotic, or different. Often we can't distinguish between the two types. Popular antagonism toward the powerful, or supposedly powerful, can generate progress, and we have expanded economic and political participation steadily through the centuries as a result. But the same impulse has also generated hatred. It's understandable. Only a democracy that believes so deeply in the freedom to associate can also believe so heartily in the possibility of conspiracy.

To shield themselves against the jealousy of the People, elites in America had to find new justification for their place in society. The Church and the king no longer had the power to sanction their elevated stations. For some elites, a Calvinist faith in the predestined success of the "elect" was a perfectly good answer. It wasn't monarchial or ecclesiastical, and it called for its believers to exhibit a sense of humility and responsibility. It was divine right democratized, brought down to the ranks of striving individuals. The Founders had a more secular method. They profoundly believed in education, and in the aristocracy of character. No less an authority than George Washington himself instructed us all on how to be gentlemen. It was not a state into which you were born, but one you could reach through self-discipline and study.

In the nineteenth century, men of means latched onto the theories of science to justify their station. "Social Darwinism" analogized the rigors of "natural selection" in the gene pools of a species to the winners and losers in the natural selection of economic competition. In the twentieth century, the IQ test took over and, eventually, a new aristocracy based on SAT scores and admission to the right schools. In the America of the early twenty-first century, we had the Ivy League, Silicon Valley, and a few other precincts of the elect. The rest was flyover country in their eyes.

Resentment of economic elites is a crimson thread woven into the oldest fabric of colonial life. It began a full century before our Revolution, in 1676, in Virginia, in the Piedmont above the fall line, and in the foothills of the Blue Ridge Mountains. The farms in that early New West were furious at the "tidewater gentry" along the Atlantic Coast, who were using their monopolistic access to seaborne trade in tobacco and other crops to squeeze their country cousins. A wealthy farmer named Nathaniel Bacon led "Bacon's Rebellion," which was soon crushed by the crown and was notable because it was a mixed-race revolt by mainly poor white farmers and their poor—and free—black brethren. Other farmer-led skirmishes arose along the periphery of the seaboard colonies in the eighteenth century, from western Massachusetts to western Pennsylvania.

The first serious reform movements materialized, not surprisingly, in response to the rise of American industry. The first of these industries was the ocean shipping industry, which reached a frenzy of activity and profit in the 1830s. The practices of the trade—specifically, the life of the men at sea—was the subject of the first great "exposé" in American journalism, *Two Years Before the Mast* by Richard Henry Dana Jr. Dana shipped out aboard the brig *Pilgrim,* and wrote vividly about the sordid conditions that common sailors faced as he chronicled his trip around Cape Horn. His account led the Massachusetts legislature to enact some of the first industrial-workplace rules in the country.

It was another mode of transportation—railroads—that led to the defining American us-versus-them reform movements in economic life: populism and the labor movement. The railroads were so vast, powerful, and all-important in the life of a continental nation that they over-whelmed the existing structures and theories of government at all levels. Without reform to control them, there would be no fair shake for any-one—for any farmer, manufacturer, or shipper—besides the owners and managers of the railroads themselves.

A new elite of railroads—strangulated unaccountable power—engendered a reaction. The first was a powerful labor union, the first of its kind in the United States. Founded by tailors in Philadelphia after the Civil War, the Knights of Labor became a national force (with a membership of 700,000) by taking on the railroads in a series of strikes in 1884 and 1885. Even Jay Gould, the ultimate railroad baron, took notice by seeking an accommodation with the union. The second strain of anti-elitist reform came from the rural South and the Plains states, where farmers saw a web of distant and imperious powers—from bankers to grain speculators—as the enemies of democracy and fair dealing. Once again, the railroads (and the telegraph and emerging telephone companies) were the galvanizing targets. Spawned by the economic panic of 1873—and the collapse of farm prices—the Populist Party by 1892 had gathered enough strength—and made common cause with the Knights of Labor—to hold a major political convention in Omaha. The proposals made there, for the most part, eventually found their way into law. They included the eight-hour workday, the graduated (or "progressive") income tax, and the direct election of senators. The Populists also demanded direct government control of the railroads. In the end, the country never went that far. Instead, from 1887 to 1995, we had the Interstate Commerce Commission, our first major regulatory body.

So that was the good that resentment of elites—of "Them"—could produce. But the same emotion could take the country, or large swatches of it, down dark and scary roads. We are always searching for conspiracies of elites. The first one we found was the Freemasons. The secret but entirely benign association of broadminded do-gooders counted most of the Founding Fathers among its members. As the Founders grew old and the new nation was buffeted by economic growing pains, the Masons became a target—and then an obsession. A political party was formed to oppose them for what the Anti-Masonic Party's 1830 proceedings called their "baneful influence on morality and religion" and their "usurpation of the rights and privileges of the people." Masons were attacked from time to time, but most of the reaction was confined to politics. A score of the party's members were elected to Congress in the 1830s and 1840s. To this day, there is lively traffic on the Internet in Masonic conspiracy theories.

In the name of seeking fairness and a more perfect union, Populist reformers have sometimes been highly selective about the people for whom they fight. A good example was "Pitchfork Ben" Tillman, the avowedly proud racist governor of South Carolina in the 1890s. He was a Populist Party ally, but his anger against the powers that be was exercised on behalf of white farmers only. He spread resentment against the usual suspects—bankers, the railroads, Yankees—but added his own state's African Americans to the mix. He supported the Populists' platform, but had his own codicil: a state constitutional convention that, in 1895, disenfranchised every black voter in the state and instituted "Jim Crow" segregation laws—all in the name of fighting the elites.

Radio is made for resentment: a semi-anonymous megaphone through which to denounce distant, aloof powers. The first tribune of broadcast populism was the template for many that followed. Father Charles Coughlin was a Catholic radio preacher in Detroit in the 1930s. He was an early supporter of Franklin Roosevelt's New Deal, which he called "Christ's Deal," as well. But he increasingly came to view the Depression—and the Roosevelt administration—as the result of secret manipulations by a conspiracy of bankers, communists, and, above all, Jews. FDR's Irish Catholic allies denounced him. The Vatican halfheartedly tried to silence him. Only Pearl Harbor and World War II finally robbed him of his stupendous influence. At his height, it was estimated that a third of the country listened to his broadcast.

It was a signal achievement of the Reagan-Bush years—and a crucial reason why they existed at all—that conservatives and Republicans were able to sanitize and redeploy radio resentment on their own behalf. Rather than featuring economic populism, these new secular evangelists attacked what they viewed as the nation's "cultural" elites—the metropolitan Democrats and liberals who favored abortion, gun control, gay marriage, bans on prayer in public school, and the like. The Founding Father of this new iteration of populism was, of course, Rush Limbaugh. It didn't matter that he broadcast from Manhattan and Palm Beach, or that he was a multimillionaire cover boy for *Cigar Afficionado* magazine. He was a serious guy with a deep grasp of the issues and a huge, loyal following. And he was not one of Them. He was one of Us.

Two Democratic parties showed up in Boston in July 2004, one at the plush Four Seasons Hotel, the other everywhere else in town. The Democrats' convention that summer was a stark display of what one of the party's presidential candidates, Senator John Edwards, had called "the two Americas." One America was rich and getting richer, the other was treading water economically; one was rising in political influence to heights unreached since the Roaring Twenties, the other was losing clout in public debate; one enjoyed access to the presidential nominee, Senator John Kerry, at fund-raisers and exclusive parties with movie stars and millionaires, the other was eating peanuts at the local bars. It all seemed somehow unfair, or at least not very Democratic.

The Democrats considered themselves the "party of the people," and they had the history and tradition to prove it. But in the early twenty-first century, they had divided themselves into upper and lower kingdoms for one fundamental reason: the need to raise cash. Modern national campaigns had become insatiable vacuums of money; more than a billion dollars would be spent on that year's election. The money was divided into different legal (and some not quite so legal) categories: "direct" and "independent," "hard" and "soft," "primary" and "general." All of it in the end was funneled into the same machine. And feeding that machine required not just small contributions, and not just the infusion of manpower from labor unions, but cold, hard cash, and lots of it.

Then, in the 2008 campaign, something very big happened. Internet fund-raising came of age. First tapped by Howard Dean in 2004, the Internet provided a gusher of support for two candidates who claimed to be outsiders. One of them was about as far outside as you could be— Libertarian Ron Paul. The other was the far more mainstream Senator Barack Obama, who raised approximately $70 million on the Internet in 2007—an astonishing total. "I'm not the establishment candidate," he told me earlier in the year. "I couldn't run without the Internet." It was changing the balance of power in American politics.

Joe Trippi made a living—a good one—as a campaign strategist, but he seemed far too disorganized and distracted to be very effective at it. His clothes were vaguely Italian—a silk shirt, perhaps, or shiny sharkskin pants—but in a bargain-basement, never-been-pressed way. He had a habit of stuffing crucial campaign documents into his overcoat and promptly forgetting about them, sometimes for weeks. In campaign season, you would see him in a hotel lobby in, say, Iowa or New Hampshire, deep in thought. He would be in what looked like a hurry, but he never seemed to disappear from view.

Instead, he would hang by the elevator and . . . talk. It was a Tiber of talk: low, friendly, conspiratorial, constant, sometimes overflowing dangerously. Details varied from campaign to campaign, but the gist was the same. Only he understood what was going on in the race—which he was now going to explain to you. Only he (and now you) understood how everything worked (or, rather, didn't), how it would all fit together in the campaign, how the insiders and the establishment had no idea what really was happening in the country, how his candidate would ride these unseen forces to victory. The theme was always the same: The big shots, the befogged of Washington and the big media, had no clue about the concerns of America. Still, America would rise up, finally, to salvage the system.

Trippi came by his disdain for the insiders honestly. It was the sum and substance of his biography. His immigrant father ran a flower shop in a hardscrabble neighborhood in east-central Los Angeles. Crime and drugs were only a few doors away in a riot-torn city. Trippi's prize possession was a television set through which he could view a wider world. There, on TV, he found his inspiration: Robert F. Kennedy. Their shared Catholic faith was one bond. So, too, was youth. Trippi was among the legion of Baby Boomers who responded to Bobby—always "Bobby"—as one of their own. Kennedy approached life and politics with an idealistic, emotional zeal that transcended, indeed seemed outside of, traditional campaigning. Bobby's campaign motto became famous: "Some men see things as they are and ask, 'Why?' I dream things that never were and ask, 'Why not?' "

Trippi had another, even more powerful connection to RFK. The candidate was murdered in April 1968 at the Ambassador Hotel, only blocks from the Trippi family apartment. "I had wanted to go see him but couldn't," he told me years later. "The thought that I was so close, and that he was killed so nearby, freaked me out."

The death of his hero inspired him. In college at San Jose State in the early 1970s, Trippi developed a knack for organizing other people to ask, "Why not?" Eager to honor the memory of RFK with a statement on race relations, Trippi chose as his target South Africa and its infamous apartheid laws. He set up a petition drive with what was then a novel aim: to change the investment policy of the public school. In what companies, he demanded to know, was the school's board of trustees investing? If any of those companies were doing business in South Africa, San Jose State should "divest" those holdings. What began as an obscure and rather arcane protest eventually shook the state higher-education system, and even got the attention of the then-governor, Democrat Jerry Brown. The governor wanted to meet the person who had put together such a media-savvy (and ultimately successful) crusade. He was astonished to find that the mastermind was a nineteen-year-old immigrant's son.

So began Trippi's life as a professional political outsider. He was a Democrat, but his views otherwise were hard to pigeonhole. He didn't have a ten-point program; his focus was on making the "system" responsive to average folks. To do so, he would find clever new organizational techniques that in themselves became part, if not the core, of his message. For Trippi, the act of inspiring people—and the use of novel communications methods to do it—was as important, if not more important, than any specific policy goal other than the one he started with in college: bet-ter relations between the races.

Over the years he worked for a wide variety of candidates, starting at ground level with local officials in San Jose. He signed on for duty in Sen-ator Ted Kennedy's 1980 presidential campaign. Not only was the candi-date a Kennedy, he was challenging a sitting president for the Democratic nomination. Perfect. When Kennedy's challenge fell short, Trippi signed on with Tom Bradley, who in 1981 became the first African American mayor of Los Angeles. The following year, gearing up to help Bradley in his statewide run for governor, Trippi bought an early generation, Paleo-lithic DEC computer for use in the campaign.

It was a pioneering technological move, widely considered one of the first in-house deployments of computers in a campaign. After Bradley lost, Trippi signed up with Walter Mondale, helping him win the 1984 Democratic nomination by using a new—and much-criticized—method of funneling union money into the campaign through independent "del-egate committees." Then it was on to Gary Hart in 1987, Dick Gephardt in 1988, and Jerry Brown in 1992. That campaign involved another techno-organizational novelty: the candidate promoting his own "800"-number contribution phone line during debates.

The vectors of Trippi's life and craft intersected dramatically in 2003, in Dr. Howard Dean's antiwar, anti-establishment—and Internet-based—campaign for the Democratic nomination. Until it fizzled (partly, Trippi's critics said, due to his chaotic nonmanagement), the Dean insur-gency was the perfect union of message and technology. The powers that be were not listening to the deep anti–Iraq War sentiment of the rank and file, Dean said; the insiders literally couldn't hear that rage, Trippi said, because they had no idea what was being said in the new grass roots of politics, the Internet. Dean rocketed to the top, fueled by $40 million in small donations solicited on his website, and by an unprecedented word-of-Web organizing campaign. After his Dean experience, Trippi wrote a book with a modest title: *The Revolution Will Not Be Televised: Democracy, the Internet, and the Overthrow of Everything.*

But he hadn't really overthrown *anything.* The election of a black mayor had been a triumph, and an important milestone in race relations in America. But all of the national candidates he had ever worked for in a serious way—Kennedy, Mondale, Hart, Gephardt, Brown, and Dean—

had lost. Still, although winning was important, Trippi was the kind of figure who relished the fight, and who thought that there would be long-range victories that perhaps he couldn't even see. The idea was to keep the blood flowing in the body politic. He had a modestly successful business advising corporate clients in San Jose, where he had extensive high-tech connections.

He couldn't resist another race, another chance to take a run at the big shots. In the spring of 2007, former senator John Edwards called. Just as important, so did Edwards's wife, Elizabeth. As a result of her various personal travails—the loss of a son in an auto accident, her own battles with cancer—she had developed something close to a sense of awe for the ability of the Internet to connect people to one another. She thought that her husband's second run for the presidency could plug into the power in the way Dean had tried, but ultimately failed, to do.

Trippi told her—and her husband agreed—that the campaign needed to change its tone and tangent. In 2004, Edwards had been a sitting senator. He had since left the Senate and returned to North Carolina. Now, in 2007 and 2008, he could be the outsider/insurgent. His target: the way Washington did business. He would decry the capital elites, the corporate lobbyists, and fellow media travelers who had anesthetized the Beltway Democrats into giving America a trade policy that was draining away jobs, a foreign policy that was spilling blood, and a tax policy that was siphoning trillions from the Treasury.

In his first campaign, in 2004, Edwards had mostly been sunlight and togetherness, flashing his Hollywood-handsome smile and talking in upbeat tones about uniting the "two Americas." He sounded at times like a conscience-stricken rich man (which he was), talking at every stop about the plight of the poor (which he had once been) in a wealthy society. Three years later he was back with a far more sweeping critique. The entire middle class was getting screwed, too—indeed, everyone in America except for the plutocrats at the top of the heap in a hedge-fund-driven economy was getting screwed. It was time for a crusade to rewire the system and take power back from the elites.

Or so Edwards said—in an angry, confrontational voice that was nothing like the Southern syrup of 2004. By the summer, Trippi had Edwards in full anti-establishment cry. Edwards's enemy: "the Washington lobbyists." The audience was an appropriate one, one that Trippi knew well from his Dean days: an annual convention of "progressive" political bloggers. The group had started as a loose association of antiwar websites but had grown into what amounted to a new constituency of reformers looking to take over and transform the Democratic Party. They were meeting in, of all places, Chicago, where a member of the old Democratic Machine had once famously declared: "This town ain't ready for reform."

Reform was Edwards's theme. Edwards noted that the Democrats in Congress had hurried to pass a new "campaign-finance" law before going home to recess. He expressed contempt for what he implied was their rear-covering efforts. "The Democrats don't have to wait for a new law," he said. "The Democratic Party can end the game today, and from this day forward, and say to Washington lobbyists: Your money is no good here."

Edwards was just getting warmed up as he spoke to a ballroom of the "netroots" activists. "The system in Washington is broken," he declared. "It's rigged to serve the interests of those with the most money to throw around, rather than the best interests of the American people." Then he went on to imply that Senator Hillary Rodham Clinton and even Senator Barack Obama were part of what was wrong with the system. "The type of change America needs will never be achieved if we just replace the insiders from one party with the insiders from another party."

Would Edwards win? It seemed unlikely, especially since Obama had elbowed his way into the role of outsider and change agent. He had established credentials—president of the *Harvard Law Review,* no less. But as an African American from the South Side of Chicago, it was hard to depict him as an insider. To Trippi, it almost didn't matter. His candidate was saying what needed to be said. As the Iowa caucuses approached, Trippi could be found one night closing down the bar at the old Hotel Fort Des Moines. The young organizers who surrounded him were not from Edwards's campaign, they were from Barack Obama's. So what? There was too much power in unaccountable hands. Voices were not being heard.

As the lights came on in the bar, he started leading the kids in Obama's signature campaign chant: "Fired up! Ready to go!" Somebody had to shout, Trippi believed, and it might as well be him.

CONCLUSION

When I first envisioned this book in the spring of 2005, I saw it as a reporter's act of explanation, an effort to map what I had come to see, after years on the politics beat, as the double-helix DNA of American public life. But in the years since, the country's mood has darkened and, without my intending it, this book acquired a second purpose: to offer reassurance and hope to readers who may need both.

Optimism is our national faith, a secular religion that forms the essence of our identity. In the fall of 2007, however, Americans were restless in the pews of the church of good news. Most of us doubted that the threat of terrorism had been quelled or that the $1 trillion war in Iraq, in which 4,000 Americans had died and 25,000 had been wounded, had made us safer. Perhaps that is why only a third of Baby Boomer adults thought that their children would enjoy lives as prosperous and contented as theirs. With gasoline prices rising and home prices falling, middle-income families were plunged into the abyss between rich and poor, which was at its widest since the 1920s. Latino immigrants, once welcomed for their sunny industry, had come to be seen in many communities as an invading force, burdening schools and hospitals and disrupting the settled ways and rhythms of American life.

The world beyond our shores looked equally bleak. In an understandable and in many ways justified response to the attacks of 9/11, we had gone to war and thrown up barriers, but rather than cheer us on, most of the rest of the world eventually concluded that we were abandoning our own values and sanity. Global geopolitics morphed into perilous new shapes. The Soviet Union was long gone, but Vladimir Putin was erecting a new, hydrocarbon-based hydra in its place. In Latin America, a Venezuelan neo-Castro arose with the oil and inclination to hector us. From Andalusia to Indonesia, Muslim clerics and terrorists who claimed to speak for a billion people cried havoc over Palestine and Iraq, and vowed to restore the continent-spanning caliphate of old.

In the worldwide marketplace, the United States faced the prospect of losing the dominant role it had played since World War II. With oil at nearly $100 a barrel and the European currency suddenly in demand as the preferred denominator of deals, the dollar fell to record modern lows as we piled up debt on the balance sheets of trade and national finance. Spending beyond our means on war and waste, we found ourselves in an economic riptide. If we raised interest rates to lure investment, we risked a recession. But the same might result if we raised taxes. And yet we needed more revenue—lots of it—to pay for a Baby Boom that was about to enter the arms of Medicare and Social Security. How much more could we borrow? How much harder would we have to work? How much of our patrimony would we have to sell?

And all of this occurred at a time when our political system, if that term was not an oxymoron, seemed unable to fulfill its basic mission, which is to generate serious debate on real issues, find common ground in workable deals, and establish capable leadership. Candidates spent most of their time raising money; playing to the "base," not the center, seemed the only route to power; the media too often served as circus impresarios, or boxing promoters, and not forums for something more, and deeper.

In response to this litany, the message of this book is this: We need to calm down, get engaged, and look for leadership. We have been here before: the seeming gridlock; the sudden, uncharacteristic loss of faith in the future; the sense that we cannot produce leaders capable of dealing with real problems. Facing dispirit and danger, we have always found in our storehouse of conflicting, paradoxical traditions a way forward. We have done so through civil war and waves of political paranoia, in the face of would-be global dictators, in times of rampant profit and smug bureaucracy.

History is hope, the evidence shows. We were born in crushing debt after the Revolution, for example, and worked our way out of it through the ferocious arguments of the Hamiltonians and Jeffersonians. We have felt overwhelmed by waves of immigration before, starting with the Germans in the early nineteenth century, followed by the Jews, Italians, and Slavs a century later. In response, we started with the Know-Nothings and ended with the settlement-house movement. Before we decided to take on Hitler and Imperial Japan—before the bombs dropped at Pearl Harbor—we spent a decade debating America's course in often-bitter terms that stretched back to the days of Monroe and Adams. We have endured bouts of political xenophobia and fear, from the anti-French riots of the Federalist days to the Palmer Raids to the paralyzing, accusatory reign of Senator Joe McCarthy's Red Scare. Existing political parties have broken down, ceasing to dig down into the bedrock of the Thirteen American Arguments. When they do, new parties emerge. The Whigs vanished and the Republican Party arose in the mid-nineteenth century; we may yet see another earthquake of that kind if the Republicans and Democrats of today do not do their part.

I will admit that perhaps we have been lucky in our leadership. This is not a book about the nature of American political leadership—though that is what I have spent most of my time doing on the campaign trail. Still, writing this book has given me a theory. Our best presidents are those who embrace and embody the contradictions and paradoxes of our country. Fate and fortitude allow them to see and even feel both (all) sides of the Thirteen American Arguments. That gift enables them to assemble pieces of enduring ideas and traditions in new ways to meet new challenges.

Consider for a moment the presidents we tend to regard as great or near-great. Noble in bearing but self-effacing, George Washington always seemed to have had responsibility thrust upon him (or was careful to make it look that way), rather than to have sought it. He made a nation in that same fashion, mixing bold military leadership with caution in executive authority. Abraham Lincoln literally lived the Arguments of his day, and not just the regional and tribal ones. He was a dirt-poor kid who became a powerful railroad lawyer. He could see the moral claims of both economic Americas. He was a Southerner by birth who led the Union against the Confederacy, a skeptic of establishments who left behind a muscular, continental industrial nation poised to exert itself on the global stage. As a backwoods boatman, he saw and loved the lonely beauty of the rivers, and knew the countryside and the states, and valued their prerogatives and frontier spirit. Yet he stood for, and wielded, awesome federal power. He kept his distance from organized religion, yet perhaps that is why his evocations of God's grace were so inspiring.

If you look, you can find that same ability to bridge and embody conflicting sides of our arguments in other presidents we admire: in Jackson, the Roosevelts, Truman, and even Ronald Reagan, who cut taxes but blessed a Social Security deal that raised them; who called out an "evil empire" and then made a realist's deal with it.

We have to hope we can find more leaders of this kind. There is no reason to believe we cannot. Back on the campaign trail, I am looking for them now.

And there is this: In a country based on individuals and their families and friends, system-wide failure is less likely. We aren't one vast, vulnerable mainframe. We are the ultimate in distributed computing.

All we have to do—and it is not easy, admittedly—is debate (frankly, even fiercely) who we are and want to be. The political genetic material is there; our gene pool, thanks to the foresight of the Founders and four hundred years' worth of immigration, is that deep. "There is nothing wrong with America," Bill Clinton declared in his first inaugural address in 1993, "that cannot be cured by what is right with America." We have to watch, and get involved—as Americans have been wont to do. Racism at the turn of the last century produced the NAACP; the Espionage Act of 1917 led to the creation of the ACLU; the antiprayer and pro-abortion court decisions of the sixties led to what we now call the "Religious Right." It's the way we work.

It is up to each of us to decide which parts of our heritage—which sides of which arguments—are the "right" ones to meet the moment. If this book in any way enhances that process, then my two aims—to define and inspire—become one.

So let the American Arguments begin—again.

AFTERWORD

We were flying from Reno to Albuquerque when Senator Barack Obama's aides waved me up to the front of the campaign plane. In the living room–like cabin, I found the candidate in a reclining chair, a pile of papers on his lap. I had interviewed him for *Newsweek* several times, but now I was on a different, more limited mission: to give him a copy of *The Thirteen American Arguments*. He glanced at the cover and took a moment to study the contents page. "I guess you've got all the answers to all the arguments here," Obama said with a smile.

I took his smile to be a wry, knowing one. As a professor of constitutional law and a shrewd politician, Obama understood the idea that had taken me years of reporting and two years of research to grasp. In this country there *are* no permanent "answers." There is no dogma, no orthodoxy. Arguing is what we were born and bred to do. It's what we need to do. No sooner do we settle an iteration of a dispute—generated by one era's facts and frictions—than we start another.

So I smiled, too. "You taught con law," I said, "so you know there are no answers in there!" Then, with his aides watching impatiently, I gave him the gist of my ambitious (and perhaps rather lunatic) attempt to explain all four hundred years of our public life in three hundred pages about the thirteen enduring debates that define and inspire us. "The conventional wisdom is that we argue too much," I concluded, "but I say in the book that we don't argue enough—about the right things, the deep things."

Obama nodded, seemingly in agreement. But he shot me a wary glance, too. Arguing wasn't what he was selling; national unity was.

Crafted and sold over two years, Obama's message was that we had endured too much combat for its own sake; that pettiness, fear mongering, and dog-eat-dog division had paralyzed our politics. He promised debate—actually listening to other views and carefully explaining one's own positions and conclusions—but not more bullying from the pulpit of the presidency.

He offered as proof of his intentions his own campaign and biography. Obama's Net-based campaign was a digital exercise in shared experience, cooperative creativity, and the desire for community. His personal life and even DNA were symbols of reconciliation: white and black, old and young, local and global. Bursting onto the scene in 2004 with a speech to Democrats in Boston, Obama had declared, "There is not a liberal America and a conservative America; there is a United States of America!"

So, on the campaign plane, he was not about to agree with my premise: that our heritage and habit of argument is what makes us unique and keeps us free. However messy (even bloody) the process, it is indispensable. "I'll take a look at the book," he promised. I happily returned to my seat in the back of the plane.

More than three months later, on a clear night by the shores of Lake Michigan, Obama stood alone on a stage before a crowd of two hundred thousand adoring supporters. He had just won the presidential election by an impressive margin. His victory speech was the exclamation point at the end of a long sermon to the country. On that day, he said, with their votes, Americans had "sent a message to the world that we have never been a collection of red states and blue states: We are, and always will be, the United States of America."

Accepting the cheers, he urged Americans to sing politics in a new key. "Let us resist the temptation," he said, "to fall back on the same partisanship and pettiness and immaturity that has poisoned our politics for so long." As if to prove his point, he reached out to foes. "And to those Americans whose support I have yet to earn," he said, "I may not have won your vote, but I hear your voices. I need your help, and I will be your president, too."

Watching the feed of the speech on a television monitor at NBC News in New York, I saw a man who seemed to believe in his words of hope and unity. But I also saw a somber, reflective character, whose writings and speeches—whose presidential campaign—bespoke a realistic sense of the American experience. I had listened to him enough, talked to him enough, and watched him on the trail enough to know that he understood the challenges he faced.

The main one was that he would now have to argue, maybe even vehemently, for his vision of how he wanted to change America.

After the 2008 election, voters might have assumed—or wanted to assume—that a season of peace and silence would descend on our public life. No way. There *was* one such moment on the calendar: Inauguration Day. That was it for quiet. The world was spinning too fast.

If you've read this book, you know that I don't mind the noise. I welcome it. The season for our arguments never ends, nor should it, and there was no chance that it would as 2008 turned into 2009. The final month of the race was run in the midst of a global economic crisis. Whatever the voters' view of the contest and its outcome, they had little choice after November but to turn their eyes and minds immediately to the task ahead: debating the course of the new Obama administration as it confronted daunting challenges at home and abroad.

There was hope in the air as Obama took center stage, but much to discuss—more, it seemed, than at almost any time in the past century. We had to deal with the seizing up of the world's credit markets and the consequent demise of private (American) ownership of Wall Street and the country's largest banks. A recession, perhaps a deep one, proved inescapable. At the same time the federal government spent vast sums on trying to bail out global capitalism, it faced colossal debt and deficits—on its own balance sheet and in everything from roads and research to health care, education, and global esteem. We faced competition from rising or renewed powers—China, India, Russia, and the European Union—and, if and when global markets recovered, a bidding war for commodities ranging from crude oil and coal to concrete and copper. Nor could Americans dismiss the nightmare visions of another terrorist attack or an unprecedented climate disaster. Beyond all the financial and the physical was the psychic. Even after the election, voters (not to mention investors) harbored a nagging sense that, as a country, we did not know, or could not quite decide, how to define ourselves in and for the twenty-first century.

All of this would (and should) fuel the next round of American argument. The idea of a respite from political contention is appealing, but unrealistic, and, I argue in this book, fatal.

And yet there are doubts—my own included. If you write a book proclaiming the virtue of argument, you had better be willing to consider carefully conflicting views and contradictory evidence and respond. I am, and now I will.

I say the following with good cheer: I should have expected British friends to genially dismiss my assertion that their American cousins are unique. Matt Frei, the BBC's Washington-based anchor, reminded me that there is no more argumentative person on earth than, say, an Italian driver on a narrow Roman street. Our mother country, he said, launched the modern idea of parliamentary debates. In that sense, and in some others (an abundance of lawyers, judges, and courts, for example), we are nothing more than a second-generation copy of the argumentative English id.

All true enough, but my thesis remains undisturbed: Other countries, including England, *evolved* into something other than what they were originally. We remain the only place that was never really choked by the grip of heaven-sent, top-down thinking.

Another BBC headliner, Katty Kay, suggested that I had erred in focusing on politics rather than Main Street culture. Americans do not really like to discuss—let alone confront each other about—profound topics, she has noticed in her years as a reporter here. The English feel freer to dissent, she said. It is the paradox of England's stratified, formerly feudal society that it prizes, because of its very history, eccentricity and principled defiance of authority. A mass democracy, by contrast, is liable to suffocate itself in its own leveling conformity. In saying this, Katty was following a line of sharp-eyed, distinguished foreigners that stretches back to Tocqueville.

I disagree, and I cite another of Tocqueville's observations for support. We are, as he pointed out, a nation of inveterate joiners. So the same social instincts that mass produce conformity can also produce engines of useful, churning conflict: our political parties, interest groups, reform movements—the vast panoply of "associations" that the observant Frenchman celebrated. True, Americans shun eccentrics. But we were not engineered to draw inspiration primarily from solitary dissidents. We're less about Solzhenitsyns than soldiers, less about Cassandras than about civil rights organizers and suffragettes. Americans generally join a group to raise a ruckus.

Even if I am right about our makeup, that doesn't answer other, equally valid, doubts about my description of our nature and its value. A crucial one is this: Do campaigns advance the cause of argument, or make a mockery of it? Do they facilitate and frame real debates that allow voters to make substantive choices? In theory, presidential elections are the zenith of our argumentative national identity. I say "in theory," however, because we all know that campaigns are a maddening mix of Chautauqua and circus, Lincoln and Douglas—but also of Laurel and Hardy and Batman and The Joker. For better or worse, campaigns are who we are, which is why we are right to ask if they work.

So did the 2008 presidential campaign in fact contribute anything useful to our endless American conversation? If you know our history, you know that we should never confuse ourselves with the Academy in Athens. (And even there, the philosopher-politicians resorted to hemlock on occasion.) At times in 2008, the campaigns took breathtaking liberties with the facts and toyed cynically with deep and dangerous emotions. John McCain's team, reflecting their boss, was brash and in-your-face about it, as if lying about his foe was a glorious, whatever-it-takes moment of combat heroism. As for Obama, Harvard Law notwithstanding, he was no innocent. His "yes we can" message was inspiring, as the election results showed. His detailed grasp of issues was impressive. And yet he imperiously waved off McCain's plea to hold ten town hall debates, a series that may have elevated the tone overall. Instead, Obama at times tried to show how tough he was by letting his folks play as rough as the Republicans. Still, the 2008 campaign was hardly our worst. We muddled through.

In spite of these obstacles, the candidates and their running mates often *did* express or embody aspects of the thirteen foundational arguments I have outlined as the essence of our national life. They *did* touch on many big questions, even if they did not always do so in edifying style. You can find evidence of all of the Thirteen American Arguments in speeches and debates, even amid the visual rubble and Net-based babble of spots about Paris Hilton or "lipstick on a pig" or in gauzy rhetoric about Change. Here are four:

The Limits of Individualism Governor Sarah Palin ridiculed Obama's career-launching work as a community organizer but, in his view and that of his supporters, the job was emblematic of his message: that rugged individualism, however deep-set in the American grain, is not the *only* Ameri-

can answer to our prayers. Government, when properly deployed, is an expression of, and delivery vehicle for, another of our core values: the duty to
give a hand up, though not a handout, so that everyone can have a fair
chance at the American Dream. Republicans offered their own traditional
but still-vital response: We do not dare trust government, especially the one
in Washington, unless we put a Republican in charge to limit its reach and
prevent it from destroying freedom, creativity, and initiative, not to mention the market.

The framework shaped the debate on how to deal with the biggest crisis in global capitalism since the Great Depression: the collapse of credit
systems. Obama's instincts were those of a community organizer, favoring
systemic change; McCain, while conceding the need for regulation, em-
phasized individuals and their mistakes.

Soon enough, the candidates' clashing instincts were overwhelmed by
the sheer magnitude of the mess, as government (not just ours but the
world's) struggled to revive markets that had crippled themselves by running wild and without rules for far too long. Obama and McCain tossed
off proposal after proposal, but none approached the awesome scope and
sweep of the actions of the Bush administration itself was forced to take.

In the end, the government had no choice but to vastly expand
its role as the last-resort guarantor of debt and credit worldwide. Party
and ideological labels, as always, meant nothing. George W. Bush—a
self-proclaimed conservative Republican—had expanded Washington's
reach, intrusiveness, and indebtedness at a greater rate than had any president since Franklin Roosevelt. Soon enough, that would start another
argument.

A Fair, "More Perfect" Union By 2008, most voters had long since
concluded that Washington was a corrupt mess. As a result, the candidates clashed over this question more than any other: Which of them was
the *real* reformer? Obama offered himself as a newbie with smarts, en-
dowed with the brains and the beyond-the-Beltway common sense to
have known that Iraq would be a disaster. Supported by grassroots, Net-
based donors, he claimed that he would ignore the capital's corrupting
cadre of lobbyists. McCain's pitch was more complicated. Years earlier, he
had made his name as a foe of moneyed interests, but that maverick history had been diluted by his more recent embrace of Bush's donors and

the business tax cuts they favored. So McCain chose to stress culture over economics. He did so by picking Palin as his running mate. She hailed from a small town in the corner of the continent and bragged about her lack of experience as if it were a virtue. Together, the GOP ticket claimed their anti-establishment bona fides by expressing scorn for eastern, Ivy League, cosmopolitan elites and their mainstream media fellow travelers.

Who Is a Person? This first and most fundamental argument was central, too. It could not have been otherwise in a year that saw the advent of the first African American major-party nominee and two top-level female candidates, Palin and Democratic senator Hillary Rodham Clinton. In the privacy of the voting booth, Americans were free to express not only their choice, but also their view of personhood.

Without saying it in so many words, Obama's campaign revived the argument in a new form: Do we believe in the idea of personhood enough to choose as president the son of an African goatherd? Ironically, but perhaps inevitably, Obama himself was forced to deal with the question of his race in defensive, negative terms: Hadn't he countenanced racism in his own black church? Rather than cry racism himself; rather than lashing out at his critics, Obama chose to distance himself from the ranting Rev. Jeremiah Wright by recounting our sad, centuries-long history of mistrust and misunderstanding, and vowing to help us surmount. It was a masterstroke of political maneuvering because it offered something more: understanding and hope.

On the night Obama declared victory, he had every right to exult—not on his own behalf, but on behalf of the country. "If there is any one out there," he declared, "who still doubts that America is a place where all things are possible, who still wonders if the dream of our Founders is alive in our time, who still questions the power of our democracy, tonight is your answer."

From that night forward, the personhood debate is settled in one of its forms. No one can argue that DNA is a bar to reaching the highest levels of American society. To be sure, there are other limits in the accidents of birth—poverty, lack of education, a crime-ridden neighborhood, poor health and health care—but not race. That one is over. The mixed-race son of Kansas and Kenya ended that one.

It only took four centuries.

War and Diplomacy Beneath the harsh, accusatory language, the candidates had a real conversation about how to answer the basic foreign policy questions: Do we need to change the world to survive in it? Or is it better to deal with the planet's powers as they are, however distasteful or dangerous? McCain, with a turbocharged boost from Palin, all but shouted the "we must change the world" mantra. Obama, the product and proponent of a more intuitively internationalist view, argued that the shrewder course was to see the world through the eyes and lives of others. In that he had the backing of his own running mate, the globetrotting senator Joe Biden. Both sides claimed to be "realists." The question was not what the world was really like—everyone agreed it was a perilous place—but how to deal with it.

So yes, the 2008 campaign reflected the architecture of American argument. And yet it often failed to be an engine of genuine, meaningful debate.

There were several reasons for this failure. Sometimes there was a fear-based conspiracy of silence on the part of the candidates. Immigration was an example. Obama didn't want to dwell on the issue because his proposal—amounting to amnesty for perhaps 12 million illegals—might alienate white working-class voters in northern industrial states. McCain shied away for the opposite demographic reason. He feared that his own proposal, which had come to rely heavily on punitive measures, would offend Hispanic voters in the Southwest. So both candidates kept quiet.

Some problems seemed so vast and insoluble that the candidates balked at suggesting a detailed line of argument about them. The more urgent and cosmic the crisis, the less they wanted to talk about it in detail, at least at first. The credit crisis was an example. Through the spring and summer of 2008, it was as if the very topic was simply too frightening to be uttered by name—the Lord Voldemort of presidential politics. Finally, in late September, the collapse of credit markets, banks, and the Dow left Obama and McCain no choice but to speak up. They pilloried their favorite villains: McCain, Democrats and Washington bureaucrats; Obama, "Wall Street greed." But events moved too swiftly for either candidate. They never proposed comprehensive answers.

The same sin of silence applied to the gargantuan federal debt. It seemed to be a sleep-inducing subject. And yet, in 2008, the government was liable, according to one reasonable estimate, for *$53 trillion* in payments to its citizens and to foreign creditors. We either had to pay, slash benefits to future generations, or let the dollar become worthless scrip. The candidates had no desire to discuss so much bad news; the solutions seemed too draconian to mention.

Until the credit crisis hit, candidates, their handlers, and their allegedly independent outriders preferred to talk about one another's personal shortcomings; manipulate symbols and moments of exultation or fear; and traffic in gossip, dirt, and innuendo.

Voters soon learned the litany and, depending on their prejudices, tended to believe what they wanted to believe. For example: Obama was a closet Muslim and a devoted friend of a retired and unrepentant American terrorist; McCain was a doddering old man, out of touch except for the sensation in his trigger finger; Palin was a pitchfork populist rube and hypocritical evangelical libertine; Biden was, well, Biden. None of the trash-talking was unprecedented in the history of campaign discourse. But that didn't make it more worthy.

Obama's campaign was paradoxical. He called for an end to division in the midst of asking the American people to choose him and reject competing men and ideas. However much he called us to a higher purpose, Obama issued a scalpel-sharp critique of the Bush years, an era Obama derided as full of selfishness, dissolute, feckless governance and wrongheaded military adventures. In his speeches, Obama deployed a civil, accommodating, even lofty tone. He always seemed to be speaking more in sorrow than in anger. His campaign machinery, meanwhile, fed the Republicans into the rhetorical wood chipper.

The politicians weren't the only ones at fault. The media was, too. There were some bright media moments—the illuminating and instructive presidential debates, which drew huge television audiences and allowed Obama to exhibit the cerebral cool that got him elected. The debates were the exception, however. Most of 2008 was a media free-for-all of ideological flavors and agendas, with no one outlet, or combination of outlets, able to play arbiter and umpire of argument.

The media's loss of authority was accompanied by a scramble for ratings and circulation. Websites, pushing their particularized slants and obsessions, dominated the conversation as they sought to grab advertising dollars. Beleaguered and confused, leaders of the staid old media assumed that they had no choice but to follow. Former senator Sam Nunn, a sober sort who had spent a decade focusing on the obscure but profound problem of "loose nukes," complained to me that the country had become "obsessed with the vivid at the expense of the vital." It took a global recession—both vivid and vital—to focus our minds.

It's fair to say that we didn't argue as well or as productively as we should have in the campaign of 2008. But that was only the half of it.

The moment the election ended, another question arose again, this one about governing as opposed to campaigning. And it went to the heart of my case for the indispensability of argument. Isn't more debate the last thing we need? That, after all, was the centerpiece of Obama's message: Yes we can all get together. Haven't we become so mired in partisanship and gridlock—with Washington becoming so immobilized—that we must cease and desist?

There are reasons to think so. In Congress, most of the arguments in recent years seemed little more than a pantomime designed to elicit campaign contributions. The artful creation of safe districts led House members to play only to their base; senators, no longer lordly independent actors of their states, became creatures of nation-spanning, vertically integrated lobbies and ideological groups. The result, concluded Nolan McCarty of Princeton, was the most gridlocked Congress in one hundred fifty years, unable to do anything but shout across the aisle and block all legislation. The last time things were this bad, McCarty pointed out, was in the aftermath of the Civil War—an interesting if disturbing parallel. Obama's victory brought with it a surge in Democratic strength, but did that mean an end to legislative paralysis? No one was ready to predict it.

In the White House, Bush administration officials had come to regard the very act of argument as a betrayal of their duty. After eight years of high-handed secrecy in the name of national security, President Bush and Vice President Dick Cheney left behind a new White House tradition: a refusal to acknowledge the need to make its case in public or even in secret. Obama promised—had been elected on the promise—to change all of that. His would be an administration of ongoing, transparent, candid conversation. We could only hope.

Washington, on the eve of the Obama years, seemed unable to make decisions—let alone the right ones.

As they waited for a new day, people who should have known better yearned for an end to all argument and for the imposition of something else: decision-making by fiat. At the Aspen Ideas Festival in the summer of 2008, I heard speakers openly wish for an overmastering force that would allow us (them) to plan our future. The prospect of catastrophic climate change was enough for author Thomas Friedman. In an amphitheater filled with two thousand of the country's best-educated and well-connected leaders, he dreamed aloud of his solution to our problems. "If only we could be China for one day," he said. I understand the instinct, but one day as China is one day too many.

No, there is no easy way out.

I appreciate Plato, but I side with Aristotle. The Founders admired the former, and assembled a republic based on his political physics. But the machine won't run unless we do what Aristotle would have us do, which is exploit to the fullest our unique destiny of freedom. We have no choice but to rely on who we are and who we must be. Arguing is what we were born to do.

The real question is: How do we do it better? If our disputes don't produce results, one reason is because we have lost a shared sense of—and pride in—ourselves as Americans. The most patriotic things we can do are to take part in the debate, and honor with all our hearts the humanity of whoever else does the same. Patriotism isn't merely a salute; it's the right to speak. Indeed, it is the very *act* of speaking.

Leadership is indispensable in making this work. Our best leaders instruct us on our own glorious if contentious history, and explain how to gather strength from our contractions in ways that meet the moment. This was the promise of Obama, an articulate man who had been a teacher, and who would have to be one again. In a world and a time of dangerous complexity, he would have to be—and wanted to be— explainer in chief.

The first speech I heard Obama give in person was at Georgetown University in the fall of 2006. His topic was energy and the environment; he had absorbed a series of mind-numbing complexities and now was playing them back in words and ideas that the rapt student audience seemed eager to hear and ingest. There was, frankly, nothing that remarkable in the content. We needed market incentive to promote efficiency, while at the same time mandating higher mileage standards; we had to promote new technology: solar, wind, biomass. It was green boilerplate.

But what mattered to the students was the sense of Obama himself. And that sense was of a reasonable man, smart enough to see all sides of all the arguments—and decent and confident enough as a person. He seemed, to them, to be the kind of fellow who would not let ego warp his view of the wise course to pursue. Obama has a judicious, even judicial quality about him, one that clearly voters found appealing after George Bush's rigid judgments.

If we need a teacher, and we do, we need an educated electorate even more. As I researched and wrote this book, simultaneously performing my daily rounds as a reporter for *Newsweek* and NBC, I came to understand that the key to our survival rests, above all, in educating ourselves and our children. We have no choice but to be the captains of our own ship, and the only way to learn how to navigate is to study the charts.

The seas are stormy. We are not philosopher kings. But I insist on asking: Is this a great country or what?

I glimpsed its maddening grandeur again, covering last year's conventions. The din in the street behind me on the *Hardball* set in Denver was so loud that I could barely hear Chris Matthews even though he was in shout mode. The MSNBC brain trust had decided to stage his show outdoors on an elevated set across from the train station during the Democratic convention. The idea was to plug him into the high-voltage current of the election season.

It worked. Americans love television, of course, but they love appearing on it more. As word spread across the Mile High City, if not the country, that MSNBC cameras were shooting live near Union Station, crowds materialized on cue. They were a rowdy lot, somewhere between cheerful, giddy, and faintly menacing: the fans and foes of the presidential contenders; the otherwise inspired or aggrieved, yelling at the top of their lungs about everything from abortion to Afghanistan; a guy with a bullhorn (not fair) who spent hours screaming that the 9/11 investigation was a coverup.

That crowd, eager and insistent, was an inspiring and unsettling sliver of our decibel democracy. Does it have to be so loud—or, worse, so nasty, divisive, and sometimes even contemptuous of the very idea of rational discourse? Only if we want to keep what God gave us.

At least that's my argument.

ACKNOWLEDGMENTS

I have many people to thank—for giving me the best job there is, that of reporter; for educating me in the headlines and history of our country; for instructing me in politics, journalism, and book writing; and for giving me the time and support I needed to turn a reporter's musings into *The Thirteen American Arguments*.

In a sense, this book is nothing more or less than a summary of what I have learned (so far) in more than two decades on the political beat at *Newsweek*. Editor Jon Meacham, my friend and confidant, counseled me on the project and made sure that I had time to complete it. The rest of *Newsweek*'s leadership was equally supportive: chairman Rick Smith; former editor Mark Whitaker (now a senior vice president at NBC), who gave me the initial go-ahead and sabbatical; also Alexis Gelber, Lally Weymouth, Dan Klaidman, Bret Begun, Debra Rosenberg, Ann McDaniel, Mark Miller, Deidre Depke, and Tom Watson.

In the magazine's Washington Bureau I am surrounded by the best of the best, starting with bureau chief Jeff Bartholet and Evan Thomas, a colleague of many years who is a historian and editor; columnist Robert Samuelson, who shared his expertise and love of big, animating ideas; Mike Isikoff and Eleanor Clift, longtime colleagues and the most inspiringly dogged of reporters; Mike Hirsh, who offered perspective on foreign policy; and Weston Kosova, whose humor, wit, and steadfast collegiality were invaluable. I also want to thank Holly Bailey, John Barry, Martha Brant, Daren Briscoe, Eve Conant, Jon Darman, Dan Ephron, Mark

Hosenball, Claudia Kalb, Gail Tacconelli, Rich Thomas, Steve Tuttle, Patricia Wingert, and Richard Wolffe. Although I have never been based at *Newsweek* headquarters in New York, I benefit from the wisdom, knowledge, and patience of many people there, chief among them Jonathan Alter, Nancy Cooper, Barbara Kantrowitz, George Hackett, and Steve Levy, as well as Allan Sloan (now of *Fortune*), Nancy Stadtman, Andrew Romano, Connie Wiley, Madeline Cohen, Barbara DiVittorio, Deborah Milan, Susan McVea, and Dave Friedman.

My other Manhattan journalistic home is 30 Rockefeller Center, headquarters of NBC and MSNBC. There, I want to thank Jeff Zucker, Steve Capus, Phil Griffin, Bill Wolff, Dan Abrams, Brian Williams, Keith Olbermann, Norah O'Donnell, Joe Scarborough, Matt Lauer, and Ann Curry. For encouragement and advice, and for accommodating my book-writing schedule, I owe thanks to the dedicated crew of *Countdown:* executive producer Izzy Povich, producers Amy Shuster and Greg Cockrell, and especially producer Katy Ramirez-Karp, who patiently listens to my off-air observations.

My editors and colleagues at MSNBC.com were considerate as well. They include Charlie Tillinghast, Russ Shaw, Jennifer Sizemore, Lauren Vicary, Mike Stuckey, Craig Staats, Tom Curry, Andrea Hamilton, and Kara Kearns.

In Washington, my second professional home is anywhere in the force field of Chris Matthews. Appearing on *Hardball* is in itself an education. His dedicated team of producers and reporters make it more so. They include David Shuster, Brooke Brower, Ann Klenk, Querry Robinson, Connie Patsalos, Vidhya Murugesan, and Tina Urbanksi. I also thank Rick Jefferson, Derbin Cabell, Robbi Blevins, George Toman, Carl Trost, Gary Lynn, Roland Woerner, and Nicole Iannucci of the *Hardball* team. I deeply value the friendship and advice of Tammy Haddad.

I have also learned from my fellow guests on the Sunday *Chris Matthews Show,* and from the show's executive producer, Nancy Nathan, and her deputies, Bill Hatfield and Mike Levine. I also thank other friends and colleagues in the Washington Bureau of NBC, including David Gregory, Andrea Mitchell, Pete Williams, and Lisa Myers.

I tip my hat (a baseball cap will have to do) to Don Imus, who first invited me on his show in 1998. He and his wife, Deirdre, are generous souls and friends.

For most reporters (certainly for me) there is no better—or instructive—company than that of colleagues in the trade. I talked to a number of them about the book and I want to mention them above the fold: E. J. Dionne of *The Washington Post* and Adam Nagourney of *The New York Times* patiently and supportively listened to me yak about this project early on. So did Jill Abramson of *The New York Times* and Arianna Huffington of *The Huffington Post*. Craig Shirley is a conservative activist, consultant, and historian of Ronald Reagan's campaigns, and he, too, listened to me early and often. Others in the legion of patience include: David Bradley, Michael Beschloss, Sally Bedell Smith, Stephen G. Smith, Tom Edsall, Mark Halperin, and Pat Buchanan.

Several friends, experts in their fields or in authorship, helped me by reading all or portions of the manuscript: Georgetown University professor James Allen Smith; American Enterprise Institute scholar Norman Ornstein; Cliff Sloan, a former White House deputy counsel and Supreme Court clerk who is now the publisher of *Slate;* former senator Robert Kerrey of Nebraska, now the president of the New School in New York; Laura Handman, a Washington attorney and one of the nation's leading experts on First Amendment issues; Carol Browner, former secretary of the Environmental Protection Agency; and Goldman Sachs partner and former Treasury official Robert Hormats.

I could not have written this book without the help of Amy Dudley, Catherine O'Connor, Daniel Ornstein, and Samuel I. Stein—four brilliant and wise-beyond-their-years researchers who compiled source material for invaluable memos that helped educate me in the history and dimensions of the Thirteen Arguments. I was optimistic about our country before I started; I am more so after working with them. I also received valuable assistance from librarian Heather Shafer and from my daughter, Meredith Claire Fineman, who did research and bibliographic work.

It took two terrific editors to turn a reporter's musings into a real book. Susan Mercandetti, my editor at Random House, is the proximate cause of *The Thirteen American Arguments*. I had the idea; she had the belief. Susan's discerning eye, indefatigable support, and firm management kept the project on track. Jonathan Jao of Random House was equally enthusiastic and helpful. Dennis Ambrose smoothed the text (to the extent possible) with superb copyediting. My agent, Robert Barnett, is deservedly praised as a Washington wise man. Gerson Zweifach and his wife, Jackie Zins, are the dearest of friends and the most trusted of advisers, and they were with me every step of the way. Al Franken, a friend for twenty years, offered constant (and constantly funny) encouragement.

When you write a book, you become so irascible that you find out who your friends really are. Here are some who survived the ordeal with me: Judy Harris, Abbe and Adam Aron, Debbie Harmon and Bob Seder, Tom Howell and Shelly Rockwell, Sara and Barkley Jones, Franni Franken, Sidney and Jane Harman, Ron and Diane Eichner, Jeff MacMillan and Lucinda Leach, Ray and Shauna Wertheim, Jim Ramey, Barb and Pete Thompson, Deborah and Michael Salzberg, Andrew Smith, Ralph Gerson and Erica Ward, and Susan and Evan Bayh and Kathleen Matthews.

If this book has value, the credit belongs to families: the one in which I grew up, and the one that my wife, Amy Nathan, and I have had the good fortune to fashion. My mother, Jean Lederman Fineman, is a retired—and justly fabled—English teacher who taught me everything I know about language, loyalty, and parental love. My late father, Charles Morton Fineman, began his career teaching high school history before he switched to business. Deeply read, he had a symphonic sense of events and (like my mom) did not hesitate to express his views about them. My sister, Elisabeth Fineman Schroeter, listened intently and has been rendering her sympathetic and incisive judgments to me ever since. (Her husband, Paul Schroeter, does the same.) Our dinner table was a font of intelligent argument—and, I realize after having written this book, the unique essence of what is best, even sacred, about our country.

Now it is my turn to hold forth at the dinner table, and the love and endless understanding shown to me there, and everywhere else, is my salvation. Our children, Meredith and Nicholas, discussed the book with me and accepted my grumpiness with wry humor and constant support. My in-laws, Patti and David Nathan, are an extra set of loving parents. Amy, my beloved wife, meant everything to this project and all else. As I write in the dedication, she makes everything possible.

NOTES

Sloan, Cliff   Trippi, Joe
Smith, James Allen   Valenti, Jack
Sperling, Gene   Wilcove, David
Sununu, Senator John   Williams, Brian

NEWSWEEK INTERVIEWS

In addition to interviews listed above, specifically conducted for this book, I rely on quo-
tations from interviews I have done over the years in the course of reporting stories
for *Newsweek*. The sources and circumstances are clear in the text. Interviewees in-
clude: President George W. Bush, President Bill Clinton, Vice President Dick
Cheney, Vice President Al Gore, Senator Hillary Rodham Clinton, Senator Barack
Obama, Dr. James Dobson, Senator Bill Frist, Senator George Allen, Rep. Dick
Gephardt, Senator John McCain, Senator Fred Thompson, White House Counselor
Karl Rove, and the late Lee Atwater.

General/Introduction

Alter, Jonathan. *The Defining Moment: FDR's Hundred Days and the Triumph of Hope*.
New York: Simon & Schuster, 2006.

Amar, Akhil Reed. *America's Constitution*. New York: Random House, 2005.

Bailyn, Bernard. *To Begin the World Anew: The Genius and Ambiguities of the American
Founders*. New York: Random House, 2004.

Barone, Michael. "Our Country: The Shaping of America from Roosevelt to Reagan." In
Democracy and the Constitution, edited by Walter Berns. Washington, D.C.: AEI
Press, 2006.

Barone, Michael and Richard E. Cohen. *The Almanac of American Politics*. Washington,
D.C.: National Journal, 1972–current.

Blackstone, Sir William. *Commentaries on the Laws of England*. New York: Banks &
Brothers, 1895.

Bowen, Catherine Drinker. *Miracle at Philadelphia: The Story of the Constitutional Convention May–September 1787*. Boston: Little, Brown and Co., 1966.

Bridges, Constance. *Great Thoughts of Great Americans*. New York: Thomas Y. Crowell
Co., 1951.

Brogan, D. W. *The American Character*. Gloucester, Mass.: Peter Smith, 1975.

Bryce, James. *The American Commonwealth*. Vols. 1–2. New York: Macmillan, 1915.

Chafee, Zechariah Jr. *Free Speech in the United States*. Cambridge, Mass.: Harvard University Press, 1967.

Collier, Christopher, and James Lincoln Collier. *Decision in Philadelphia: The Constitutional Convention of 1787*. New York: Random House, 1986.

Commager, Henry Steele. *Living Ideas in America*. New York: Harper & Row, 1951.

Cook, Alistair. *Letter from America, 1946–2004*. New York: Knopf, 2004.

Danforth, Sen. John. *Faith and Politics*. New York: Viking, 2006.

Dionne, E. J. *Why Americans Hate Politics*. New York: Touchstone Books, 1992.

Ellis, Joseph J. *Founding Brothers: The Revolutionary Generation.* New York: Vintage Books, 2000.

Etzioni, Amitai. *The New Golden Rule: Community and Morality in a Democratic Society.* New York: Basic Books, 1996.

Fischer, David Hackett. *Albion's Seed: Four British Folkways in America.* New York: Oxford University Press, 1989.

Friedman, Lawrence M. *A History of American Law.* New York: Simon & Schuster, 1973.

Gordon, John Steele. *An Empire of Wealth.* New York: HarperCollins, 2004.

Greene, Jack P. *Encyclopedia of American Political History.* Vols. 1–3. New York: Scribner's, 1984.

Gribben, John. *The Fellowship and the Story of a Scientific Revolution.* New York: Overlook Press, 2007.

Gunther, Gerald, and Noel T. Dowling. *Constitutional Law: Cases and Materials.* Mineola, N.Y.: Foundation Press, Inc., 1970.

Hamilton, Alexander, et al. *The Federalist.* New York: Modern Library, 1937.

Heffner, Richard D. *A Documentary History of the United States.* New York: New American Library, 1999.

Hitchens, Christopher. *Thomas Jefferson: Author of America.* New York: HarperCollins, 2005.

Hofstadter, Richard. *The American Political Tradition.* New York: Vintage Books, 1989.

Hofstadter, Richard, and Clarence Lester Ver Steeg, eds. *Great Issues in American History from Reconstruction to the Present Day, 1864–1969.* New York: Vintage Books, 1969.

Holton, Woody. *Unruly Americans and the Origins of the Constitution.* New York: Hill and Wang, 2007.

Jamieson, Kathleen Hall. *Dirty Politics.* New York: Oxford University Press, 1993.

Johnson, Paul. *A History of the American People.* New York: HarperCollins, 1999.

Kazin, Michael, and Joseph A. McCartin, ed. *Americanism: New Perspectives on the History of an Ideal.* Chapel Hill N.C.: University of North Carolina Press, 2006.

Kennedy, Caroline. *A Patriot's Handbook.* New York: Hyperion, 2003.

Kennedy, Caroline, and David Eisenhower. *The United States Constitution: What It Says, What It Means.* New York: Oxford University Press, 2005.

Lamb, Brian. *Booknotes: Stories from American History.* New York: Public Affairs, 2001.

Lewis, R.W.B. *The American Adam.* Chicago: University of Chicago Press, 1955.

Malone, Dumas. *Jefferson and His Time.* Vols. 1–6. Boston: Little, Brown and Co., 1948–81.

Mann, Thomas E., and Norman J. Ornstein. *The Broken Branch: How Congress Is Failing America and How to Get It Back on Track.* New York: Oxford University Press, 2006.

McDougal, Walter A. *Freedom Just Around the Corner: A New American History 1585–1828.* New York: HarperCollins, 2004.

Meacham, Jon. *American Gospel: God, the Founding Fathers, and the Making of a Nation.* New York: Random House, 2004.

Milton, John. *Complete Poems and Major Prose.* Edited by Merritt Yerkes Hughes. Indianapolis: Hackett Publishing Co., Inc., 2003.

Morison, Samuel Eliot. *The Oxford History of the American People.* New York: Oxford University Press, 1965.

Morris, Edmund. *The Rise of Theodore Roosevelt.* New York: Modern Library, 2001.

———. *Theodore Rex.* New York: Modern Library, 2002.

Paine, Thomas. *Common Sense.* New York: Penguin, 2005.

Phillips, Kevin. *The Emerging Republican Majority.* New York: Arlington House, 1969.

Rand, Ayn. *Atlas Shrugged.* New York: Random House, 1957.

Ravitch, Diane, ed. *The American Reader: Words That Moved a Nation.* New York: HarperCollins, 1991.

Schlesinger, Arthur M., Jr. *The Cycles of American History.* New York: Houghton Mifflin, 1999.

Shorto, Russell. *The Island at the Center of the World.* New York: Doubleday, 2004.

Solotaroff, Ted. *Alfred Kazin's America, Critical and Personal Writings.* New York: HarperCollins, 2003.

"Stamp Act of 1765." Avalon Project of Yale Law School. http://www.yale.edu.lawweb/-avalon/england/htm.

Tocqueville, Alexis de. *Democracy in America.* Toronto: Random House of Canada, 1945.

Ungar, Roberto and Cornel West. *The Future of American Progressivism.* Boston: Beacon Press, 1999.

Weinstein, Allen, and David Reubel. *The Story of America: Freedom and Crisis from Settlement to Superpower.* New York: DK Publishing, Inc., 2002.

Whitman, Walt. *The Complete Poems.* New York: Penguin Classics, 1986.

Wilentz, Sean. *The Rise of American Democracy: Jefferson to Lincoln.* New York: W. W. Norton & Co., 2005.

Wood, Gordon S. *The American Revolution: A History.* New York: Modern Library, 2002.

Woolley, Peter J., and Albert R. Papa. *American Politics: Core Argument/Current Controversy.* Upper Saddle River, N.J.: Pearson Education, Inc., 2002.

Zinn, Howard. *A People's History of the United States.* New York: HarperCollins, 2003.

Zolberg, Aristide R. *A Nation by Design: Immigration Policy in the Fashioning of America.* Cambridge, Mass.: Harvard University Press, 2006.

One: Who Is a Person?

Ackerman, Bruce. *We the People.* Cambridge, Mass.: Belknap Press of Harvard University Press, 1991.

Amar, Akhil. *America's Constitution: A Biography.* New York: Random House, 2005.

An Act to Provide for the Allotment of Lands in Severalty to Indians on the Various Reservations (General Allotment Act or Dawes Act), Statutes at Large 24, 388–91, NADP Document A1887.

Armitage, David. *The Declaration of Independence: A Global History.* Cambridge, Mass.: Harvard University Press, 2007.

Bender, Thomas, ed. *The Antislavery Debate: Capitalism and Abolitionism as a Problem in Historical Interpretation.* Berkeley, Calif.: University of California Press, 1992.

Berkhofer R. *The White Man's Indian: Images of the American Indian from Columbus to the Present.* New York: Vintage Books, 1978.

Berkhofer, Robert F., Jr. *Salvation and the Savage: An Analysis of Protestant Missions and*

American Indian Response, 1787–1862. Lexington: University Press of Kentucky, 1965.

Blight, David. *Race and Reunion and Beyond the Battlefield.* Cambridge, Mass.: Harvard University Press, 2001.

Burke Act of 1906.

Carmichael, Stokely, and Charles V. Hamilton. *Black Power: The Politics of Liberation in America.* New York: Vintage Books, 1967.

Cohen, Felix S. *Handbook of Federal Indian Law.* New York: AMS Press, 1972.

Davis, David Brion. *The Problem of Slavery in the Age of Revolution, 1770–1823.* New York: Oxford University Press, 1999.

Diggins, John. "Slavery, Race, and Equality: Jefferson and the Pathos of the Enlightenment." *American Quarterly* 28, no. 2 (Summer 1976).

Dippie, Brian W. *The Vanishing American: White Attitudes and U.S. Indian Policy.* Lawrence, Kans.: University Press of Kansas, 1991.

Donald, David Herbert. *Lincoln.* New York: Touchstone Books, 1995.

Dred Scott v. Sandford, 60 U.S. 393 (1856).

DuBois, W.E.B. "The Freedmen's Bureau," *Atlantic Monthly* 87 (1901): 354–65.

Finkelman, Paul, and Peter Wallenstein, eds. *The Encyclopedia of American Political History.* Washington, D.C.: CQ Press, 2000.

Foner, Eric. *Reconstruction: America's Unfinished Revolution, 1863–1877.* New York: HarperCollins, 1988.

———. *Forever Free: The Story of Emancipation and Reconstruction.* New York: Knopf, 2005.

Goodwin, Doris Kearns. *Team of Rivals: The Political Genius of Abraham Lincoln.* New York: Simon & Schuster, 2005.

Gottmacher Institute, Facts on Abortion, 2006, http://guttmacher.org/pubs/fb_abortion.html

Greene, Jack P., ed. *Encyclopedia of American Political History.* New York: Scribner's, 1984.

Humes, James C. *The Wit and Wisdom of Abraham Lincoln.* New York: Gramercy Books, 1996.

Kim, Claire Jean. "Clinton's Race Initiative: Recasting the American Dilemma," *Polity* 33, no. 2 (Winter 2000): 175–97.

King, Martin Luther, Jr. "Letter from a Birmingham Jail," in *Why We Can't Wait.* New York: Harper & Row, 1963.

Levin, Phyllis Lee. *Abigail Adams: A Biography.* New York: St. Martin's Press, 1987.

Lewis, David Levering. *W.E.B. DuBois: The Fight for Equality and the American Century, 1919–1963.* New York: Henry Holt, 2000.

Litwack, Leon F. *Been in the Storm So Long: The Aftermath of Slavery.* New York: Knopf, 1979.

Meier, August. "Negro Thought in America, 1880–1915: Racial Ideologies in the Age of Booker T. Washington." *American Sociological Review* 30, no. 2 (April 1965): 329–30.

Moore, John Leo. *Elections A to Z.* Washington, D.C.: CQ Press, 2003.

Myrdal, Gunnar. *An American Dilemma: The Negro Problem and Democracy.* New York: Harper & Row, 1962.

National Conference of State Legislatures. "State Embryonic and Fetal Research Laws." http://www.ncsl.org/programs/health/genetics/embfet.htm.

National Research Act. July 12, 1974.

NIH Revitalization Act of 1993. Public Law 103–43 (1993).

Obama, Barack. Announcement for President. February 10, 2007.

Onuf, Peter S. " 'To Declare Them a Free and Independent People': Race, Slavery and National Identity in Jefferson's Thought." *Journal of the Early Republic* 18, no. 1 (Spring 1998): 1–46.

Oubre, Claude F. *Forty Acres and a Mule: The Freedmen's Bureau and Black Land Ownership.* Baton Rouge, La.: Louisiana State University Press, 1978.

Planned Parenthood v. Casey. 505 U.S. 833 (1992).

Plessy v. Ferguson. 163 U.S. 537 (1896).

Prucha, Francis Paul. *A Bibliographical Guide to the History of Indian-White Relations in the U.S.* Chicago: University of Chicago Press, 1977.

————. *American Indian Policy in the Formative Years: The Indian Trade and Intercourse Acts, 1790–1834.* Cambridge, Mass.: Harvard University Press, 1962.

————. *Documents of United States Indian Policy.* Lincoln, Neb.: University of Nebraska Press, 1990.

Roe v. Wade. 410 U.S. 113 (1973).

Satz, Ronald. *American Indian Policy in the Jacksonian Era.* Lincoln, Neb.: University of Nebraska Press, 1975.

Sheehan, Bernard W. *Seeds of Extinction: Jeffersonian Philanthropy and the American.* New York: W. W. Norton & Co., 1974.

Shklar, Judith. *American Citizenship: The Quest for Inclusion.* Cambridge, Mass.: Harvard University Press, 2001.

Smedley, Audrey. *Race in North America: Origins of a Worldview.* Boulder, Colo.: Westview Press, 2007.

Smith, William. "William Jennings Bryan and Racism." *The Journal of Negro History* 54, no. 2 (April 1969): 127–49.

Spencer, Martin E. "Multiculturalism, 'Political Correctness' and the Politics of Identity." *Sociological Forum* 9, no. 4 (December 1994): 547–67.

Stokes, Curtis. "Tocqueville and the Problem of Racial Inequality." *Journal of Negro History* 75, no. ½ (winter–spring 1990): 1–15.

Taylor, Graham D. *The New Deal and American Indian Tribalism: The Administration of the Indian Reorganization Act, 1934–45.* Lincoln, Neb.: University of Nebraska Press, 1980.

Thomas, Benjamin P. *Abraham Lincoln.* New York: Knopf, 1952.

U.S. Congress. House. *Certificates of Citizenship to Indians.* HR 222. 68th Congress, 1st sess. (February 22, 1924).

Two: Who Is an American?

Amar, Akhil. *America's Constitution: A Biography.* New York: Random House, 2005.

Anbinder, Tyler. *Nativism and Slavery: The Northern Know Nothings and the Politics of the 1850s.* New York: Oxford University Press, 1973.

Barabak, Mark Z. "Campaign 2000; Bush Softens Sharp Edges of Republican Platform; Politics: Draft Retains Tough Anti-Abortion Stand, but Harsh Rhetoric of Past Document Gone." *Los Angeles Times,* July 28, 2000.

"Chinese Immigration." *The New York Times,* December 18, 1877.

Chy Lung v. Freeman. 92 U.S. 275 (1875).

Clancy, Herbert John. *The Presidential Election of 1880.* Chicago: Loyola University Press, 1958.

Divine, Robert A. *American Immigration Policy 1924–1952.* New Haven, Conn.: Yale University Press, 1957.

Finkelman, Paul, and Peter Wallenstein, eds. *The Encyclopedia of American Political History.* Washington, D.C.: CQ Press, 2000.

Franklin, Benjamin. "Observations Concerning the Increase of Mankind." *Autobiography and Other Writings.* New York: Penguin, 2001.

Greene, Jack P. *Encyclopedia of American Political History.* Vols. 1–3. New York: Scribner's, 1984.

Guzman, Betsy. 2001. "The Hispanic Population." Census 2000 Brief.

Higham, John. *Strangers in the Land: Patterns of American Nativism, 1860–1925.* New Brunswick, N.J.: Rutgers University Press, 1955.

Hutchinson, Edward P. *Legislative History of American Immigration Policy, 1798–1965.* Philadelphia: University of Pennsylvania Press, 1981.

Institute of International Education. "International Student Enrollment in U.S. Rebounds." Nov. 12, 2007, http://opendoors.iienetwork.org.

Isaacson, Walter. *Benjamin Franklin: An American Life.* New York: Simon & Schuster, 2003.

Jones, Maldwyn Allen. *American Immigration.* Chicago: University of Chicago Press, 1960.

Kettner, James H. *The Development of American Citizenship, 1608–1870.* Chapel Hill: University of North Carolina Press, 1978.

LeMay, Michael C., and Elliot R. Barkan. *U.S. Immigration and Naturalization Laws and Issues: A Documentary History.* Westport, Conn.: Greenwood Press, 1999.

Miller, Willard, and Ruby M. Miller. *United States Immigration: A Reference Handbook.* New York: ABC-CLIO, 1996.

Moore, John Leo. *Elections A to Z.* Washington, D.C.: CQ Press, 2003.

Scherer, Michael. "Salon Person of the Year: S. R. Sidarth." *Salon,* December 16, 2007. http://www.salon.com/opinion/feature/2006/12/16/sidarth/index_np.html.

University of Virginia Library. "Historical Census Browser." http://fisher.lib.virginia.edu/collections/stats/histcensus/.

U.S. Census Bureau. "Population and Household Economics Topics." http://www.census.gov/population/www/index.html.

———. "Selected Historical Decennial Census Population and Housing Counts." http://www.census.gov/population/www/censusdata/hiscendata.html.

U.S. Citizenship and Immigration Services, DHS. "Who Gets In: Four Main Immigration Laws."

Weigley, Russell Frank, Nicholas B. Wainwright, and Edwin Wolf. *Philadelphia: A 300-year History.* New York: W. W. Norton & Co., 1982.

Zolberg, Aristide R. *A Nation by Design.* Cambridge, Mass.: Harvard University Press, 2006.

Three: The Role of Faith

Ahlstrom, Sidney E. *A Religious History of the American People.* New Haven, Conn.: Yale University Press, 1972.

Amar, Akhil. *America's Constitution: A Biography.* New York: Random House, 2005.

Butler, Jon. *Awash in a Sea of Faith: Christianizing the American People.* Cambridge, Mass.: Harvard University Press, 1990.

Carroll, Jackson W., Douglas W. Johnson, and Martin E. Marty. *Religion in America, 1950 to the Present.* San Francisco: Harper & Row, 1979.

CBS "Religion" Poll. June 26–28, 2007. http://www.pollingreport.com/religion.htm.

Church, Forrest. *The Separation of Church and State: Writings on a Fundamental Freedom by America's Founders.* Boston: Beacon Press, 2004.

Dionne, E. J., and John J. Dilulio Jr., eds. *What's God Got to Do with the American Experiment?: Essays on Religion and Politics.* Washington, D.C.: Brookings Institution Press, 2000.

Dionne, E. J., Jean Bethke Elshtain, and Kayla M. Drogosz, eds. *One Electorate Under God: A Dialogue on Religion and American Politics.* Washington, D.C.: Brookings Institution Press, 2004.

Djupe, Paul, and Laura Olson, eds. *Encyclopedia of American Religion and Politics.* New York: Facts on File, 2003.

Everson v. Board of Education. 330 U.S. 1 (1947).

Feldman, Noah. *Divided by God: America's Church–State Problem—and What We Should Do about It.* New York: Farrar, Straus and Giroux, 2005.

Finkelman, Paul, and Peter Wallenstein, eds. *The Encyclopedia of American Political History.* Washington, D.C.: CQ Press, 2000.

Gallup, George. *The Next American Spirituality: Finding God in the Twenty-First Century.* Washington, D.C.: Gallup, 2000.

Gallup, George, and D. Michael Lindsay. *The Gallup Guide: Reality Check for 21st Century Churches.* Washington, D.C.: Gallup, 2002.

Gilgoff, Dan. "John McCain: Constitution Established a 'Christian Nation.' " *Beliefnet .com.* September 2007.

Greene, Jack P. *Encyclopedia of American Political History.* Vols. 1–3. New York: Scribner's, 1984.

Hamburger, Philip. *Separation of Church and State.* Cambridge, Mass.: Harvard University Press, 2002.

Hudson, Winthrop S. *Religion in America.* New York: Scribner's, 1965.

Jefferson, Thomas. "Virginia's Statute for Religious Freedom." 1786.

———. "Letter to the Danbury Baptists," 1802.

Johnson, Paul. *A History of the American People.* New York: HarperCollins, 1997.

Knoll, Mark A. *America's God: From Jonathan Edwards to Abraham Lincoln.* New York: Oxford University Press, 2002.

Kosmin, Barry A., and Seymour P. Lachman. *One Nation Under God: Religion in Contemporary American Society.* New York: Harmony Books, 1993.

Lambert, Frank. *The Founding Fathers and the Place of Religion in America.* Princeton, N.J.: Princeton University Press, 2003.

Lemon v. Kurtzman. 403 U.S. 602 (1971).

Lippy, Charles H., and Peter W. Williams, eds. *Encyclopedia of the American Religious Experience.* New York: Scribner's, 1988.

Malone, Dumas. *Jefferson and the Rights of Man.* Boston: Little, Brown and Co., 1951.

Meacham, Jon. *American Gospel.* New York: Random House, 2006.

Moore, John Leo. *Elections A to Z.* Washington, D.C.: CQ Press, 2003.

Moore, Robert Laurence. *Selling God: American Religion in the Marketplace of Culture.* New York: Oxford University Press, 1994.

———. *Touchdown Jesus: The Mixing of Sacred and Secular in American History.* Louisville, Ky.: Westminster John Knox Press, 2003.

Odegard, Peter, ed. *Religion and Politics.* New York: Oceana Publications, 1960.

Peterson, Merrill D., and Robert C. Vaughan, eds. *Virginia Statute for Religious Freedom: Its Evolution and Consequences in American History.* Cambridge and New York: Cambridge University Press, 1988.

Pew Research Center for the People & the Press. "Religion and the Presidential Vote," December 6, 2004.

Phillips, Kevin. *American Theocracy.* New York: Viking, 2006.

Reynolds v. U.S. 98 U.S. 145 (1879).

Sanford, Charles B. *The Religious Life of Thomas Jefferson.* Charlottesville, Va.: University of Virginia Press, 1984.

Smith, Donald Eugene, ed. *Religion and Political Modernization.* New Haven, Conn.: Yale University Press, 1974.

Sorauf, Frank J. *The Wall of Separation: The Constitutional Politics of Church and State.* Princeton, N.J.: Princeton University Press, 1976.

Thomas Prince. "Chronological History of New England" (simply how he begins his narrative with the Genesis account of creation).

Tocqueville, Alexis de. *Democracy in America.* Toronto: Random House of Canada, 1945.

Wills, Garry. *Under God: Religion and Politics in America.* New York: Simon & Schuster, 1990.

Wilson, John F., ed. *Church and State in America: A Bibliographical Guide.* Vols. 1–2. New York: Greenwood Press, 1986–1987.

Wilson, John F. and Donald L. Drakeman, eds. *Church and State in American History.* Boston: Health, 1965.

Winthrop, John. "City Upon a Hill" sermon, 1630.

Wood, Gordon S. *The American Revolution: A History.* New York: Modern Library, 2002.

Four: What Can We Know and Say?

Abrams v. U.S. 250 U.S. 616 (1919).

ACLU et al. v. NSA et al. U.S. District Court, Eastern District of Michigan, Case No. 06-CV-10204 (2006).

Amar, Akhil. *America's Constitution: A Biography.* New York: Random House, 2005.

Alexa Global Top 500, January 1, 2008. http://www.alexa.com/site/as/top_500.

Chafee, Zechariah, Jr. *Free Speech in the United States.* Cambridge, Mass.: Harvard University Press, 1967.

De Grazia, Edward. *Censorship Landmarks.* New York: Bowker, 1969.

Dempsey, James X., and David Cole. *Terrorism and the Constitution: Sacrificing Civil Liberties in the Name of National Security.* Washington, D.C.: First Amendment Foundation, 2002.

Donner, Frank J. "The Age of Surveillance: The Aims and Methods of the American Political Intelligence System." *Political Science Quarterly* 95, no. 4 (Winter 1980–1981): 699–700.

Etzioni, Amitai. *How Patriotic Is the Patriot Act? Freedom Versus Security in the Age of Terrorism.* New York: Routledge, 2004.

Federation of American Scientists. "Project on Government Secrecy." http://www.fas.org/sgp/index.html).

Finkelman, Paul, and Peter Wallenstein, eds. *The Encyclopedia of American Political History.* Washington, D.C.: CQ Press, 2000.

Foerstel, Herbert N. *Free Expression and Censorship in America: An Encyclopedia.* Westport, Conn.: Greenwood Press, 1998.

———. *Freedom of Information and the Right to Know: The Origins and Applications of the Freedom of Information Act.* Westport, Conn.: Greenwood Press, 1999.

George Washington University. "The National Security Archive." http://www.gwu.edu/~nsarchiv/.

Greene, Jack P., ed. *Encyclopedia of American Political History.* New York: Scribner's, 1984.

Gup, Ted. *Nation of Secrets: The Threat to Democracy and the American Way of Life.* New York: Doubleday, 2007.

Hagedorn, Ann. *Savage Peace: Hope and Fear in America, 1919.* New York: Simon & Schuster, 2007.

Hohenberg, John. *Free Press/Free People.* New York: Columbia University Press, 1971.

Jaspers, James M. *Restless Nation: Starting Over in America.* Chicago: University of Chicago Press, 2000.

Levy, Leonard W. *Legacy of Suppression: Freedom of Speech and Press in Early American History.* Cambridge, Mass.: Harvard University Press, 1960.

Madison, James. "Report to the Virginia House of Delegates," 1800.

———. *The Federalist No. 10,* 1787.

Melanson, Philip. *Secrecy Wars: National Security, Privacy and the Public's Right to Know.* Washington, D.C.: Potomac Books, 2002.

Milton, John. "Areopagitica," in *Complete Poems and Major Prose.* New York: Prentice Hall, 1957.

Moore, John Leo. *Elections A to Z.* Washington, D.C.: CQ Press, 2003.

Moynihan, Daniel Patrick. *Secrecy.* New Haven, Conn.: Yale University Press, 1998.

Mullen, William E. *Presidential Power and Politics.* New York: St. Martin's Press, 1976.

Murray, Robert K. *Red Scare: A Study in National Hysteria, 1919–1920.* Minneapolis: University of Minnesota Press, 1955.

New York Times v. Sullivan. 376 U.S. 254 (1964).

New York Times v. U.S. and U.S. v. Washington Post. 403 U.S. 713 (1971).

Reagan, Ronald. "Presidential Directive on Safeguarding National Security Information." 1983.

Rozell, Mark. *Executive Privilege: Presidential Power, Secrecy, and Accountability.* Lawrence, Kans.: University Press of Kansas, 2002.

Schenck v. U.S. 249 U.S. 47 (1919).

Stone, Geoffrey R. *Perilous Times: Free Speech in Wartime from the Sedition Act of 1798 to the War on Terrorism.* New York: W. W. Norton & Co., 2004.

Sunstein, Cass. *Democracy and the Problem of Free Speech.* New York: Free Press, 1995.

Torr, James D., ed. *Homeland Security.* San Diego: Greenhaven Press, 2004.

U.S. Congress. House. Subcommittee on National Security, Emerging Threats, and International Relations of the Committee on Government Reform. *Too Many Secrets: Overclassification as a Barrier to Critical Information Sharing.* 108th Cong., 2nd sess., August 24, 2004.

Five: The Limits of Individualism

Allen, Mike, and Jonathan Wiseman. "Bush to Present His Agenda for a Second Term; President to Tout 'Ownership Society.'" *Washington Post,* September 2, 2004.

Becker, Robert A. *Revolution, Reform and the Politics of American Taxation, 1763–1783.* Baton Rouge, La.: Louisiana State University Press, 1980.

Bergsten, C. Fred. "The Problem." *Foreign Policy* 59, 1985.

Berkowitz, Peter, ed. *Varieties of Conservatism in America.* Stanford, Calif.: Hoover Institution Press, 2004.

Boaz, David. *The Libertarian Reader.* New York: Free Press, 1997.

Brooks, David. "The Ownership Society." *New York Times,* December 20, 2003.

Brownlee, W. Elliott. *Federal Taxation in America.* Cambridge: Cambridge University Press, 2004.

Buckley, William F. *Up from Liberalism.* New York: Stein and Day, 1984.

Clift, Eleanor and Mary Hager. "Covert Operation." *Newsweek,* March 15, 2003.

Clinton, Hillary R. *Living History.* New York: Simon & Schuster, 2003.

Clinton, William J. *My Life.* New York: Knopf, 2004.

Demos, John. *A Little Commonwealth: Family Life in Plymouth Colony.* New York: Oxford University Press, 1970.

Dubovsky, Melvyn, and Warren R. Van Tine. *John L. Lewis: A Biography.* Urbana-Champaign, Ill.: University of Illinois Press, 1986.

Dunn, Charles W. and J. David Woodward. *The Conservative Tradition in America.* Lanham, Md.: Rowman and Littlefield, 1996.

Dworkin, Ronald. "Sovereign Virtue Revisited." *Ethics* 113, 2002: 106–43.

Emanuel, Rahm, and Bruce Reed. *The Plan.* New York: Public Affairs, 2006.

Etzioni, Amitai. *The New Golden Rule: Community and Morality in a Democratic Society.* New York: Basic Books, 1996.

Friedman, Milton. *Capitalism and Freedom.* Chicago: University of Chicago Press, 1982.

Galbraith, John Kenneth. *The Culture of Contentment.* New York: Houghton Mifflin, 1992.

Gilbert, Neil. *Capitalism and the Welfare State: Dilemmas of Social Benevolence.* New Haven, Conn.: Yale University Press, 1983.

Goldwater, Barry. *Conscience of a Conservative.* Washington, D.C.: Regnery Publishing, 1994.

Gross, Daniel. "Asking Big Spenders to Be Big Savers, Too." *New York Times,* October 17, 2004.

Gutman, Amy. *Democracy and the Welfare State.* Princeton, N.J.: Princeton University Press, 1988.

Hacker, Jacob S. *The Divided Welfare State.* Cambridge: Cambridge University Press, 2002.

Hayek, F. A. *The Road to Serfdom.* Florence, Ky.: Routledge, 2001.

Kadlec, Daniel, Eric Roston, and Jyoti Thottam. "Taking the Plunge; On the Way to His Vision of an 'Ownership Society,' President Bush Picks a Big Fight Over Social Security." *Time,* November 22, 2004.

Kirk, Russell. *A Conservative Mind: From Burke to Eliot.* Washington, D.C.: Regnery Publishing, 1986.

Kranish, Michael. "Bush Expected to Reintroduce 2000 Proposal." *Boston Globe,* August 31, 2004.

Krugman, Paul. "Bush's Own Goal." *New York Times,* August 13, 2004.

Kymlicka, Will. *Contemporary Political Philosophy.* Oxford, U.K.: Clarendon Press, 1990.

Levitan, Sar. "Budgeting States' Rights." *Society* 14, no. 5 (1982).

Lowe, Carl. *Reaganomics: The New Federalism.* New York: The H. H. Wilson Company, 1984.

Moynihan, David Patrick. *Miles to Go: A Personal History of Social Policy.* Cambridge, Mass.: Harvard University Press, 1996.

Murray, Charles. *The Bell Curve: Intelligence and Class Structure in American Life.* New York: Free Press, 1994.

———. *What It Means to Be a Libertarian.* New York: Broadway Books, 1997.

Niskanen, William A. *Reaganomics: An Insider's Account of the Policies and the People.* New York: Oxford University Press, 1988.

Nozick, Robert. *Anarchy, State and Utopia.* New York: Basic Books, 1974.

Orloff, Ann Shola, Theda Skocpol, and Margaret Weir. *The Politics of Social Policy in the United States.* Princeton, N.J.: Princeton University Press, 1988.

Palmer, John, and Isabella Sawhill. *The Reagan Experiment.* Washington, D.C.: Urban Institute Press, 1982.

Rand, Ayn. *Atlas Shrugged.* New York: New American Library, 1996.

Rawls, John. *Theory of Justice.* Cambridge, Mass.: The President and Fellows of Harvard College, 1971.

Rosenbaum, David. "Bush to Return to 'Ownership Society' Theme in Push for Social Security Changes." *New York Times,* January 16, 2005.

Russell, Dean. "Who Is a Libertarian?" *Ideas on Liberty* 5, no. 5 (May 1955).

Schlesinger, Arthur M. *The Age of Roosevelt: The Politics of Upheaval.* Boston: Houghton Mifflin, 1960.

Smith, Adam. *An Inquiry into the Nature and Causes of the Wealth of Nations.* New York: Modern Library, 1937.

Starr, Paul. "What Happened to Health Care Reform?" *The American Prospect,* no. 20 (Winter 1995).

Stein, Charles. "Moving Toward an 'Ownership Society.' " *Boston Globe,* September 12, 2004.

Surowiecki, James. "The Risk Society." *The New Yorker,* November 15, 2004.

Walczak, Lee, Richard Dunham, and Mike McNamee. "I Want My Safety Net: Why So Many Americans Aren't Buying Into Bush's Ownership Society." *Business Week,* May 16, 2005.

———. "Selling the Ownership Society." *Business Week,* September 6, 2004.

Walzer, Michael. "The Community." *The New Republic,* March 31, 1982.

Washington, George. "Farewell Address," 1796. http://www.earlyamerica.com/earlyamerica/milestones/farewell/.

Westphal, David. "The Republican Convention: Bush to Focus on His Vision of 'Ownership Society.' " *Star Tribune,* September 2, 2004.

Will, George. "It's Ownership vs. Welfare State: The Contrasting Conservative and Liberal Emphases on Freedom and Equality Are Clear." *Chicago Sun-Times,* October 17, 2004.

Six: Who Judges the Law?

Abrams v. United States. 250 U.S. 616 (1919).

Ackerman, Bruce. *Reconstructing American Law.* Cambridge, Mass.: Harvard University Press, 1984.

Amar, Akhil. *America's Constitution: A Biography.* New York: Random House, 2005.

Bolick, Clint. *David's Hammer: The Case for an Activist Judiciary.* Washington, D.C.: Cato Institute, 2007.

Brest, Paul, and Sanford Levinson. *Processes of Constitutional Decision-Making.* Aspen, Colo.: Aspen Publishers, 2000.

Breyer, Stephen. *Active Liberty: Interpreting Our Democratic Constitution.* New York: Knopf, 2005.

Bush v. Gore. 531 U.S. 98 (2000).

Cohen v. California. 403 U.S. 15 (1971).

Cray, Ed. *Chief Justice: A Biography of Earl Warren.* New York: Simon & Schuster, 1997.

Dworkin, Ronald. *Taking Rights Seriously.* Cambridge, Mass.: Harvard University Press, 1977.

Ely, John Hart. *Democracy and Distrust: A Theory of Judicial Review.* Cambridge, Mass.: Harvard University Press, 1980.

Feinberg, Joel. "The Nature and Value of Rights." In *Rights,* edited by Carlos Santiago Nino. New York: New York University Press, 1992.

Finkelman, Paul, and Peter Wallenstein, eds. *The Encyclopedia of American Political History.* Washington, D.C.: CQ Press, 2000.

Friedman, Lawrence M. *A History of American Law.* New York: Simon & Schuster, 1973.

Golding, Martin A., and William A. Edmundson, eds. *The Blackwell Guide to Philosophy of Law and Legal Theory.* Malden, Mass.: Blackwell, 2005.

Griswold v. Connecticut. 381 U.S. 479 (1965).

Hamilton, Alexander, et al. *The Federalist.* Nos. 78–83. Cambridge, Mass.: Belknap Press of Harvard University Press, 1961.

Katcher, Leo. *Earl Warren: A Political Biography.* New York: McGraw-Hill, 1967.

Kennedy, Duncan. "American Constitutionalism as a Civil Religion: Notes of an Atheist." *Nova Law Review,* 1995.

Leoni, Bruno. *Freedom and the Law.* Princeton, N.J.: Van Nostrand, 1961.

Lewis, Frederick P. *The Context of Judicial Activism.* Lanham, Md.: Rowman & Littlefield, 1999.

Marbury v. Madison. 5 U.S. (1 Cranch) 137 (1803).

Mason, Alpheus Thomas. *Brandeis: Lawyer and Judge in the Modern State.* Princeton, N.J.: Princeton University Press, 1933.

McCulloch v. Maryland. 17 U.S. 316 (1819).

Moore, John L., ed. *Elections A to Z.* Washington, D.C.: CQ Press, 2003.

Peretti, Terri Jennings. *In Defense of a Political Court.* Princeton, N.J.: Princeton University Press, 1999.

Posner, Richard. *Breaking the Deadlock: The 2000 Election, the Constitution and the Courts.* Princeton, N.J.: Princeton University Press, 2001.

Rackleff, Robert. "Are Money and Special Interests Tipping the Balance in the Process of Electing Judges?" *Carnegie Reporter,* Vol. 3, No. 4, 2006.

Rakove, Jack. *Original Meanings.* New York: Vintage Books, 1997.

Regents of the University of California v. Bakke. 438 U.S. 265 (1978).

Scalia, Antonin. *A Matter of Interpretation: Federal Courts and the Law.* Princeton, N.J.: Princeton University Press, 1998.

Smith, Mark W. *Disrobed: The New Battle Plan to Break the Left's Stranglehold on the Courts.* New York: Crown Forum, 2006.

Strum, Philippa. *Brandeis: Beyond Progressivism.* Lawrence, Kans.: University Press of Kansas, 1995.

Toobin, Jeffrey. *The Nine: Inside the Secret World of the Supreme Court.* New York: Doubleday, 2007.

Wellington, Harry. *Interpreting the Constitution: The Supreme Court and the Process of Adjudication.* New Haven, Conn.: Yale University Press, 1990.

White, Edward. *Earl Warren: A Public Life.* New York: Oxford University Press, 1987.

Woodward, Bob, and Scott Armstrong. *The Brethren.* New York: Simon & Schuster, 1979.

Seven: Debt and the Dollar

Bartlett, Bruce. "Politics at the Fed." *National Review Online,* April 28, 2004.

Brands, H. W. *Andrew Jackson: His Life and Times.* New York: Doubleday, 2005.

————. *The Money Men: Capitalism, Democracy, and the Hundred Years' War over the American Dollar.* New York: W. W. Norton & Co., 2006.

Brownlee, W. Elliot. *Federal Taxation in America.* Cambridge: Cambridge University Press, 2004.

Bryan, William Jennings. *The First Battle: A Story of the Campaign of 1896.* Chicago: W. B. Conkey Company, 1896.

Bureau of the Public Debt. "Historical Debt Outstanding." http://www.publicdebt.treas .gov/opd/opdhisto1.htm.

Carroll, Richard. *An Economic Record of Presidential Performance.* Wesport, Conn.: Greenwood Press, 1995.

Cencini, Alvaro. *Monetary Theory: National and International.* London: Routledge, 1996.

Chernow, Ron. *Alexander Hamilton.* New York: Penguin, 2004.

Clinton, Bill. *Between Hope and History: Meeting America's Challenges for the 21st Century.* New York: Random House, 1996.

Dalrymple, Theodore. *Our Culture, What's Left of It: The Mandarins and the Masses.* Chicago: Ivan R. Dee Publisher, 2007.

Dean, John. *Warren G. Harding: The American Presidents Series.* New York: Times Books, 2004.

Dougherty, Keith L. *Collective Action Under the Articles of Confederation.* Cambridge: Cambridge University Press, 2000.

Downs, Hugh. *Odder than Oz.* American Monetary Institute, 1998.

Eisenhower, Dwight. *State of the Union Address.* Whitefish, Mont.: Kessinger Publishing, 2004.

Fausold, Martin. *The Hoover Presidency: A Reappraisal.* Albany, N.Y.: SUNY Press, 1974.

Foner, Eric. *Reconstruction: America's Unfinished Revolution, 1863–1877.* New York: HarperCollins, 2002.

Foner, Eric, and John Garraty. *The Reader's Companion to American History.* New York: Houghton Mifflin, 1991.

Franklin, Benjamin. "A Modest Enquiry into the Nature and Necessity of Paper Currency." In *The Writings of Benjamin Franklin.* New York: Macmillan, 1907.

Fremantle, Richard. *God and Money: Florence and the Medici in the Renaissance.* Florence: Private Press, 2005.

Friedman, Milton. *Capitalism and Freedom.* Chicago: University of Chicago Press, 1982.

Gerring, John. *Party Ideologies in America, 1828–1996.* Cambridge: Cambridge University Press, 2001.

Gnazzo, Douglas V. *Honest Money, Part VII: The Moneychangers—Secrets of the Temple.* November 30, 2004. http://www.financialsense.com/fsu/editorials/gnazzo/2004/part7.html.

Gordon, John Steele. *An Empire of Wealth: The Epic History of American Economic Power.* New York: HarperCollins, 2004.

Greenspan, Alan. *The Age of Turbulence: Adventures in a New World.* New York: Penguin, 2007.

Hamilton, Alexander. *Report on a National Bank,* 1790.

———. *Report on the Public Credit,* January 9, 1790.

Havrilesky, Thomas. *The Pressures on American Monetary Policy.* New York: Springer, 1995.

Heilbroner, Robert, and Peter Bernstein. *The Debt and the Deficit.* New York: W. W. Norton & Co., 1989.

Johnson, Lyndon. "Renunciation Speech," March 31, 1968.

Kennedy, John. "Commencement Address at Yale University," June 11, 1962.

Letwin, William, ed. *A Documentary History of American Economic Policy Since 1789.* New York: W. W. Norton & Co., 1972.

Mackin, John. *Debt and Taxes: How America Got Into Its Budget Mess.* Washington, D.C.: AEI Press, 1994.

Markham, Jeffrey W. *A Financial History of the United States.* Armonk, N.Y.: M. E. Sharpe, 1999.

Mayer, Thomas. *Monetary Policy and the Great Inflation in the United States. The Federal Reserve and the Failure of Macroeconomic Policy, 1965–1979.* Northampton, Mass.: Edward Elgar, 1999.

McFeely, William S. *Grant: A Biography.* New York: W. W. Norton & Co., 2002.

Meltzer, Allan. *A History of the Federal Reserve: Volume 1: 1813–1951.* Chicago: University of Chicago Free Press, 2002.

Morris, Irwin. *Congress, the President, and the Federal Reserve.* Ann Arbor, Mich.: University of Michigan Press, 2002.

Phillips, Kevin. *Wealth and Democracy.* New York: Broadway Books, 2002.

———. *William McKinley.* New York: Times Books, 2003.

Pine, Josly. *American Presidents' Wit and Wisdom.* Mineola, N.Y.: Dover Publications, 2002.

Polenberg, Richard. *The Era of Franklin D. Roosevelt, 1933–1945: A Brief History with Documents.* New York: Palgrave, 2000.

Polk, James. *State of the Union Addresses.* Whitefish, Mont.: Kessinger Publishing, 2004.

Poor, Henry V. *The Money Question.* New York: H. V. Poor, 1896.

Reagan, Ronald. *State of the Union Address.* Whitefish, Mont.: Kessinger Publishing, 2004.

Rodden, Jonathan A. *Hamilton's Paradox: The Promise and Peril of Fiscal Federalism.* Cambridge: Cambridge University Press, 2005.

Romer, Christina. *Reducing Inflation: Motivation and Strategy.* Chicago: University of Chicago Press, 1997.

Roosevelt, Franklin D. *Great Speeches.* Mineola, N.Y.: Dover Publications, 1999.

Sargent, Epes. *The Life and Public Services of Henry Clay.* Whitefish, Mont.: Kessinger Publishing, 2004.

Sargent, Thomas. *Ambiguity in American Monetary and Fiscal Policy.* New York: New York University Press, May 2005.

Saxton, Jim. *U.S. Dollar Policy: A Need for Clarification.* Joint Economic Committee Study, November 1998.

Scott, Charles. *William McKinley: Part 1, American Statesman.* Whitefish, Mont.: Kessinger Publishing, 2004.

Sellars, Charles. *The Market Revolution: Jacksonian America.* New York: Oxford University Press, 1994.

Sperling, Gene. *The Pro-Growth Progressive: An Economic Strategy for Shared Prosperity.* New York: Simon & Schuster, 2005.

Steeples, Douglas, and David Whitten. *Democracy in Desperation: The Depression of 1893.* Westport, Conn.: Greenwood Press, 1998.

Stevens, C. M. *Free Silver and the People.* New York: F. T. Neely, 1896.

Timberlake, Richard H. *Monetary Policy in the United States.* Chicago: University of Chicago Press, 1993.

Tobin, James. "Fiscal Policy: Its Macroeconomic Perspective." *Yale Journal of Politics* 1, no. 1 (Spring 2001).

Truman, Harry. *State of the Union Address.* Whitefish, Mont.: Kessinger Publishing, 2004.

U.S. Department of State. *Monetary and Fiscal Policy.* (International Information Programs.)

Wanniski, Jude. *The Way the World Works.* Washington, D.C.: Regnery Publishing, 1998.

Webster, Daniel. *The Works of Daniel Webster.* Boston: Little, Brown and Co., 1853.

Wilentz, Sean. *Andrew Jackson.* New York: Times Books, 2005.

Wills, Garry. *Henry Adams and the Making of America.* New York: Houghton Mifflin, 2005.

Woodward, Bob. *Maestro.* New York: Simon & Schuster, 2001.

Eight: Local v. National Authority

Altenburg, Eric, and Bill Swinford, eds. *Litigating Federalism: The States Before the US Supreme Court.* Westport, Conn.: Greenwood Press, 1999.

Amar, Akhil Reed. *America's Constitution.* New York: Random House, Inc., 2005.

Barth, Gunther. *City People: The Rise of Modern City Culture in Nineteenth-Century America.* New York: Oxford University Press, 1981.

Bensel, Richard Franklin. *Sectionalism and American Political Development, 1880–1980.* Madison, Wis.: University of Wisconsin Press, 1984.

Bradshaw, Michael. *Regions and Regionalism in the United States.* Jackson, Miss.: University Press of Mississippi, 1988.

Cayton, Mary Kupiec, and Peter W. Williams. *Encyclopedia of American Cultural and Intellectual History.* New York: Scribner's, 2001.

Conkin, Paul. *The Southern Agrarians.* Nashville, Tenn.: Vanderbilt University Press, 1988.

Cronon, William, George Miles, and Jay Gitlin, eds. *Under an Open Sky: Rethinking America's Western Past.* New York: W. W. Norton & Co., 1992.

Current, Richard. "Northernizing the South." *The Journal of Southern History* 50, no. 3 (August 1984): 461–62.

Davidson, Donald. *The Attack on Leviathan: Regionalism and Nationalism in the U.S.* Chapel Hill, N.C.: University of North Carolina Press, 1938.

Degler, Carl N. "Thesis, Antithesis, Synthesis: The South, the North, and the Nation," *Journal of Southern History* 53 (February 1987): 3–18.

Donaldson, Susan V. Introduction to *I'll Take My Stand: The South and the Agrarian Tradition,* by Twelve Southerners. New York: Harper & Row, 1962.

Drake, Frederick, and Lynn Nelson, eds. *States' Rights and American Federalism: A Documentary History.* Westport, Conn.: Greenwood Press, 1999.

Farragher, John Mack, ed. *Rereading Frederick Jackson Turner.* New York: Henry Holt, 1994.

Finkelman, Paul, and Peter Wallenstein, eds. *The Encyclopedia of American Political History.* Washington, D.C.: CQ Press, 2000.

Foner, Eric. *Politics and Ideology in the Age of the Civil War.* New York: Oxford University Press, 1980.

Foster, George. *New York by Gaslight and Other Urban Sketches.* Chapel Hill, N.C.: University of North Carolina Press, 1850.

Frady, Marshall. *Wallace.* Cleveland: World Publishing Co., 1968.

Freehling, William. *The Road to Disunion.* New York: Oxford University Press, 1990.

Gannon, Kevin. "Escaping 'Mr. Jefferson's Plan of Destruction': New England Federalists and the Idea of a Northern Confederacy, 1803–1804." *Journal of the Early Republic* 21 (Fall 2001): 413–41.

Gienapp, William, ed. *War and Reconstruction: A Documentary Collection.* New York: W. W. Norton & Co., 2001.

Gimpel, James, and Jason Schuknecht. 2002. "Reconsidering Regionalism in American State Politics." *State Politics and Policy Quarterly* 2, no. 4 (Winter 2002): 325–52.

———. *Patchwork Nation: Sectionalism and Political Change in American Politics.* Ann Arbor, Mich.: University of Michigan Press, 2003.

Hayward, Clarissa Rile. "The Difference States Make: Democracy, Identity, and the American City." *American Political Science Review* 97, no. 4 (November 2003): 501–14.

Howe, Frederick. *The City: The Hope of Democracy.* New York: Scribner's, 1905.

Jefferson, Thomas. *Notes on the State of Virginia.* Chapel Hill, N.C.: University of North Carolina Press, 1996.

Jensen, Merrill, ed. *Regionalism in America.* Madison, Wis.: University of Wisconsin Press, 1964.

John Edgerton. *The Americanization of Dixie.* New York: Harper's Magazine Press, 1974.

Key, V. O. *Southern Politics in State and Nation.* New York: Knopf, 1949.

Kirby, Jack Temple. *Media Made Dixie.* Athens, Ga.: University of Georgia Press, 1986.

———. *The Countercultural South.* Athens, Ga.: University of Georgia Press, 1995.

Levine, Bruce. *Half Slave and Half Free: The Roots of the Civil War.* New York: Hill and Wang, 2005.

Madison, James. *Federalist No. 10.* New York: Modern Library, 1955.

McWhiney, Grady. *Southerners and Other Americans.* New York: Basic Books, 1973.

Moore, John Leo. *Elections A to Z.* Washington, D.C.: CQ Press, 2003.

Morrison, Chaplain W. *Democratic Politics and Sectionalism: The Wilmot Proviso Controversy.* Chapel Hill, N.C.: University of North Carolina Press, 1967.

Nagel, Robert F. *The Implosion of American Federalism.* New York: Oxford University Press, 2002.

O'Brien, Michael. *The Idea of the American South, 1920–1941.* Baltimore: Johns Hopkins University Press, 1990.

O'Toole, Laurence J., ed. *American Intergovernmental Relations: Foundations, Perspectives and Issues.* Washington, D.C.: Congressional Quarterly, 2000.

Paquette, Robert. *Slavery, Secession, and Southern History.* Charlottesville, Va.: University of Virginia Press, 2000.

Phillips, Kevin. *The Emerging Republican Majority.* New York: Arlington House, 1969.

Potter, David. *Division and the Stresses of Reunion.* New York: Scott Foresman, 1973.

Pred, Allen Richard. *Urban Growth and the Circulation of Information, 1790–1840.* Cambridge, Mass.: Harvard University Press, 1973.

Reed, John Shelton. *The Enduring South: Subcultural Persistence in Mass Society.* Chapel Hill, N.C.: University of North Carolina Press, 1972.

Riker, William H. *Federalism: Origins, Operations, Significance.* Boston: Little, Brown and Co., 1964.

Sellers, Charles G. *The Southerner as American.* Chapel Hill, N.C.: University of North Carolina Press, 1960.

Steiner, Michael, and Clarence Mondale. *Region and Regionalism in the United States: A Source Book for the Humanities and Social Sciences.* Ypsilanti, Mich.: Garland Publishing, 1988.

Susman, Warren. "The City in American Culture." In *Culture as History: The Transformation of American Society in the 20th Century,* edited by Warren Susman. New York: Oxford University Press, 1980.

Turner, Frederick Jackson. *The Significance of Sections in American History.* New York: Henry Holt, 1932.

White, Morton, and Lucia White. *The Intellectual Versus the City.* Cambridge, Mass.: Harvard University Press, 1962.

William, Charles. *Encyclopedia of Southern Culture.* Chapel Hill, N.C.: University of North Carolina Press, 1989.

Wilson, Charles Reagan, ed. *The New Regionalism.* Jackson, Miss.: University Press of Mississippi, 1998.

Woodward, Vann C. *Origins of the New South, 1877–1913.* Baton Rouge, La.: Louisiana State University Press, 1951.

Zelinsky, Wilbur. *The Cultural Geography of the United States.* Englewood Cliffs, N.J.: Prentice Hall, 1992.

Zimmerman, Joseph F. *Contemporary American Federalism: The Growth of National Power.* Westport, Conn.: Greenwood Press, 1992.

Nine: Presidential Power

"Articles of Confederation." Avalon Project of Yale Law School. http://www.yale.edu/lawweb/avalon/artconf.htm.

"The Presidents." *American Experience,* PBS. http://www.pbs.org/wgbh/amex/presidents/ 38_ford/index.html.

"War Powers Resolution." Avalon Project of Yale Law School http://www.yale.edu/ lawweb/avalon/warpower.htm.

Adams, Henry. *The Education of Henry Adams.* New York: Penguin Classics, 1995.

Aldrich, J. H., and Thomas Weko. *The Presidency and the Election Campaign: Framing the Choice.* Washington, D.C.: CQ Press, 2000.

Alter, Jonathan. *The Defining Moment: FDR's Hundred Days and the Triumph of Hope.* New York: Simon & Schuster, 2006.

Angle, Paul M., and Earl S. Miers. *The Living Lincoln.* New York: Barnes & Noble Publishing, 1992.

Bernard, Andre, and Clifton Fadiman. *Bartlett's Book of Anecdotes.* Boston: Little, Brown and Co., 2000.

Beschloss, Michael. "Presidential Power." *NewsHour,* PBS, December 24, 2001.

Boller, Paul F., Jr. *Presidential Anecdotes.* New York: Oxford University Press, 2007.

Brodsky, Alyn. *Grover Cleveland.* New York: St. Martin's Press, 2000.

Brown, Seyom. *The Illusion of Control: Force and Foreign Policy in the Twenty-First Century.* Washington, D.C.: Brookings Institution Press, 2003.

Bryce, James. *The American Commonwealth.* London: Macmillan, 1893.

Cannon, Lou. *President Reagan: The Role of a Lifetime.* New York: Public Affairs, 2000.

———. *Ronald Reagan: The Presidential Portfolio.* New York: Public Affairs, 2001.

Carter, Jimmy. "The Crisis of Confidence Speech." *American Experience,* PBS. http://www.pbs.org/wgbh/amex/carter/filmmore/ps_crisis.html.

Currie, David P. *The Constitution in Congress: The Federalist Period, 1789–1801.* Chicago: University of Chicago Press, 1997.

Detz, Joan. *It's Not What You Say, It's How You Say It.* New York: St. Martin's Press, 2000.

DuBose, Lou, and Jack Bernstein. *Dick Cheney and the Hijacking of the American Presidency.* New York: Random House, 2006.

Ebrahim, Margaret. "Papers: Ford White House Weighed Wiretaps." *Associated Press,* February 4, 2006.

Favor, Lesli J. *The Iroquois Constitution.* New York: Rosen Publishing Group, 2003.

Flexner, James Thomas. *Washington: The Indispensable Man.* New York: Back Bay Books, 1974.

Frum, David. *The Right Man.* New York: Random House, 2003.

Gardner, Michael. *Harry Truman and Civil Rights: Moral Courage and Political Risks.* Carbondale, Ill.: Southern Illinois University Press, 2002.

Genovese, Michael. *The Power of the American Presidency: 1789–2000.* New York: Oxford University Press, 2000.

Grinde, Donald A. "The Iroquois and the Origins of American Democracy." CNN, March 18, 2003.

Haynes, Richard. *The Awesome Power: Harry S. Truman as Commander in Chief.* Baton Rouge, La.: Louisiana State University Press, 1973.

Isaacson, Walter. *Benjamin Franklin: An American Life.* New York: Simon & Schuster, 2003.

Israel, Fred, and J. F. Watts, eds. *Presidential Documents: The Speeches, Proclamations and Policies That Have Shaped the Nation.* Oxford: Routledge, 2000.

Jackson, Percival. *Dissent in the Supreme Court.* Buffalo, N.Y.: William S. Hein, 1969.

Jamieson, Kathleen H. *Packaging the Presidency: A History and Criticism of Presidential Campaign Advertising.* New York: Oxford University Press, 1996.

Kagan, Elena. *Presidential Administration. Harvard Law Review* 114, no. 8 (June 2001).

Kennedy, John F. *State of the Union Addresses.* Fairfield, Iowa: 1st World Library, 2004.

Kent, Harold. *Presidential Powers.* New York: New York University Press, 2005.

Kernell, Sam. *Going Public.* Washington, D.C.: CQ Press, 1997.

Klein, Joe. *The Natural: The Misunderstood Presidency of Bill Clinton.* New York: Doubleday, 2002.

Korn, Jessica. *The Power of Separation: American Constitutionalism and the Myth of the Legislative Veto.* Princeton, N.J.: Princeton University Press, 1996.

Korzi, Michael. *Seat of Popular Leadership: The Presidency, Political Parties, and Democratic Leadership.* Amherst, Mass.: University of Massachusetts Press, 2004.

Kutler, Stanley. *Wars of Watergate: The Last Crisis of Richard Nixon.* W. W. Norton & Co., 1990.

Light, Paul C. *The New Public Service.* Washington, D.C.: Brookings Institution Press, 1999.

Madison, James. *The Federalist No. 49.* New York: Modern Library, 1955.

Mann, Thomas E., and Norman J. Ornstein. *The Broken Branch: How Congress Is Failing America and How to Get It Back on Track.* New York: Oxford University Press, 2006.

Marcus, Maeva. *Truman and the Steel Seizure Case: The Limits of Presidential Power.* Durham, N.C.: Duke University Press, 1994.

Mathis, Mark. *Feeding the Media Beast.* West Lafayette, Ind.: Purdue University Press, 2002.

Mayer, David N. *The Constitutional Thought of Thomas Jefferson.* Charlottesville, Va.: University of Virginia Press, 1994.

Mayer, Kenneth. *With the Stroke of a Pen: Executive Orders and Presidential Power.* Princeton, N.J.: Princeton University Press, 2001.

Meese, Edwin. *With Reagan: The Inside Story.* Washington, D.C.: Regnery Publishing, 1992.

Miller, Anita, ed. *George W. Bush versus the U.S. Constitution.* Chicago: Academy Chicago Publishers, 2006.

Morris, Edmund. *Dutch: A Memoir of Ronald Reagan.* New York: Random House, 1999.

Nelson, Michael. "Evaluating the Presidency." In *The Presidency and the Political System,* edited by Michael Nelson. Washington, D.C.: CQ Press, 1990.

Neustadt, Richard. *Presidential Power and the Modern Presidents.* New York: Free Press, 1990.

Newmyer, R. Kent. *John Marshall and the Heroic Age of the Supreme Court.* Baton Rouge, La.: Louisiana State University Press, 2001.

Noonan, Peggy. *When Character Was King.* New York: Viking, 2002.

Novak, Michael. *Choosing Presidents: Symbols of Political Leadership.* Piscataway, N.J.: Transaction Publishers, 1992.

Paine, Thomas, *Common Sense.* New York: Penguin, 1776.

Parmet, Herbert. *George Bush: The Life of a Lone Star Yankee*. New York: Scribner's, 2000.

Polenberg, Richard. *The Era of Franklin D. Roosevelt, 1933–1945*. New York: Palgrave, 2000.

Richardson, James. *James Monroe: A Compilation of the Messages and Papers of the Presidents*. Whitefish, Mont.: Kessinger Publishing, 2004.

Robert, Remini. *Andrew Jackson*. New York: HarperCollins, 1999.

Robinson, Peter. *How Ronald Reagan Changed My Life*. New York: HarperCollins, 2004.

Roosevelt, Theodore. *Theodore Roosevelt: An Autobiography*. Whitefish, Mont.: Kessinger Publishing, 2004.

Ross, Irwin, *The Loneliest Campaign: The Truman Victory of 1948*. Westport, Conn.: Greenwood Press, 1968.

Schlesinger, Arthur M. *The Cycles of American History*. New York: Houghton Mifflin, 1999.

———. *The Imperial Presidency*. Tampa, Fla.: Mariner Books, 2004.

———. *War and the American Presidency*. New York: W. W. Norton & Co., 2004.

Schultze, Charles. "Interview." *Jimmy Carter Presidential Oral History Project*. January 8–9, 1982.

Simendinger, Alexis. "Results-Oriented President Uses Levers of Powers." *Government Executive Magazine,* January 25, 2002.

Smith, Steve, Jason Roberts, and Ryan Vander Weilan. *The American Congress*. Cambridge: Cambridge University Press, 2006.

Spitzer, Robert J. *Presidential Veto*. Albany, N.Y.: SUNY Press, 1988.

Starobin, Paul. "Imperial presidency has long history." *National Journal,* February 22, 2006.

Stephanopoulos, George. *All Too Human*. Boston: Little, Brown and Co., 1999.

Sundquist, James L. *Decline and Resurgence of Congress*. Washington, D.C.: Brookings Institution Press, 1981.

Suskind, Ron. *The Price of Royalty*. New York: Simon & Schuster, 2004.

Tocqueville, Alexis de. *Democracy in America*. Toronto: Random House of Canada, 1945.

Tower, John G. "Congress Versus the President." *Foreign Affairs* (Winter 1981).

Warren, Robert Penn. *All the King's Men*. New York: Harcourt, Inc., 2001.

White, Theodore. *America in Search of Itself: The Making of the President 1856–1980*. New York: Harper & Row, 1982.

Woodward, Bob. *Bush at War*. New York: Simon & Schuster, 2003.

———. *Plan of Attack*. New York: Simon & Schuster, 2004.

———. *State of Denial: Bush at War, Part III*. New York: Simon & Schuster, 2007.

Ten: The Terms of Trade

"An Illustrated History of Free Trade," BBC News, February 12, 2003.

"President Jackson's Proclamation Regarding Nullification, December 10, 1832." Avalon Project of Yale University, 1999.

"South Carolina Ordinance of Nullification, November 24, 1832." Avalon Project of Yale University, 1999.

Auerbach, Stuart. "Gephardt Stand Is Making Trade Campaign Issue" *Washington Post,* March 6, 1988.

Bauer, Raymond A., and Lewis Anthony Dexter. *American Business and Public Policy: The Politics of Foreign Trade.* Chicago: Aldine-Atherton, 1972.

Bensel, Richard F. *The Political Economy of American Industrialization, 1877–1900.* Cambridge: Cambridge University Press, 2000.

Bordo, Michael D., Claudia Goldin, and Eugene N. White. *The Defining Moment: The Great Depression and the American Economy in the Twentieth Century.* Chicago: University of Chicago Press, 1998.

Brands, H. W. *Woodrow Wilson: The American President Series.* New York: Times Books, 2003.

Brinkley, Douglas, and Richard T. Griffiths. *John Kennedy and Europe.* Baton Rouge, La.: Louisiana State University Press, 1999.

Brodsky, Alyn. *Grover Cleveland.* New York: St. Martin's Press, 2000.

Buchanan, Pat. "Riding the Free Trade Raft over the Falls." *American Cause,* April 18, 2005.

Bush, George H. W. "Transcript of State of the Union." CSPAN, January 28, 1992.

Calhoun, Charles W. *Benjamin Harrison.* New York: Times Books, 2005.

Cameron, Fraser. *U.S. Foreign Policy after the Cold War.* Oxford: Routledge, 2002.

Carter, Jimmy. *State of the Union Addresses.* Whitefish, Mont.: Kessinger Publishing, 2004.

Clinton, Bill. *Between Hope and Histoy.* New York: Times Books, 1996.

———. *My Life.* New York: Knopf, 2004.

Cohen, Richard. ". . . and the Gephardtmobile." *Washington Post,* February 8, 1988.

Cramer, Richard B. *What It Takes: The Way to the White House.* New York: Random House, 1992.

Crowley, Michael. "The Case for Dick Gephardt: Old Faithful." *The New Republic,* January 19, 2004.

Crucini, Mario J. "Sources of Variation in Real Tariff Rates: The United States, 1900–1940." *American Economic Review* 84, no. 3, June 1994.

DeConde, Alexander, Richard Dean Burns, and Frederik D. Logevall, eds. *Encyclopedia of American Foreign Policy.* New York: Simon & Schuster, 2002.

Dester, I. M. *American Trade Politics.* Washington, D.C.: Institute for International Economics, 2005.

Eckes, Alfred. *Opening America's Market: U.S. Foreign Trade Policy Since 1776.* Chapel Hill, N.C.: University of North Carolina Press, 1995.

Eckes, Alfred E. *Revisiting U.S. Trade Policy.* Athens, Ohio: Ohio University Press, 2000.

Eichengreen, Barry. "The Political Economy of the Smoot-Hawley Tariff." *Research in Economic History* 12 (1989).

Eisenhower, Dwight D. *State of the Union Addresses.* Whitefish, Mont.: Kessinger Publishing, 2004.

Eisner, Marc Allen. *From Warfare State to Welfare State.* State College, Pa.: Penn State Press, 2000.

Everett, Marshall. *Complete Life of William McKinley.* Whitefish, Mont.: Kessinger Publishing, 2003.

Feldstein, Martin. *American Economic Policy in the 1980s.* Chicago: University of Chicago Press, 1994.

Ferguson, Thomas. "Dick and Trade; Richard Gephardt Commercial Policy." *The Nation* 246, no. 7 (February 20, 1988): 221.

Fowler, Cornell. "Gephardt takes it to the farm." *United Press International,* February 6, 1988.

Franklin, Benjamin. *The Works of Benjamin Franklin.* New York: T. MacCoun, 1882.

———. "Observations Concerning the Increase of Mankind, Peopling of Countries." In *Memoirs in the Life and Writings of Benjamin Franklin.* Boston: E. P. Dutton and Co., 1910.

Friedman, Milton. "The Case for Free Trade." *Hoover Digest* 4 (1997).

Gaddis, John L. *The United States and the Origins of the Cold War.* New York: Columbia University Press, 2000.

Giunta, Mary A., ed. *The Emerging Nation: A Documentary History.* Vol. 3. Washington, D.C.: Government Printing Office, 1996.

Gordon, John S. *Empire of Wealth.* New York: HarperCollins, 2004.

Green, John R. *The Presidency of George Bush.* Lawrence, Kans.: University Press of Kansas, 2000.

Greenberg, Stan. *Middle Class Dreams.* New York: Random House, 1995.

Gresser, Edward. "Hoover and Roosevelt, 70 Years Later: Toward a New Progressive Framework for Trade and Labor Links." Progressive Policy Institute Paper, September 27, 2001.

Haberler, Gottfried von. *The Theory of International Trade.* London: William Hodge, 1936.

Hamilton, Alexander, James Madison, and John Jay. *Federalist Papers.* New York: Sterling Publishing Company, 1992.

Hill, William. *The First Stages of the Tariff Policy of the United States.* New York: Guggenheimer, Weil & Co., 1898.

Hofstadter, Richard. *Social Darwinism in American Thought.* Boston: Beacon Press, 1992.

Huston, James L. *The Panic of 1857 and the Coming of the Civil War.* Baton Rouge, La.: Louisiana State University Press, 1987.

Keylor, William R. *The Twentieth-Century World: An International History.* New York: Oxford University Press, 2001.

Kindleberger, Charles P. *The World in Depression, 1929–1939.* Berkeley, Calif.: University of California Press, 1973.

Klein, Joe. *The Natural: The Misunderstood Presidency of Bill Clinton.* New York: Doubleday, 2002.

Kuttner, Robert. *Everything for Sale: The Virtues and Limits of Markets.* Chicago: University of Chicago Press, 1996.

Lovett, William A., Alfred E. Eckes, and Richard L. Brinkman. *U.S. Trade Policy: History, Theory, and the WTO.* Armonk, N.Y.: M. E. Sharpe, 2004.

Marrison, Andrew. *Free Trade and Its Reception 1815–1960: Freedom and Trade.* London: Routledge, 1998.

Monroe, James. *State of the Union Addresses.* Whitefish, Mont.: Kessinger Publishing, 2004.

———. *The Writings of James Monroe.* New York: G. P. Putnam, 1903.

Montgomery, William M. *The Life of John Caldwell Calhoun.* New York: Neale Publishing, 1917.

Nixon, Richard. *Public Messages, Speeches and Statements of the President.* Washington, D.C.: Government Printing Office, 1975.

———. *State of the Union Addresses.* Whitefish, Mont.: Kessinger Publishing, 2004.

O'Driscoll, Gerald P. *Free Trade Within North America: Expanding Trade for Prosperity.* New York: Springer, 1993.

Pollack, Sheldon D. *The Failure of U.S. Tax Policy.* State College, Pa.: Penn State Press, 1996.

Prestowitz, Clyde. *Three Billion Capitalists: The Great Shift of Wealth and Power to the East.* New York: Perseus Books, 2006.

Reitano, Joanne R. *The Tariff Question in the Gilded Age.* State College, Pa.: Penn State Press, 1994.

Remini, Robert V. *Henry Clay: Statesman of the Union.* New York: W. W. Norton & Co., 1991.

Roberts, Paul C. "Conservative Dogma Pulling Marx Out of His Grave," September 4, 2005. http://www.vdare.com/roberts/050904_marx.htm.

Roosevelt, Franklin D. *State of the Union Addresses.* Whitefish, Mont.: Kessinger Publishing, 2004.

Roosevelt, Franklin. *My Friends: Twenty-Eight History Making Speeches.* Whitefish, Mont.: Kessinger Publishing, 2005.

Roosevelt, Theodore. *The Roosevelt Policy.* Whitefish, Mont.: Kessinger Publishing, 2004.

Runkel, David R. *Campaign for President: The Managers Look at '88.* Westport, Conn.: Greenwood Press, 1989.

Saletan, William, and Ben Jacobs. "The Worst of Dick Gephardt: A troubling tale from his past. Is it true?" *Slate,* September 3, 2003.

Schattschneider, E. E. *Politics, Pressures and the Tariff.* Upper Saddle River, N.J.: Prentice Hall, 1935.

Schlesinger, Arthur M. *A Thousand Days: John F. Kennedy in the White House.* New York: Houghton Mifflin, 2002.

The Shanghai Communiqué. Episode 15. *CNN.com.*

Shoch, James. *Trading Blows: Party Competition and U.S. Trade Policy in a Globalizing Era.* Chapel Hill, N.C.: University of North Carolina Press, 2001.

Simmons, Richard. *The American Colonies: From Settlement to Independence.* New York: W. W. Norton & Co., 1976.

Sklansky, Jeffrey. *The Soul's Economy: Market Society and Selfhood in American Thought.* Chapel Hill, N.C.: University of North Carolina Press, 2002.

Stengel, Richard. "Pilloried for Pandering; By Changing His Tune, Gephardt Found the Rhythm." *Time,* February 22, 1988.

Taft, William H. *Four Aspects of Civic Duty.* Athens, Ohio: University of Ohio Press, 2001.

Taussig, F. W. *The Tariff History of the United States.* 8th ed. New York: G. P. Putnam, 1931.

Temin, Peter. *Lessons from the Great Depression: The Lionel Robbins Lectures of 1989.* Cambridge, Mass.: MIT Press, 1989.

U.S. Department of State. *President Bush Imposes Safeguards on Steel Imports,* March 5, 2002.

U.S. Department of State. *Smoot-Hawley Tariff Act,* 1930.

United States Tariff Commission. *The Tariff and Its History.* Washington, D.C.: Government Printing Office, 1934.

Van Dyk, Ted. "A Dose of Protectionism Is Bad Medicine." *U.S. News & World Report,* March 28, 1988.

Wallison, Peter J. *Ronald Reagan: The Power of Conviction and the Restoration of the Presidency.* Boulder, Colo.: Westview Press, 2003.

Walsh, Edward, and David S. Broder. "Democrats Spar Over Paying for Programs; Debate Roadshow Visits New Hampshire." *Washington Post,* January 25, 1988.

Wanniski, Jude. *The Way the World Works.* Washington, D.C.: Regnery Publishing, 1998.

Washington, George. *State of the Union Addresses.* Whitefish, Mont.: Kessinger Publishing, 2004.

Weeks, William E. *John Quincy Adams and American Global Empire.* Lexington, Ky.: University Press of Kentucky, 1992.

White, Donald. *The American Century: The Rise and Decline of the United States as a World Power.* New Haven, Conn.: Yale University Press, 1996.

Zeiler, Thomas, and Alfred Eckes. *Globalization and the American Century.* Cambridge: Cambridge University Press, 2003.

Eleven: War and Diplomacy

"Documents reveal U.S. funding for Chile coup." CNN, November 13, 2000.

"The Gulf War: An In-depth Examination of the 1990–1991 Persian Gulf Crisis." *Frontline,* PBS, February 4, 1997.

"The Unfinished War: A Decade Since Desert Storm." *CNN.com.* http://www.cnn.com/SPECIALS/2001/gulf.war/facts/gulfwar/.

"Thomas Jefferson on Foreign Affairs." http://etext.virginia.edu/jefferson/quotations/jeff1400.htm.

Ambrosius, Lloyd E. *Wilsonianism: Woodrow Wilson and His Legacy in American Foreign Relations.* New York: Palgrave Macmillan, 2002.

Ammon, Henry. *James Monroe.* Charlottesville, Va.: University of Virginia Press, 1990.

Andrew, Christopher. *For the President's Eyes Only.* New York: HarperCollins, 1995.

Andrews, Roberts. *The Columbia Dictionary of Quotations.* New York: Columbia University Press, 1993.

Barnet, Richard J. *The Rockets' Red Glare.* New York: Touchstone Books, 1990.

Brands, H. W. *The Devil We Knew: Americans and the Cold War.* New York: Oxford University Press, 1993.

———. *What America Owes the World: The Struggle for the Soul of Foreign Policy.* Cambridge: Cambridge University Press, 1998.

Brzezinski, Zbigniew. *The Choice: Global Domination or Global Leadership.* New York: Basic Books, 2004.

Bukowski, Douglas, ed. *American History: A Concise Documents Collection.* Boston: Bedford St. Martin's, 1999.

Carter, John J. *Covert Operations as a Tool of Presidential Foreign Policy in American History.* New York: Edwin Mellen Press, 2000.

Crocker, H. W. *Don't Tread on Me: A 400-Year History of America at War, from Indian Fighting to Terrorist Hunting.* New York: Crown Forum, 2006.

DeConde, Alexander, Richard Dean Burns, and Frederik D. Logevall, eds. *Encyclopedia of American Foreign Policy.* New York: Simon & Schuster, 2002.

Dulles, John F. *War or Peace.* New York: Macmillan, 1950.

Dumbrell, John. *American Foreign Policy: Carter to Clinton.* New York: Palgrave, 1997.

Ellis, Joseph. *Founding Brothers.* New York: Knopf, 2000.

Erisman, Michael. *Cuba's Foreign Relations in a Post-Soviet World.* Gainesville, Fla.: University of Florida Press, 2000.

Fromkin, David. "Lyndon Johnson and Foreign Policy: What the New Documents Show." *Foreign Affairs,* Winter 1995.

Gaddis, John L. *Strategies of Containment: A Critical Appraisal of Postwar American National Security.* New York: Oxford University Press, 1982.

Goldzwig, Steven R., and George N. Dionisopoulos, eds. *In a Perilous Hour: The Public Address of John F. Kennedy.* Westport, Conn.: Greenwood Press, 1995.

Graebner, Norman A. *Ideas and Diplomacy: Readings in the Intellectual Tradition of American Foreign Policy.* New York: Oxford University Press, 1964.

Greenberg, David. *Nixon's Shadow: The History of an Image.* New York: W. W. Norton & Co., 2003.

Haass, Richard N. *The Opportunity: America's Moment to Alter History's Course.* New York: Public Affairs, 2005.

Hickley, Donald. *The War of 1812: A Forgotten Conflict.* Urbana-Champaign, Ill.: University of Illinois Press, 1989.

Hitchens, Christopher. *Jefferson: Author of America.* New York: HarperCollins, 2007.

Holsti, Ole R. *Public Opinion and American Foreign Policy.* Ann Arbor, Mich.: University of Michigan Press, 2004.

Isaacson, Walter. *Kissinger.* New York: Touchstone Books, 1992.

Isserman, Maurice, and Michael Kazin. *America Divided: The Civil War of the 1960s.* New York: Oxford University Press, 2004.

Johnson, Chalmers. *Nemesis: The Last Days of the American Republic.* New York: Henry Holt, 2006.

Johnson, Lyndon. "Message to Congress August 5, 1964." Department of State Bulletin, August 24, 1964.

Judis, John B. *Folly of Empire.* New York: Oxford University Press, 2004.

Kennedy, John F. "Towards a Strategy of Peace." Speech to American University, June 10, 1963.

———. "Special Message to Congress, May 25, 1961. The Pentagon Papers, Gravel Edition, 1964.

Kipling, Rudyard. "The White Man's Burden." *McClure's Magazine,* February 12, 1899.

Kirkpatrick, Jeane. *Legitimacy and Force: Political and Moral Dimensions.* Piscataway, N.J.: Transaction Publishers, 1988.

Kissinger, Henry. *Crisis: The Anatomy of Two Major Foreign Policy Crises.* New York: Simon & Schuster, 2003.

———. *Diplomacy.* New York: Touchstone Books, 1994.

LaFeber, Walter. *John Quincy Adams and American Continental Empire.* Chicago: Quadrangle Books, 1965.

Lens, Sidney. *The Forging of the American Empire.* Chicago: Haymarket Books, 2003.

Lind, Michael. *The American Way of Strategy.* New York: Oxford University Press, 2006.

Looze, Helene Johnson. *Alexander Hamilton and the British Orientation of American Foreign Policy, 1783–1803.* The Hague: Mouton, 1969.

Lycan, Gilbert L. *Alexander Hamilton and American Foreign Policy: A Design for Greatness.* Norman, Okla.: University of Oklahoma Press, 1970.

Mahin, Dean. *One War at a Time: The International Dimensions of the American Civil War.* London: Brasey's, 1999.

Mann, James. *The Rise of the Vulcans: The History of Bush's War Cabinet.* New York: Viking, 2004.

Marks, Frederick. *Velvet on Iron: The Diplomacy of Theodore Roosevelt.* Lincoln, Neb.: University of Nebraska Press, 1979.

McDougall, Walter. *Promised Land, Crusader State: The American Encounter with the World Since 1776.* New York: Houghton Mifflin, 1997.

Mead, Walter Russell. *Special Providence: American Foreign Policy and How It Changed the World.* New York: Knopf, 2001.

Melanson, Richard A. *American Foreign Policy Since the Vietnam War.* Armonk, N.Y.: M. E. Sharpe, 2000.

Monaghan, Jay. *Abraham Lincoln Deals with Foreign Affairs.* Lincoln, Neb.: University of Nebraska Press, 1997.

Morison, Samuel E. *A Concise History of the American Republic.* New York: Oxford University Press, 1980.

Ninkovich, Frank. *The Wilsonian Century: U.S. Foreign Policy Since 1900.* Chicago: University of Chicago Press, 1999.

Nordlinger, Eric. *Isolationism Reconfigured.* Princeton, N.J.: Princeton University Press, 1996.

Pike, Frederick. *FDR's Good Neighbor Policy: Sixty Years of Generally Gentle Chaos.* Austin, Tex.: University of Texas Press, 1995.

Power, Samantha. *"A Problem from Hell": America and the Age of Genocide.* New York: HarperPerennial, 2003.

Ramsay, David. *The Life of George Washington.* Vol. 2. New York: M. D. & C., 1807.

Reagan, Ronald. "National Radio Address on Foreign Policy." October 20, 1984.

———. "Remarks at the Brandenburg Gate." West Berlin, Germany, June 12, 1987.

———. *Reagan's Path to Victory.* New York: Simon & Schuster, 2004.

Richardson, James, ed. *A Compilation of the Messages and Papers of the Presidents.* Washington, D.C.: Bureau of National Literature and Art, 1908.

Rutland, Thomas A., et al., eds. *Madison, James. The Papers of James Madison: Presidential Series.* 3 vols. Charlottesville Va.: University of Virginia Press, 1983–1996.

Ryan, David. *U.S. Foreign Policy in World History.* London: Routledge, 2000.

Schlesinger, Arthur, Jr. *The Cycles of American History.* New York: Houghton Mifflin, 1999.

———. *A Thousand Days.* New York: Houghton Mifflin, 2002.

Schlesinger, Arthur M. *The Imperial Presidency.* Tampa, Fla.: Mariner Books, 2004.

Scripps Library and Multimedia Archive. Miller Center of Public Affairs. Charlottesville, Va.: University of Virginia Press, 2005.

Shogan, Robert. *The Double-Edged Sword: How Character Makes and Ruins Presidents from Washington to Clinton.* Boulder, Colo.: Westview Press, 2000.

Sorenson, Theodore. "JFK's Strategy of Peace." *World Policy Journal* 10, no. 3 (Fall 2003).

Soros, George. *The Age of Fallibility.* New York: Public Affairs, 2006.

Steele, Ronald. *Walter Lippmann and the American Century.* Boston: Little, Brown and Co., 1999.

Stevenson, Adlai. *Putting First Things First.* New York: Random House, 1960.

Tocqueville, Alexis de. *Democracy in America.* Toronto: Random House of Canada, 1945.

Tucker, Robert W. *Empire of Liberty: The Statecraft of Thomas Jefferson.* New York: Oxford University Press, 1992.

Woodward, Bob. *Bush at War.* New York: Simon & Schuster, 2003.

———. *Plan of Attack.* New York: Simon & Schuster, 2004.

———. *State of Denial: Bush at War, Part III.* New York: Simon & Schuster, 2007.

Zimmerman, Warren. *First Great Triumph: How Five Americans Made Their Country a World Power.* New York: Farrar, Straus and Giroux, 2002.

Twelve: The Environment

Baarschers, William H. *Eco-facts and Eco-fiction: Understanding the Environmental Debate.* London: Routledge, 1996.

Barnett, Harold J., and Chandler Morse. *Scarcity and Growth: The Economics of Natural Resource Availability.* Baltimore: Johns Hopkins University Press, 1963.

Barton, Gregory. *Empire Forestry and the Origins of Environmentalism.* Cambridge: Cambridge University Press, 2002.

Bates, Marston. *Forest and the Sea.* New York: Vintage Books, 1973.

Bradford, William. *Of Plymouth Plantation, 1620–1647.* New York: Knopf, 1952.

Bramwell, Anna C. *The Fading of the Greens: The Decline of Environmental Politics in the West.* New Haven, Conn.: Yale University Press, 1994.

Brick, Philip D., and R. McGreggor Cawley. *A Wolf in the Garden: The Land Rights Movement and the New Environmental Debate.* Lanham, Md.: Rowman & Littlefield, 1996.

Brower, David. *Let the Mountains Talk, Let the Rivers Run: A Call to Those Who Would Save the Earth.* San Francisco: HarperCollins West, 1995.

Callicott, J. Baird, and Michael P. Nelson. *The Great New Wilderness Debate.* Athens, Ga.: University of Georgia Press, 1998.

Carson, Rachel. *Silent Spring.* New York: Houghton Mifflin, 1962.

Carter, Jimmy. *Keeping Faith: Memoirs of a President.* New York: Bantam Books, 1985.

Carter, Neil. *The Politics of the Environment: Ideas, Activism, Policy.* Cambridge: Cambridge University Press, 2003.

Clifford, Frank. "Alarmed by 'Cycle of Anti-Environmentalism.' " *Los Angeles Times,* November 15, 2005.

Cockburn, Alexander, and Jeffrey St. Clair. *Al Gore: A User's Manual.* London: Verso, 2000.

Commoner, Barry. *The Closing Circle.* New York: Knopf, 1971.

Cronon, William. *Changes in the Land.* New York: Hill and Wang, 2003.

Dowie, Mark. *Losing Ground.* Cambridge, Mass.: MIT Press, 1995.

Duffy, Michael, and Dan Goodgame. *Marching in Place: The Status Quo Presidency of George Bush.* New York: Simon & Schuster, 1992.

Edwards, Jonathan. "True Christian's Life." In *The Works of President Edwards.* 4 vols. New York: B. Franklin, 1968.

Feldman, Leslie, and Rosanna Perotti. *Honor and Loyalty: Inside the Politics of the George H. W. Bush White House.* Westport, Conn.: Greenwood Press, 2002.

Fox, Stephen R. *John Muir and His Legacy: The American Conservation Movement.* Boston: Little, Brown and Co., 1981.

Freyfogle, Eric T. *The Land We Share: Private Property and the Common Good.* Washington, D.C.: Island Press, 2003.

Gore, Al. "Leadership to Renew The American Spirit." Al Gore for President 1988 Campaign Brochure, 1988.

———. *Earth in the Balance: Ecology and the Human Spirit.* New York: Houghton Mifflin, 1992.

———. *An Inconvenient Truth.* New York: Viking, 2007.

Gottlieb, Robert. *Forcing the Spring.* Washington, D.C.: Island Press, 1993.

Hahn, Robert W., Sheila M. Cavanagh, and Robert N. Stavins. "National Environmental Policy During the Clinton Years." AEI-Brookings Joint Center Working Paper No. 01-09 (April 2002).

Hargrove, Erwin. *Jimmy Carter as President: Leadership and the Politics of the Public Good.* Baton Rouge, La.: Louisiana State University Press, 1998.

Isikoff, Michael, and Bill Turque. "Gore's Pollution Problem: In Washington, Al Gore is Mr. Environment. But Back Home, a Smelly River May Hurt Him in 2000." *Newsweek,* November 24, 1997.

Jefferson, Thomas. *Notes on the State of Virginia.* New York: Penguin, 2001.

Koppes, Clayton R. "Efficiency, Equity, Esthetics: Shifting Themes in American Conservation." In *The Ends of the Earth: Perspectives on Modern Environmental History.* Cambridge: Cambridge University Press, 1988.

Lomborg, Bjørn. *The Skeptical Environmentalist: Measuring the Real State of the World.* Cambridge: Cambridge University Press, 1998.

Marsh, George Perkins. *Man and Nature.* Cambridge, Mass.: Belknap Press of Harvard University Press, 1965.

Marx, Leo. *The Machine in the Garden: Technology and the Pastoral Ideal in America.* New York: Oxford University Press, 2000.

Mencimer, Stephanie. "Weather 'tis nobler in the mind: Al Gore lost in 2000 by going soft on the environment. He can win in 2004 by getting tough." *Washington Monthly,* July–August 2002.

Morris, Kenneth. *Jimmy Carter, American Moralist.* Athens, Ga.: University of Georgia Press, 1997.

Muir, John. *A Thousand-Mile Walk to the Gulf.* New York: Houghton Mifflin, 1998.

Nash, Roderick. *The American Environment: Readings in the History of Conservation.* New Haven, Conn.: Yale University Press, 1967.

Nash, Roderick. *Wilderness and the American Mind.* New Haven, Conn.: Yale University Press, 1967.

Neimark, Peninati, and Peter M. Rhoades. *The Environmental Debate.* Westport, Conn.: Greenwood Press, 1999.

Pinchot, Gifford. *Breaking New Ground.* Washington, D.C.: Island Press, 1998.

Radcliffe, Florence. "Private Interests Trying to Grab Off Yellowstone Park." *Washington Post,* February 3, 1930.

Ridley, Matt, and Bobbi S. Low. "Can Selfishness Save the Environment?" *The Atlantic Monthly* 272 (1993): 76–86.

Rowell, Andrew. *Green Backlash: Global Subversion of the Environment Movement.* London: Routledge, 1996.

Sale, Kirkpatrick. *The Green Revolution: The American Environmental Movement, 1962–1999.* New York: Hill and Wang, 1993.

Sax, Joseph L. *Mountains Without Handrails.* Ann Arbor, Mich.: University of Michigan Press, 1980.

Soden, Dennis L. *The Environmental Presidency.* Albany, N.Y.: SUNY Press, 1999.

Steinbeck, John. *The Log from the Sea of Cortez.* New York: Penguin Modern Classics, 1977.

Suskind, Ron. *The Price of Royalty.* New York: Simon & Schuster, 2004.

Taylor, Bob Pepperman. *Our Limits Transgressed: Environmental Political Thought in America.* Lawrence, Kans.: University Press of Kansas, 1992.

Thomas, John L. *A Country in the Mind: Wallace Stegner, Bernard DeVoto, History and the American Land.* London: Routledge, 2000.

Thoreau, Henry David. *The Maine Woods.* Princeton, N.J.: Princeton University Press, 2004.

Tocqueville, Alexis de. *Journey to America.* Westport, Conn.: Greenwood Press, 1981.

Udall, Stewart. *The Quiet Crisis.* New York: Holt, Rinehart and Winston, 1963.

Vogt, William. *Road to Survival.* London: Victor Gollancz Ltd., 1947.

Weinberg, Albert K. *Manifest Destiny: A Study of Nationalist Expansionism in America History.* Baltimore: Johns Hopkins University Press, 1935.

Williams, George Huntston. *Wilderness and Paradise.* New York: HarperCollins, 1962.

Zahniser, Howard, ed. *Where Wilderness Preservation Began: The Adirondack Writings of Howard Zahniser.* Utica, N.Y.: North Country Books, Inc., 1992.

Zaslowsky, Dyan. *These American Lands.* Washington, D.C.: Island Press, 1994.

Zelnick, Bob. "Al Gore: A Case Study." *Hoover Institution Digest,* no. 3 (1999).

Thirteen: A Fair, "More Perfect" Union

"Father Coughlin: The Radio Priest." The Detroit News, Rearview Mirror, http://info
.detnews.com/history/story/index.cfm?id=43&category=people.

"The Great Strike." *Harper's Weekly,* August 11, 1877.

"The Growth of the Christian Counter-Culture." *PublicEye.org.* http://www.publiceye
.org/magazine/v15n1/State_of_Christian_Rt-10.html.

"President Bill Clinton accepts his nomination at the Democratic National Convention."
PBS *NewsHour,* August 29, 1996.

"The Weather Underground." PBS News. http://www.pbs.org/independentlens/
weatherunderground/movement.html.

"U.S. Info on State Government." *Discontent and Reform,* November 2005.

Addams, Jane. *A New Conscience and an Ancient Evil.* New York: Macmillan, 1923.

Alexander, Jeffrey C., Bernhard Giesen, and Jason L. Jason. *Social Performance: Symbolic
Action, Cultural Pragmatics, and Ritual.* Cambridge: Cambridge University Press, 2006.

Berlet, Chip, and Matthew N. Lyons. *Right-Wing Populism in America: Too Close for Comfort.* New York: Guilford Press, 2000.

Bloom, Alexander. *Taking It to the Streets: A Sixties Reader.* New York: Oxford University
Press, 2002.

Brands, H. W. *The Reckless Decade: America in the 1890s.* Chicago: University of Chicago
Press, 2002.

Breitman, George. *Malcolm X Speaks: Selected Speeches and Statements.* New York: Grove
Press, 1990.

Brodsky, Alyn. *Grover Cleveland.* New York: St. Martin's Press, 2000.

Bryan, William J. *Speeches of William Jennings Bryan.* London: Funk & Wagnalls Co., 1909.

———. *The First Battle: A Story of the Campaign of 1896.* Whitefish, Mont.: Kessinger
Publishing, 2005.

Buchanan, Patrick. *The Great Betrayal.* Boston: Little, Brown and Co., 1998.

Carr, Steven Alan. *Hollywood and Anti-Semitism: A Cultural History up to World War II.*
Cambridge: Cambridge University Press, 2001.

Chace, James. *1912: Wilson, Roosevelt, Taft & Debs—The Election That Changed the Country.* New York: Simon & Schuster, 2004.

Chneirov, Richard, Nick Salvatore, and Shelton Stromquist. *The Pullman Strike and the
Crisis of the 1890s.* Urbana-Champaign, Ill.: University of Illinois Press, 1999.

CNN Transcripts. "Presidential Candidates Racing Across the Country as Election Day
Approaches." November 6, 2000.

Cohen, Robert, and Reginald E. Zelnik. *The Free Speech Movement: Reflections on Berkeley in the 1960s.* Berkeley, Calif.: University of California Press, 2002.

Digital History. *The Farmers Revolt,* http://www.digitalhistory.uh.edu/historyonline/
us25.cfm.

Duncan, Clark. *Wallace Joins the Ghost Brigade* (The Progressive Populist, 1998), http://www.populist.com/wallace.duncan.html.

Farber, David, and Beth Bailey. *The Columbia Guide to America in the 1960s.* New York: Columbia University Press, 2003.

Farmer, Brian R. *American Conservatism: History, Theory and Practice.* Cambridge: Cambridge Scholars Press, 2005.

Fogarty, Thomas. "Freedom Too Far? Not Likely." *USA Today,* January 1, 2002.

George, Henry. "The Functions of Government." In *Social Problems.* Chicago: Belford, Clarke and Co., 1884.

Gingrich, Newt. *Winning the Future: A 21st Century Contract with America.* Washington, D.C.: Regnery Publishing, 2005.

Goodwin, Lawrence. *The Populist Movement: A Short History of the Agrarian Revolt in America.* New York: Oxford University Press, 1978.

Hamilton, Alexander. *The Federalist No. 15.* New York: Modern Library, 1955.

Harkin, Tom. "Why I Am a Progressive Populist." *The Progressive Populist* 1, no. 1 (November 1995).

Heer, Jeet. "The Anti-Populist." *Boston Globe,* March 6, 2005.

Hilliard, David, and Donald Wiese. *The Huey Newton Reader.* New York: Seven Stories Press, 2002.

Hofstadter, Richard. *The Paranoid Style in American Politics.* Cambridge, Mass.: Harvard University Press, 1996.

Hovey, Pauline. "Conference Brings Gospel Message into Public Arena." *Catholic Herald,* January 19, 2006.

Janowitz, Morris. *The Last Half-Century: Societal Change and Politics in America.* Chicago: University of Chicago Press, 1984.

Jefferson, Thomas. *Memoirs, Correspondence and Private Papers.* London: H. Colburn and R. Bentley, 1829.

Jefferson, Thomas. *Notes on the State of Virginia.* New York: Penguin Classics, 1998.

Johnson, Tom. *My Story,* edited by Elizabeth Hauser. Kent, Ohio: Kent State University Press.

Kay, Harvey J. *Why Do Ruling Classes Fear History?* New York: Palgrave, 1997.

Kazin, Michael. *The Populist Persuasion: An American History.* Ithaca, N.Y.: Cornell University Press, 1998.

King, Martin Luther, Jr. *A Testament of Hope: The Essential Writings and Speeches of Martin Luther King, Jr.* New York: HarperCollins, 1990.

———. *Martin Luther King Jr. Companion.* New York: St. Martin's Press, 1998.

Lasch, Christopher. *The Revolt of the Elites and the Betrayal of Democracy.* New York: W. W. Norton & Co., 1996.

Long, Huey. "Share the Wealth." Radio address, 1934.

Madison, James. *The Federalist No. 10.* New York: Modern Library, 1955.

May, Patrick. "Either revered or reviled, cap on property taxes has changed lives, reshaped state government." *The Mercury News,* May 12, 2003.

McGuigan, Jim. *Cultural Populism.* London: Routledge, 1992.

McKay, Claude. *Harlem Shadows.* Urbana-Champaign, Ill.: University of Illinois Press, 2004.

McMath, Robert. *American Populism: A Social History 1877–1898.* New York: Hill and Wang, 1990.

Mercer, Kobena. "Identity and Diversity in Postmodern Politics." In *Theories of Race and Racism,* edited by John Solomos and Les Back. London: Routledge, 2000.

Paine, Thomas. *Common Sense.* New York: Penguin, 1982.

Roosevelt, Franklin. *Great Speeches.* New York: Courier Dover Publications, 1999.

Schlesinger, Arthur. *The Politics of Upheaval.* New York: Houghton Mifflin, 2003.

Serrin, William. *Homestead: The Glory and Tragedy of an American Steel Town.* New York: Vintage Books, 1992.

Singer, Mark. "Running on Instinct." *The New Yorker,* January 12, 2004.

Sirota, David. *Hostile Takeover: How Big Money and Corruption Conquered Our Government—and How to Take It Back.* New York: Crown Publishers, 2006.

Smith, Sam. "The Corporation and America." In *Shadows of Hope.* Bloomington, Ind.: Indiana University Press, 1994.

Stanton, Elizabeth C. *The Selected Papers of Elizabeth Cady Stanton.* New Brunswick, N.J.: Rutgers University Press, 1997.

Steinem, Gloria. " 'Women's Liberation' Aims to Free Men, Too." *Washington Post,* June 7, 1970.

Sumner, William Graham. *What Social Classes Owe to Each Other.* Whitefish, Mont.: Kessinger Publishing, 2006.

Twitchell, James B. "Jesus Christ's Superflock." *Mother Jones,* March/April 2005.

Watson, Justin. *The Christian Coalition: Dreams of Restoration, Demands for Recognition.* New York: Palgrave, 1999.

White, William Allen. *What's the Matter with Kansas?* New York: Gazette, 1910.

Williams, T. Harry. *Huey Long.* New York: Knopf, 1969.

Wolfe, Alan. *Does American Democracy Still Work?* New Haven, Conn.: Yale University Press, 2006.

Zinn, Howard. *A People's History of the United States.* New York: HarperCollins, 2003.

Conclusion

Pew Research Center. "Once Again, the Future Ain't What It Used to Be." May 2, 2006.

Wolfe, Alan. *Does American Democracy Still Work?* New Haven, Conn.: Yale University Press, 2006.

INDEX

PHOTO: © JEFFREY MACMILLAN

HOWARD FINEMAN is *Newsweek*'s senior Washington correspondent and columnist. An award-winning reporter and writer, Fineman is also an NBC news analyst, contributing reports to that network as well as MSNBC. His column, "Living Politics," appears in *Newsweek,* on Newsweek.com, and on MSNBC.com. Fineman's work has also appeared in *The New York Times, The Washington Post,* and *The New Republic.* He lives in Washington, D.C., with his wife and two children.